BESTSELLING
BOOK SERIES
FROM IDG

Internet Searching
For Dummies®

P9-DBU-819

Get Today's News

News Source	Address
The New York Times	www.nytimes.com
MSNBC	www.msnbc.com
The Washington Post	washingtonpost.com
AP Update (politics)	www.newsday.com/ap/washingt.htm
The Weather Channel	www.weather.com
Time Magazine	cgi.pathfinder.com/time
CNN	www.cnn.com
Yahoo! Sports	sports.yahoo.com
Wired News	www.wired.com/news

Ten Fun and Useful Web Directories

Directory	Address
Achoo	www.achoo.com
The Huge List	thehugelist.com
Starting Point	www.stpt.com
Virtual Library Directory	www.alexandria-home.com/directory.asp
WWWomen	www.wwwomen.com
World Wide Web Pavilion	www.catalog.com/tsw/Pavilion/pavilion.htm
WebWise Library	webwise.walcoff.com/library/index.html
The Mining Company	www.miningco.com
LookSmart	www.looksmart.com
Family Safe Startup Page	www.startup-page.com
Yecch!	www.yeeeoww.com/yecch/yecchhome.html

Web Site Password Reminders

Name of Web Site	Your User Name	Your Password
_____	_____	_____
_____	_____	_____
_____	_____	_____
_____	_____	_____
_____	_____	_____
_____	_____	_____

...For Dummies: Bestselling Book Series for Beginners

Internet Searching For Dummies®

Cheat Sheet

Bookmark These Search Sites!

Search Site	Address
Yahoo!	www.yahoo.com
HotBot	www.hotbot.com
Infoseek	www.infoseek.com
Lycos	www.lycos.com
Excite	www.excite.com
AltaVista	www.altavista.digital.com
Internet Sleuth	www.isleuth.com
Deja News	www.dejanews.com
Northern Light	www.northernlight.com

Essential Search Operators

Using This Search Operator	Gives This Result
AND	Includes both (or all) keywords in search results Example: cleveland AND indians
OR	Includes either keyword in search results Example: cleveland OR indians
NOT	Excludes a keyword from search results Example: indians NOT baseball
( )	Groups keywords together using other operators Example: cleveland AND (indians OR tribe)
*	Wildcard Example: legislat* (returns "legislature" and "legislation")

IDG BOOKS WORLDWIDE

...For Dummies: Bestselling Book Series for Beginners

INTERNET SEARCHING FOR DUMMIES®

INTERNET SEARCHING FOR DUMMIES®

by Brad Hill

IDG Books Worldwide, Inc.
An International Data Group Company

Foster City, CA ◆ Chicago, IL ◆ Indianapolis, IN ◆ New York, NY

Internet Searching For Dummies®

Published by
IDG Books Worldwide, Inc.
An International Data Group Company
919 E. Hillsdale Blvd.
Suite 400
Foster City, CA 94404
www.idgbooks.com (IDG Books Worldwide Web site)
www.dummies.com (Dummies Press Web site)

Library of Congress Catalog Card No.: 98-88387

ISBN: 0-7645-0478-9

Printed in the United States of America

10 9 8 7 6 5 4 3 2 1

1O/QW/RR/ZY/IN

Distributed in the United States by IDG Books Worldwide, Inc.

Distributed by Macmillan Canada for Canada; by Transworld Publishers Limited in the United Kingdom; by IDG Norge Books for Norway; by IDG Sweden Books for Sweden; by Woodslane Pty. Ltd. for Australia; by Woodslane (NZ) Ltd. for New Zealand; by Addison Wesley Longman Singapore Pte Ltd. for Singapore, Malaysia, Thailand, Indonesia and Korea; by Norma Comunicaciones S.A. for Colombia; by Intersoft for South Africa; by International Thomson Publishing for Germany, Austria and Switzerland; by Toppan Company Ltd. for Japan; by Distribuidora Cuspide for Argentina; by Livraria Cultura for Brazil; by Ediciencia S.A. for Ecuador; by Ediciones ZETA S.C.R. Ltda. for Peru; by WS Computer Publishing Corporation, Inc., for the Philippines; by Unalis Corporation for Taiwan; by Contemporanea de Ediciones for Venezuela; by Computer Book & Magazine Store for Puerto Rico; by Express Computer Distributors for the Caribbean and West Indies. Authorized Sales Agent: Anthony Rudkin Associates for the Middle East and North Africa.

For general information on IDG Books Worldwide's books in the U.S., please call our Consumer Customer Service department at 800-762-2974. For reseller information, including discounts and premium sales, please call our Reseller Customer Service department at 800-434-3422.

For information on where to purchase IDG Books Worldwide's books outside the U.S., please contact our International Sales department at 317-596-5530 or fax 317-596-5692.

For information on foreign language translations, please contact our Foreign & Subsidiary Rights department at 650-655-3021 or fax 650-655-3281.

For sales inquiries and special prices for bulk quantities, please contact our Sales department at 650-655-3200 or write to the address above.

For information on using IDG Books Worldwide's books in the classroom or for ordering examination copies, please contact our Educational Sales department at 800-434-2086 or fax 317-596-5499.

For press review copies, author interviews, or other publicity information, please contact our Public Relations department at 650-655-3000 or fax 650-655-3299.

For authorization to photocopy items for corporate, personal, or educational use, please contact Copyright Clearance Center, 222 Rosewood Drive, Danvers, MA 01923, or fax 978-750-4470.

About the Author

Brad Hill spends most of his time with computers and considers them living creatures with personalities. For this reason alone, he should be treated with caution. Nevertheless, this affinity with digital life forms has led him to the far corners of cyberspace.

Brad is the author of nine books about the Internet and personal technology. His titles include a *Publishers Weekly* bestseller (*World Wide Web Searching For Dummies,* published by IDG Books Worldwide, Inc.), a Book of the Month Club catalog selection *(Internet Directory For Dummies),* and several Amazon.com Recommended Books. Brad is often quoted in magazines carrying articles about the Internet, and has been a guest in more than 50 radio interviews. Brad has also appeared extensively on network television to promote the online experience.

For many years, Brad developed and managed some of the most prominent online communities in cyberspace. He has owned several CompuServe Forums and was instrumental in the WOW! consumer online service created by CompuServe. Currently, Brad consults to Web companies establishing virtual communities and is teaching his online *Investing on the Web* course for ZDU. He writes the "On the Infobahn" column for *ComputerEdge Magazine.*

Brad Hill is listed in *Who's Who* and is a member of the Author's Guild. Brad enjoys hearing from readers and invites visitors to his Web site: www.bradhill.com.

ABOUT IDG BOOKS WORLDWIDE

Welcome to the world of IDG Books Worldwide.

IDG Books Worldwide, Inc., is a subsidiary of International Data Group, the world's largest publisher of computer-related information and the leading global provider of information services on information technology. IDG was founded more than 25 years ago and now employs more than 8,500 people worldwide. IDG publishes more than 275 computer publications in over 75 countries (see listing below). More than 90 million people read one or more IDG publications each month.

Launched in 1990, IDG Books Worldwide is today the #1 publisher of best-selling computer books in the United States. We are proud to have received eight awards from the Computer Press Association in recognition of editorial excellence and three from *Computer Currents'* First Annual Readers' Choice Awards. Our best-selling *...For Dummies*® series has more than 50 million copies in print with translations in 38 languages. IDG Books Worldwide, through a joint venture with IDG's Hi-Tech Beijing, became the first U.S. publisher to publish a computer book in the People's Republic of China. In record time, IDG Books Worldwide has become the first choice for millions of readers around the world who want to learn how to better manage their businesses.

Our mission is simple: Every one of our books is designed to bring extra value and skill-building instructions to the reader. Our books are written by experts who understand and care about our readers. The knowledge base of our editorial staff comes from years of experience in publishing, education, and journalism — experience we use to produce books for the '90s. In short, we care about books, so we attract the best people. We devote special attention to details such as audience, interior design, use of icons, and illustrations. And because we use an efficient process of authoring, editing, and desktop publishing our books electronically, we can spend more time ensuring superior content and spend less time on the technicalities of making books.

You can count on our commitment to deliver high-quality books at competitive prices on topics you want to read about. At IDG Books Worldwide, we continue in the IDG tradition of delivering quality for more than 25 years. You'll find no better book on a subject than one from IDG Books Worldwide.

John Kilcullen
CEO
IDG Books Worldwide, Inc.

Steven Berkowitz
President and Publisher
IDG Books Worldwide, Inc.

Eighth Annual Computer Press Awards ≥1992

Ninth Annual Computer Press Awards ≥1993

Tenth Annual Computer Press Awards ≥1994

Eleventh Annual Computer Press Awards ≥1995

IDG Books Worldwide, Inc., is a subsidiary of International Data Group, the world's largest publisher of computer-related information and the leading global provider of information services on information technology. International Data Group publishes over 275 computer publications in over 75 countries. More than 90 million people read one or more International Data Group publications each month. International Data Group's publications include: **ARGENTINA:** Buyer's Guide, Computerworld Argentina, PC World Argentina; **AUSTRALIA:** Australian Macworld, Australian PC World, Australian Reseller News, Computerworld, IT Casebook, Network World, Publish, Webmaster; **AUSTRIA:** Computerwelt Osterreich, Networks Austria, PC Tip Austria; **BANGLADESH:** PC World Bangladesh; **BELARUS:** PC World Belarus; **BELGIUM:** Data News; **BRAZIL:** Annuário de Informática, Computerworld, Connections, Macworld, PC Player, PC World, Publish, Reseller News, Supergamepower; **BULGARIA:** Computerworld Bulgaria, Network World Bulgaria, PC & MacWorld Bulgaria; **CANADA:** CIO Canada, Client/Server World, ComputerWorld Canada, InfoWorld Canada, NetworkWorld Canada, WebWorld; **CHILE:** Computerworld Chile, PC World Chile; **COLOMBIA:** Computerworld Colombia, PC World Colombia; **COSTA RICA:** PC World Centro America; **THE CZECH AND SLOVAK REPUBLICS:** Computerworld Czechoslovakia, Macworld Czech Republic, PC World Czechoslovakia; **DENMARK:** Communications World Danmark, Computerworld Danmark, Macworld Danmark, PC World Danmark, Techworld Denmark; **DOMINICAN REPUBLIC:** PC World Republica Dominicana; **ECUADOR:** PC World Ecuador; **EGYPT:** Computerworld Middle East, PC World Middle East; **EL SALVADOR:** PC World Centro America; **FINLAND:** MikroPC, Tietoverkko, Tietoviikko; **FRANCE:** Distributique, Hebdo, Info PC, Le Monde Informatique, Macworld, Reseaux & Telecoms, WebMaster France; **GERMANY:** Computer Partner, Computerwoche, Computerwoche Extra, Computerwoche FOCUS, Global Online, Macwelt, PC Welt; **GREECE:** Amiga Computing, GamePro Greece, Multimedia World; **GUATEMALA:** PC World Centro America; **HONDURAS:** PC World Centro America; **HONG KONG:** Computerworld Hong Kong, PC World Hong Kong, Publish in Asia; **HUNGARY:** ABCD CD-ROM, Computerworld Szamitastechnika, Internetto online Magazine, PC World Hungary, PC-X Magazin Hungary; **ICELAND:** Tolvuheimur PC World Island; **INDIA:** Information Communications World, Information Systems Computerworld, PC World India, Publish in Asia; **INDONESIA:** InfoKomputer PC World, Komputek Computerworld, Publish in Asia; **IRELAND:** ComputerScope, PC Live!; **ISRAEL:** Macworld Israel, People & Computers/Computerworld; **ITALY:** Computerworld Italia, Macworld Italia, Networking Italia, PC World Italia; **JAPAN:** DTP World, Macworld Japan, Nikkei Personal Computing, OS/2 World Japan, SunWorld Japan, Windows NT World, Windows World Japan; **KENYA:** PC World East African; **KOREA:** Hi-Tech Information, Macworld Korea, PC World Korea; **MACEDONIA:** PC World Macedonia; **MALAYSIA:** Computerworld Malaysia, PC World Malaysia, Publish in Asia; **MALTA:** PC World Malta; **MEXICO:** Computerworld Mexico, PC World Mexico; **MYANMAR:** PC World Myanmar; **NETHERLANDS:** Computer! Totaal, LAN Internetworking Magazine, LAN World Buyers Guide, Macworld Netherlands, Net, WebWereld; **NEW ZEALAND:** Absolute Beginners Guide and Plain & Simple Series, Computer Buyer, Computer Industry Directory, Computerworld New Zealand, MTB, Network World, PC World New Zealand; **NICARAGUA:** PC World Centro America; **NORWAY:** Computerworld Norge, CW Rapport, Datamagasinet, Financial Rapport, Kursguide Norge, Macworld Norge, Multimediaworld Norge, PC World Ekspress Norge, PC World Nettverk, PC World Norge, PC World ProduktGuide Norge; **PAKISTAN:** Computerworld Pakistan; **PANAMA:** PC World Panama; **PEOPLE'S REPUBLIC OF CHINA:** China Computer Users, China Computerworld, China InfoWorld, China Telecom World Weekly, Computer & Communication, Electronic Design China, Electronics Today, Electronics Weekly, Game Software, PC World China, Popular Computer Week, Software Weekly, Software World, Telecom World; **PERU:** Computerworld Peru, PC World Profesional Peru, PC World SoHo Peru; **PHILIPPINES:** Click!, Computerworld Philippines, PC World Philippines, Publish in Asia; **POLAND:** Computerworld Poland, Computerworld Special Report Poland, Cyber, Macworld Poland, Networld Poland, PC World Komputer; **PORTUGAL:** Cerebro/PC World, Computerworld/Correio Informático, Dealer World Portugal, Mac*In/PC*In Portugal, Multimedia World; **PUERTO RICO:** PC World Puerto Rico; **ROMANIA:** Computerworld Romania, PC World Romania, Telecom Romania; **RUSSIA:** Computerworld Russia, Mir PK, Publish, Seti; **SINGAPORE:** Computerworld Singapore, PC World Singapore, Publish in Asia; **SLOVENIA:** Monitor; **SOUTH AFRICA:** Computing SA, Network World SA, Software World SA; **SPAIN:** Communicaciones World España, Computerworld España, Dealer World España, Macworld España, PC World España; **SRI LANKA:** Infolink PC World; **SWEDEN:** CAP&Design, Computer Sweden, Corporate Computing Sweden, Internetworld Sweden, it.branschen, Macworld Sweden, MaxiData Sweden, MikroDatorn, Nätverk & Kommunikation, PC World Sweden, PCaktiv, Windows World Sweden; **SWITZERLAND:** Computerworld Schweiz, Macworld Schweiz, PCtip; **TAIWAN:** Computerworld Taiwan, Macworld Taiwan, NEW ViSiON/Publish, PC World Taiwan, Windows World Taiwan; **THAILAND:** Publish in Asia, Thai Computerworld; **TURKEY:** Computerworld Turkiye, Macworld Turkiye, Network World Turkiye, PC World Turkiye; **UKRAINE:** Computerworld Kiev, Multimedia World Ukraine, PC World Ukraine; **UNITED KINGDOM:** Acorn User UK, Amiga Action UK, Amiga Computing UK, Apple Talk UK, Computing, Macworld, Parents and Computers UK, PC Advisor, PC Home, PSX Pro, The WEB; **UNITED STATES:** Cable in the Classroom, CIO Magazine, Computerworld, DOS World, Federal Computer Week, GamePro Magazine, InfoWorld, I-Way, Macworld, Network World, PC Games, PC World, Publish, Video Event, THE WEB Magazine, and WebMaster; online webzines: JavaWorld, NetscapeWorld, and SunWorld Online; **URUGUAY:** InfoWorld Uruguay; **VENEZUELA:** Computerworld Venezuela, PC World Venezuela; and **VIETNAM:** PC World Vietnam.   5/7/98

Dedication

This book is for my parents, Betty and Russ, with love and admiration. From my mother I've learned persistence; from my father, self-reliance. They continue to be my greatest influences.

Acknowledgments

Susan Pink is the editor of this book, and she is the best creative partner an author could have. Her thoroughness and attention to detail are legendary, and her calm in the face of deadline crisis is unearthly. Thanks for your patience and hard work, Susan. Don't edit this paragraph.

I wouldn't be involved in the ... *For Dummies* venture if it weren't for Mary Corder, who encouraged me from our very first conversation.

Many thanks to all the editors at IDG Books Worldwide who contribute sharp-eyed effort to each ...*For Dummies* manuscript.

Finally, I acknowledge the entire, vast community of souls who inhabit, even sporadically, the global Internet that is under construction. They are the pioneers of a new frontier.

Publisher's Acknowledgments

We're proud of this book; please register your comments through our IDG Books Worldwide Online Registration Form located at http://my2cents.dummies.com.

Some of the people who helped bring this book to market include the following:

Acquisitions, Editorial, and Media Development

Project Editor: Susan Pink

Acquisitions Editor: Joyce Pepple

Technical Editor: Allen Wyatt, Discovery Computing, Inc.

Associate Technical Editor: Joell Smith

Associate Permissions Editor: Carmen Krikorian

Media Development Coordinator: Megan Roney

Editorial Manager: Mary Corder

Media Development Manager: Heather Heath Dismore

Editorial Assistant: Donna Love

Production

Associate Project Coordinator: Tom Missler

Layout and Graphics: Lou Boudreau, Maridee V. Ennis, Angela F. Hunckler, Brent Savage, Janet Seib, Kate Snell

Proofreaders: Christine Berman, Laura Bowman, Nancy Price, Rebecca Senninger, Janet M. Withers

Indexer: Ty Koontz

Special Help

Suzanne Thomas, Publication Services, Inc.

General and Administrative

IDG Books Worldwide, Inc.: John Kilcullen, CEO; Steven Berkowitz, President and Publisher

IDG Books Technology Publishing: Brenda McLaughlin, Senior Vice President and Group Publisher

Dummies Technology Press and Dummies Editorial: Diane Graves Steele, Vice President and Associate Publisher; Mary Bednarek, Director of Acquisitions and Product Development; Kristin A. Cocks, Editorial Director

Dummies Trade Press: Kathleen A. Welton, Vice President and Publisher; Kevin Thornton, Acquisitions Manager

IDG Books Production for Dummies Press: Michael R. Britton, Vice President of Production and Creative Services; Cindy L. Phipps, Manager of Project Coordination, Production Proofreading, and Indexing; Kathie S. Schutte, Supervisor of Page Layout; Shelley Lea, Supervisor of Graphics and Design; Debbie J. Gates, Production Systems Specialist; Robert Springer, Supervisor of Proofreading; Debbie Stailey, Special Projects Coordinator; Tony Augsburger, Supervisor of Reprints and Bluelines

Dummies Packaging and Book Design: Robin Seaman, Creative Director; Kavish + Kavish, Cover Design

♦

The publisher would like to give special thanks to Patrick J. McGovern, without whom this book would not have been possible.

♦

Contents at a Glance

Cartoons at a Glance

By Rich Tennant

page 249

page 159

page 7

page 285

page 65

Fax: 978-546-7747 • E-mail: the5wave@tiac.net

Table of Contents

Introduction

● ●

*T*he Internet. It sometimes seems that the entire digital revolution boils down to those two words. The Internet has garnered so much hype for a few main reasons:

- ✔ It's a tremendous information source.
- ✔ It's a great community (people) resource.
- ✔ Almost everything online is free.
- ✔ Anybody can contribute to it.

It's a winning combination: informative, social, affordable, and inviting. Add to this the dazzling variety, the awesome exponential growth, and the Net's planet-shrinking capacity for making connections around the globe in a flash, and it's no wonder that you've given up the rest of your life to surf online. (I'm not the only one, am I?)

What effect has wild popularity had on the Internet? Utter chaos! You heard me — it's a mess. It's as if the whole planet discovered gardening at once. Things are sprouting all over; there are thousands of turnip beds, each a little different; tomatoes are here, there, and everywhere; and nobody knows who's going to do the weeding. The World Wide Web can get away with being chaotic because going from one of its garden plots (sites) to another is as easy as a mouse click, whether the site is located down the street or on another continent. This has led to an entire culture of browsing — people sitting at home into the night, clicking their way around the world and back again, gleaning information, meeting people, looking at pictures, listening to music, networking on message boards. Getting lost on the Web is such a delightful adventure that the disorganization is almost an advantage.

Until, that is, you want to find something fast. Or until you get sick of surfing and are ready for the Internet to become practical and useful. The Internet is an astounding resource of information, software, and people. But you need tools to search it effectively. Two kinds of tools are available:

- ✔ Online tools, such as directories and search engines
- ✔ Tools of understanding

This book gives you tools of understanding to make the most of directories and search engines.

About This Book

Internet Searching For Dummies gives you searching alternatives and tells you how to use them in detail. In these pages, you can discover which of the online searching services are currently the best, where they're located, and how their advanced features work. You may be asking yourself "But isn't Internet searching easy?" The answer is: yes and no. At the simplest level, using a Web directory or entering a keyword in a search engine is easy if you've been online before. You may not get satisfactory results, however, by taking only the simplest steps. If the Internet remains an unwieldy, impenetrable resource, you may get discouraged about using it at all.

My goal is to guide you step by step through search operations from the easy to the more complicated (and rewarding), giving you sound searching principles in the process. Furthermore, I want this book to be practical in a different way. Not only does it show you different directories and search engines, but the chapters in Part III, called "Embarking on Search Expeditions," show you how to attain typical search goals by using *all* the online tools that you'll be reading about. You discover how Internet searching works on two levels: First you look at the online tools individually, and then you conduct searches using all those tools.

As you explore Internet searching, you discover some online help when you have a question. Each directory and search engine (at least, the ones covered in this book) offers some explanations about its features and requirements. But, like much help (also called *documentation*) in the computer world, these explanations assume a certain amount of experience, or even expertise, on the user's part. This book assumes nothing of the sort! My hope is that you fall back on this book for rock-solid, start-at-the-beginning-please, take-it-slow-and-don't-rush-me explanations of how Internet searching works.

To top it off, I've thrown in many self-serving jokes (I'll do anything for a cheap laugh) to remind you that all this is supposed to be *fun!*

Conventions Used in This Book

Normally, I don't like conventions. Thousands of people all stuffed into one giant room, noisy displays, bad food. . . . Oh, sorry, wrong type of convention. This book uses certain typefaces and other layout properties to indicate particular things that appear on your screen. To make it easy to follow along with the book online, I've been consistent with these conventions. Consistent conventions create continuous clarity. (That's an old Swahili proverb.)

URLs (Uniform Resource Locators) — the addresses of Web pages — are indicated with this kind of type:

```
www.webpage.com
```

Sometimes I show really long addresses, like this:

```
www.careerpath.com/cp/owa/cp_ads_ocs.display_keyword_
        search?session_id=&status=
```

Each successive chunk of the Web address indicates a deeper level of the Web site. If you have trouble getting to an individual Web site, drop the last chunk or two of the address. (The chunks are delineated by slashes.) You should end up at a screen that allows you to get to the desired screen by simply clicking a button or two.

Whenever I refer to hypertext, whether a single word or a phrase, it appears like this: <u>This is a hypertext link</u> (just as it appears on your screen, except without the colors).

From time to time I refer to keywords that can be entered into search engines. Whenever I give an example of such a keyword, it appears like this: *keyword*. (How's that for an imaginative example? Thank you very much.)

When I introduce a new term for the first time, I *italicize* it to get your attention and to reassure you that there's no reason you should know what it means.

Foolish Assumptions

Who do I think you are? You're no dummy, regardless of the cute title slapped on the cover of this book. You may *feel* like a dummy sometimes when trying to understand the intricacies of computers, but that's not your fault. Most computer stuff is badly explained, without regard for the questions that occur to a smart beginner. If you've bought this book, you have some interest in taming the Internet, which is an ambitious and intelligent goal.

This book has a lot to offer beginners, of course, but it also has a thing or three to teach Internet veterans. In fact, I discovered quite a bit myself while writing it. If you don't yet have an online account and don't enjoy computer access to the Internet, you won't be able to follow along with the instructions in this book. If you're planning to get on the Net soon, this book prepares you with background to help cut through the online jungle. If you're already venturing online, you're set — you can start using these pages immediately. And if you are a confident Internet searcher already, you're bound to find some advanced Net-searching features that you didn't know about and some great sites that you haven't bookmarked yet.

Do you know anyone who complains about how hard it is to find things on the Web? Giving this book to that person is a good way of saying, "You're *not* a dummy!"

How to Read This Book

The best way to read this book is with one copy in each hand and another on the shelf in case you spill coffee on the others. But if that seems extreme, just having one near the computer will do. This book is a reference companion, not a novel. Don't try to read it from cover to cover — it'll only make you dizzy and boring at parties. All the chapters are self-contained — if something in another chapter is helpful, the chapter you're in tells you where to turn in the book. You can surf the book like surfing the Web, in fact, and still pick up a lot. But the best advice is to look at the Table of Contents, choose a chapter that strikes your interest, and start your explorations there.

I've divided the book into big chunks called *parts.* The Pulitzer committee is considering giving me an award for such an evocative name. In this section, I tell you what's in the parts.

Part I: Searching with Directories and Keywords

Part I is where you hear about online megadirectories that attempt to organize the entire World Wide Web. A few major, seriously ambitious directory systems exist that work daily to catalog the Web's growth, impossible though that may seem. I focus my descriptions and instructions on a few of the most popular and comprehensive directories. Each directory is different, but they all have similarities, and the first two chapters in this part tell you how to cope with their differences and likenesses.

Chapters 3 and 4 describe how keywords work. Keywords work with search engines — the workhorses of the Internet that are sometimes attached to directories. Keywords are hints you give the search engine to find what you want. However, because search engines are rather stupid, despite their hardworking nature, using keywords to the best result is a tricky matter. It's easy to get started, but finding out the tricks and complexities of keywords takes a couple of chapters to describe.

Part II: Starting Up the Search Engines

The chapters in Part II detail the features and lurking complexities of individual search engines (as they're called), such as Lycos, HotBot, Excite, InfoSeek, AltaVista, and others that you may have heard of and even visited. The chapter on Deja News walks you through the process of searching the Usenet newsgroups, which is incredibly useful, often overlooked, and can even be lots of fun. Finally, a roundup chapter brings you up to speed with a few other keyword sites that don't get as much publicity but are still pretty darn useful.

Part III: Embarking on Search Expeditions

Go straight to Part III if you know how to use keywords and directories and you're eager to find Web sites on certain subjects. This part contains chapters on finding information about money, health, education, software, and current events. These chapters show you how to put together a whole repertoire of searching techniques to zero in on a subject. Each chapter tells you how to use directories, keywords, and Usenet newsgroups to uncover good sites, and even points you toward the best Web locations in each field. Chapter 17 explains how to find people — perhaps the greatest resource the Web has to offer.

Part IV: The Part of Tens

Don't you love lists? I do. But don't confuse the lists in the Part of Tens with top-ten lists because they're not rated in any way. These chapters just contain collections of tips and sites that I want you to know about. Browse through them when you're looking for ideas, or to glean new locations if you get bored during a Web session, or when you get tired of staring at your screen saver, or for no reason whatsoever.

Part V: Appendixes

After the chapters were finished, I was still itching to put in additional information that I think is useful. Appendix A describes how to choose a Web browser.

Internet Searching For Dummies has a Frisbee attached to it! Appendix B tells you what to expect from the Frisbee . . . oh, wait — sorry, that's a CD-ROM. Now, in addition to simply reading about searching the Web, you can boot up software tools from the CD-ROM that actually help you do it. Don't throw the CD-ROM through the air. It isn't a toy. Besides, it has lousy stability and doesn't float well.

Icons Used in This Book

Because I can't stand next to you waving my arms every time you use this book, I use icons to get your attention.

This icon appears whenever a paragraph is trying to awaken your inner nerd. It notifies you that I have flaunted the geekish side of my nature by degenerating into techno-babble. For your own protection, try to avoid all such paragraphs.

If you don't heed the information associated with this icon, I may have to send you e-mailed reprimands. The Web is not a dangerous place, but these warnings let you know that you may waste your time with something or complicate your session unnecessarily.

I've stuffed this book with tips worth their weight in gold. Of course, they don't weigh anything. Still, you may find them useful. If not, it's time to send *me* e-mailed reprimands.

This icon means . . . umm . . . well, I don't recall *what* it means. But it probably has something to do with reminding you of an important point.

Where to Go from Here

I may live much of my life on the Web, but I'm a real person (at least, my computer thinks so). And I love getting mail of the electronic persuasion (e-mail). Fire up your modem, boot up your software, visit my Web site, and click the e-mail link to say hello at this site:

```
www.bradhill.com
```

In the meantime, happy searching, and may you always find the unexpected jewel.

Part I
Searching with Directories and Keywords

The 5th Wave — By Rich Tennant

"From now on, let's confine our exploration of ancient Egypt to the computer program."

In this part . . .

Mapping the vast terrain of the Internet is a task best left to fearless explorers. Fortunately, brave cyber-cartographers have stepped forward to meet the challenge. These hardy individuals have created Web directory services that can chart your way through the tangled growth of the ever-expanding Internet.

This part introduces you to the main Internet directories — but before those introductions, the first chapter gives you a general tutorial about what directories are, how they work, why they're useful, and what you should wear when using them. Just kidding about that last part.

You're about to discover the locations, differences, similarities, and quirks of some of the most useful destinations in cyberspace: Internet directories.

Chapter 1

Getting the Big Picture

· ·

· ·

*I*magine that you're an archaeologist and you need to travel to a foreign country for research. (If you really are an archaeologist, substitute an even more glamorous scenario.) To locate the site of your dig, you use a series of maps. First, you use a global atlas to situate the country of your destination in an international context. Then you use a map of the country to acquaint yourself with regions, geographical features, and main highways. To further narrow the perspective, you use a local map to familiarize yourself with the roadways and towns of the area. A town map may come into play, if it exists, to identify all the streets, shops, and local attributes.

Locating something on the Internet can prove as complex as locating a certain spot in any country. With either destination, maps help you find your way around. This chapter describes how the maps of the Internet — the directories — work. Every Internet directory is different, and other chapters explore those differences. Here, you find out how all directories work, and gain a few tips for using them well.

Directories: Your Internet Maps

The Internet has attained popularity as an environment for browsing and surfing. Many people think of the World Wide Web (a portion of the Internet) as a place of unfocused wandering, following trails of information from one Web page to another. The popular term *Web surfing* implies a superficial, ride-the-crest approach to the Internet. The Web's easy point-and-click hyperlinks are conducive to information grazing. But those same user-friendly hyperlinks make power searching for information easier than it has ever been. The Web browser, most people's interface to the Internet, is an all-purpose vehicle for recreation and research. As a result, searching the Internet can be both productive and fun as all get-out.

With a few well-directed clicks of the mouse, your Web browser delivers maps to virtually everything on the Internet. These Web maps are called *directories* (not to be confused with *indexes, crawlers, search engines, spiders, robots,* or other unsavory online creatures that you don't need to deal with right now). Like the maps used by the imaginary archaeologist, some directories cover broader areas than others. Some serve as global Web atlases and others consolidate information about certain local areas on the Internet.

Most Internet directories concentrate on Web sites, and are known as *Web directories*, appropriately enough. Usenet newsgroups may or may not appear in Web directories. (See the sidebar titled "The Internet and the Web: Not quite the same" for a description of Usenet newsgroups.) When they do, something special happens if you click on a link to a Usenet newsgroup. Assuming you have a fully installed Web browser suite (Appendix A explains what that means), the newsgroup reader window pops open and takes you to that newsgroup. (If that window is already open, it automatically moves to the front of your screen.)

Directories work like a restaurant menu that divides dishes into soups, appetizers, salads, entrees, and (save room for it!) desserts. Within these meal categories, you can find selections of specific dishes. In the same way, Web directories start with broad topics and then enable you to click your way deeper into each topic, finding more specialized subjects. Then you can go deeper still until the directory points you towards exactly the type of information you need. You can get an idea of how directories work by visiting Yahoo!, one of the most popular directories and certainly the directory with the happiest name. You can get there by typing this World Wide Web address (called a *URL*, or *Uniform Resource Locator*):

```
www.yahoo.com
```

After you use a directory to reach a site of interest, you can use specialized tools to dig for more information. Web directories have more levels than restaurant menus — and you don't have to call ahead for a reservation. (Does that mean people are hungrier for information than for food?)

Web directories are the best place to begin searching the World Wide Web. Keep the following points in mind about Web directories:

- Many Web directories exist for searching the Net.
- Each Web directory differs from the other directories.
- Each Web directory is accurate in its own way.

The Internet and the Web: Not quite the same

Many people equate the Internet with the World Wide Web. This is understandable because the Web has received such huge publicity, for good and bad, since its inception. In truth, the Internet is much larger than the Web.

The World Wide Web is a software invention that enables people and companies to share text and pictures over the Internet. Basically, the Web is an enormous (and growing) collection of computer files (called Web pages) that link to each other when you use a program called a Web browser to view them on your screen. These Web pages live on computers all over the world and contain hyperlinks. A *hyperlink* can be a word, a group of words, a picture, or a part of a picture. When you click a hyperlink, it tells your Web browser to display another Web page, gives the browser the location of that page (which you see embedded in the hyperlink), and sends you off to your new destination.

The World Wide Web makes up just part of the Internet. The Internet is a whole bunch (millions, actually) of computers called *servers* that are connected by telephone lines. It's a planetary network of computer systems. This global network wasn't built according to any grand design; it just evolved over time, and crosses national boundaries as easily as a phone call does.

The Internet also includes *Usenet newsgroups,* which are electronic bulletin boards for conducting discussions by means of typed and posted messages. (You can find about 20,000 newsgroups on the Internet!) The Internet also includes file libraries, where people store software and texts, called *FTP sites.* (FTP stands for File Transfer Protocol, but forget I said that.) The final big part of the Internet is e-mail, the most-used feature of the whole online realm.

As mentioned, you view Web sites through a piece of software called a *Web browser.* (See Appendix A for a survey of browser choices.) The browser interprets the special codes that make up Web page files and displays those pages on your screen in an attractive way. It also knows exactly what to do when you click a hyperlink. (You click hyperlinks to get around on the Web.) The browser acts like a magic carpet that takes you right to the Web location embedded in the hyperlink you just clicked, whether the server for the destination page sits across town or on the next continent. The most popular Web browsers are actually *software suites,* meaning they contain sibling programs for viewing Usenet newsgroups and e-mail and sometimes for performing more obscure Internet functions. (Appendix A fills in the gaps.)

If you're on the Web, you hear a lot about Web sites. You also hear the term *home page.* In the early days of the Web, some people were taking advantage of the unrestricted Internet by putting up a Web page describing personal interests and linking to favorite locations on the brand new World Wide Web. These home-grown efforts were called *home pages* because they represented the online home of their authors. Then people quickly learned how to create several related pages and link them together with the Web's hyperlinks. Home pages were suddenly more than one page, and everyone began referring to multipage destinations on the Web as *sites.* (You can think of a site as any location on the Web, however, even if it's only one page.) Then corporations got involved, and you can imagine what happened. Big isn't the word. Some corporate Web sites are humongous affairs with hundreds — even thousands — of pages. However, the term home page still sometimes indicates the main, front page of such megasites. I use *home page* in this book to refer to the first, main page of Web search engines.

The Internet is an enormous, constantly changing, ever-growing, continually evolving, deeply complex living landscape of information and resources that is virtually impossible to catalog exhaustively. Each Internet directory takes its own approach to what is worth searching for — and each approach is legitimate, just as several newspapers may have different editorial perspectives on the news. After sampling many directories, you may settle on some favorites and return to them habitually to chart your searches. Despite their differences in content, all Web directories operate pretty much the same way.

Can a Web directory ever be a complete map of everything on the World Wide Web? Probably not, for a few reasons. First, the Web grows and expands every hour. Web directories add new Web pages to their databases pretty quickly, but accurately indexing a constantly shifting situation presents a difficult task. (The task resembles taking a picture of a moving object.) Also, no central clearinghouse exists for new Web pages. Anyone can put a page on the Web, but no one has to register a page. A directory does not necessarily find new pages on its own, if nobody manually enters it into the directory (which many directories enable you to do).

Directories versus search engines

In my quest to eliminate all possible confusion from the Web searching process, I want to introduce you to a V.I.D. — a Very Important Distinction. I want to make a VID between a directory and a search engine. Directories and search engines are both Web-searching features, and this book covers both of them at great length. Stands to reason, then, that you should know what these two things are, right?

Directories provide maps of the World Wide Web. Their multilevel structures enable you to investigate the Web sites available in both broad and finely tuned categories, as I describe in this chapter. Web directories are meant to be browsed and are organized coherently to make browsing easy and productive.

Search engines work differently, allowing you to type in keywords that indicate what you're trying to find. The engine searches and displays the results as a list of hyperlinks to Web sites that match your search request. *Keywords* are summary words that represent your search goal. (Chapters 3 and 4 explain keywords at such length that you may be sorry I brought them up.)

Now here's the tricky part. Web directories may contain search engines, but not necessarily. By the same token, search engines don't necessarily come with directories. (Did you follow that?)

A search engine without a directory is like a library without a card catalog. But imagine if such a library had workers who scurried around finding books related to what you need: That's what a search engine does. A directory without a search engine, on the other hand, is like a library with no librarians. The stacks are well-organized, but you're on your own.

Another reason why directories aren't a complete map of all existing Web sites is that some directories deliberately try *not* to be complete! These directories, such as Excite and Lycos (which you can read about in Chapter 2) edit their directories according to quality standards, so they present only approved sites. Such an editorial policy is for your benefit, when you don't want to face enormous menus of thousands of Web sites on a particular topic. When you want a more complete directory, you can always turn to Yahoo! (which is also described in Chapter 2).

Viewing a Directory Page

A Web directory consists of many levels. The top level gives you the broadest overview of the Internet; it provides you with the global atlas. Web directories don't look very maplike, however, when it comes to graphics. Rather than relying on pictures of the cyberterrain, most directory pages basically offer a glorified list. Not very glitzy but definitely useful. On the Web, where the local mode of transportation is a mouse riding on a hyperlink, these lists are charged and ready to take you places. To check out a typical top-level directory page, go to this address:

```
a2z.lycos.com
```

Web directories work like any other Web page. *Live* (hyperlinked) words are underlined, and they appear in a different color than the color of the other text on the screen. When you position the mouse cursor over one of these words, the cursor changes shape (usually from an arrow to a pointing finger). When you click your mouse button, the Web directory interacts with your Web browser to show you a new page of directory options.

Everybody seems hyper about *hyper* words: *hyperlink, hypertext, hyperspace* — well, *hyperspace* has nothing to do with the Web. But hyperlinks and hypertext have everything to do with the Web. Without them, the Web isn't much of anything at all. Anytime your mouse cursor changes to a pointing finger when resting on a screen object, whether a picture or a word, the object is a hyperlink. Hyperlinks that are words can be called *hypertext.* Several years ago, before there were many pictures (graphics) on computer screens, hypertext was the only kind of hyperlink. Now, with all the graphics in multimedia computing, *hyperlink* is a common term, and it includes text links as well as pictorial links. In this book, I refer to all Web links as either *hyperlinks* or simply *links.*

You find the top-level directory page always divided into the widest, most general possible subject areas. Usually about 12 to 15 of these subjects appear — for example, entertainment, computers, government, and sports — each linked to a second directory level (on a separate page) that divides that topic into subtopics.

Some top-level categories appear in virtually all Web directories. The following topics make up the global attractions of the big online map:

- ✔ **Business:** This top-page link, which is sometimes called Money or Finance, leads to online brokerages, stock market information, financial software download sites, and all kinds of other business-related Internet sites.

- ✔ **Computers:** One single common denominator links every person who has ever logged into a Web directory: They have all used a computer or some computing device. Not surprisingly, you can find a great deal of computer-related information on the World Wide Web.

- ✔ **Current Events:** This category may also be called Politics, World, or News. Whatever it's called, the category enables you to link your way to the kind of current news information you see in the front section of a newspaper.

- ✔ **Entertainment:** Because entertainment subjects, especially movies, music, and television, make up many of the most popular sites in the online universe, you almost always find this category in the top-menu.

- ✔ **Sports:** Fan sites and sports news services are the two most common types of Web sites in this category. Most directories separate sports from general news in the top level of a Web directory.

Directories usually contain other main topics as well. The subjects for these topics depend on how the particular directory organizes its links to the Web.

Venturing Downward

After you make a top-level selection by clicking a hyperlink, you begin a process known as *drilling down* through the directory levels. In other words, you trade in your global atlas for local maps.

After clicking a top-level topic link, the next page to appear on your screen looks similar to the top-level page, though perhaps much larger and with more choices. Differences in design between the various directory services become apparent at lower directory levels.

In some cases, the second page looks identical to the first, with a short list of subcategories. Other sites provide that short list, but in addition, list many hyperlinks that jump to specific Web locations outside the directory. Providing these outside links in the second directory level cuts to the chase in many situations. You may find a site of interest from the second level, or you may need to drill down to lower levels before leaving the directory to visit specific sites.

As you continue delving deeper into your chosen topic, the pages contain more links to outside Web sites, and the menu selections within the directory become fewer as your search becomes more specific. To see how this process works, imagine a directory search that takes you four levels down before you leave the directory to explore some actual Web pages. Here's an overview of what the levels offer. (Feel free to follow along with your Web browser.)

✔ **Top level:** You log into the Yahoo! directory (one of the most popular Web directories, found at the following address) to find some Web pages of movie actors:

www.yahoo.com

The Yahoo! top page contains a general menu of 14 subject categories (Figure 1-1 shows some of them). You click <u>Entertainment</u>, and you go to the second level.

✔ **Second level:** Here, the directory splits the broad Entertainment topic into more than 25 subtopic links (see Figure 1-2), including <u>Comics and Animation</u>, <u>Radio</u>, <u>Television</u>, and the one you're interested in, <u>Movies and Film</u>. Pleased by your progress, you click the <u>Movies and Film</u> hyperlink.

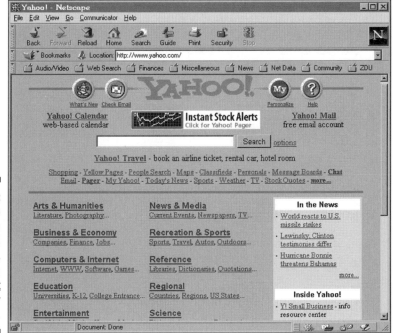

Figure 1-1:
The top level of the Yahoo! directory, showing <u>Entertainment</u> as a major link.

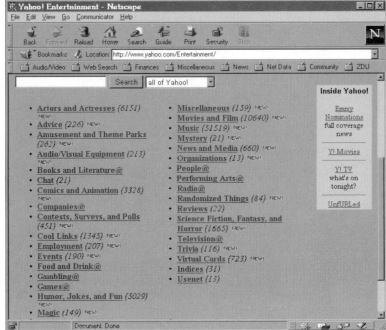

Figure 1-2:
The second
level of a
Yahoo!
directory
search for
movie
actors.

✔ **Third level:** At this level, the subject splinters into topical links such as Film Schools, Home Video, Reviews, Screenplays, Studios, and Actors and Actresses. Furthermore, the page has a second section below these divisions that lists hyperlinks to Web pages outside the directory you're using (see Figure 1-3). These links include such intriguing names as Cinemania, Film.com, Hollywood Online, and the Internet Movie Database. Still, they don't include the pages for the actors and actresses you want to find. Undeterred, you go back up to the top of the third-level page and click Actors and Actresses.

✔ **Fourth level:** Because the complete list of Internet sites about actors and actresses is intimidatingly long, the fourth-level page (Figure 1-4) gives you ways of breaking it down into manageable chunks. The alphabetical guide invites you to click the initial of an actor's last name, if you're searching for a particular actor. If you'd rather browse the complete list, click the Complete Listing link — it may take a minute to load the whole thing into your browser.

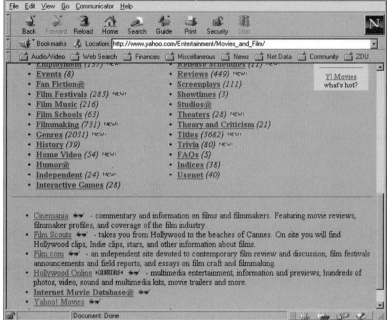

Figure 1-3:
A third-level
page of the
Yahoo!
Entertainment
directory,
showing
subtopics
and page
links.

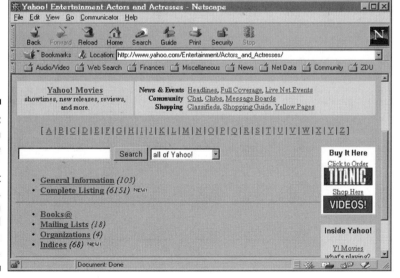

Figure 1-4:
A fourth
level in the
Yahoo!
Entertainment
directory,
offering an
alphabetical
breakdown
of sites.

✔ **Fifth level:** Assuming for the moment that this is a search for Internet pages about Sean Connery, the resilient, durable, ex-007 British actor, you clicked the C̲ alphabetical listing up at level four. You now see a long list of Web sites about actors and actresses whose last name begins with C, including Sean Connery (Figure 1-5). The link to Sean Connery, however, doesn't go outside the directory — that's because so many Sean Connery pages exist that he has his own Yahoo! directory page. (That's what the little @ means in the Yahoo! directory listing.) So you must click the <u>Connery, Sean@</u> link to go down one more level.

✔ **Sixth level:** Bingo! As you can see in Figure 1-6, Sean Connery has at least a dozen Web sites devoted to him, and you can link to them from this level.

How many levels do directories have? The number depends on the directory. Some descend to as many as eight levels below the top page. The number also depends on the category you started with. In some cases, depending on the specific service and the subject, only two or three levels can plumb a subject's depth. Some services give an indication of what's ahead by placing numbers next to their menu selections. For example, Yahoo! recently grouped 10,640 listings under the <u>Movies and Films</u> category (the number changes frequently); on the same page, the <u>Reviews</u> link promises only 22 items. So you know you have a lot of browsing ahead of you in the first case, but you're near the end of the road in the second.

Figure 1-5:
You've
found Sean
Connery,
and clicking
his name
displays a
page of his
many site
links.

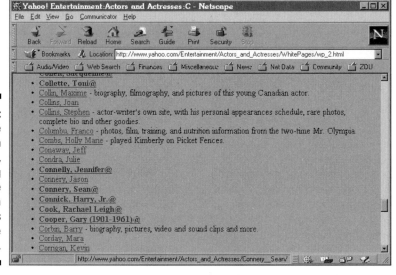

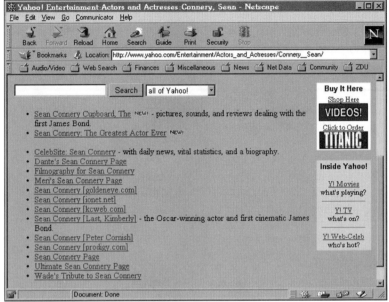

Figure 1-6:
Finally, links
to several
sites about
Sean
Connery.

Basic Lessons in Using Directories

Directories seem simple to use, and in fact they are. That's one thing that makes them so appealing — anyone able to use a mouse can begin making sense of the Internet through one of its directories. What's that? You want to be a power-user of Web directories? I can't promise unearthly directory skills, but the following tips may at least help you avoid potential tangles.

Choosing the right map

It stands to reason that if you're traveling to Spain, a map of Africa won't help you much. By the same token, if you're looking for online information about your favorite baseball team, you won't get far by choosing the Science category of your favorite Web directory. That much is obvious. But not all selections are so clear cut. For example, if you're searching for financial investment software, should you follow the <u>Business/Investments</u> or <u>Computers/Software</u> directory path? In many cases, the quickest method is to simply dive in and try all the possibilities. But I want to give you a few guidelines so that you can avoid dealing with typical categorization confusion. Remember — each Web directory differs from the others, and each one groups topics according to its own editorial viewpoint.

Entertainment versus Arts

Entertainment topics tend to be popular show-business subjects that change daily. Entertainment topics include items about movies, television, actors, humor, radio, and theater. Art subjects are usually more static and refined, such as photography, painting, sculpture, architecture, dance, museums, and drama. Intellectual and spiritual arts are sometimes represented by philosophy and religion links. Sometimes you can find artistic spinoffs, such as science fiction (literature) and pop music, on the Entertainment directory pages.

Government versus World Affairs versus Social Sciences

The Government, World Affairs, and Social Sciences category types often have quite a bit of overlap, and their subtopics vary in each directory service. Government categories usually list political, international, law, military, and official Unites States Government pages, such as the page for the Internal Revenue Service. World Affairs generally refers to regional information, almanacs, cultural sites, and language resources. Choices for the Social Sciences link you to advocacy sites, social services locations, community organizations, and minority affairs issues.

Social Sciences versus Society and Culture

When the Social Sciences category and the Society and Culture category appear in the same Web directory, the directory divides the categories by whether their subtopics are more scientific or more cultural. Under Social Sciences, you're likely to find humanities, economics, regional studies, political science, gender studies, and anthropology. Society and Culture links can include civil rights, environmental concerns, sexual issues, race relations, and abortion platforms.

Reference versus Regional

The Reference and Regional top-level categories can contain some topic overlap, thanks to the many statistical sites often found in the Regional area. In particular, almanac-style Web pages devoted to countries or states can include lists and numbers that you may normally associate with the Reference category.

Elusive topics

Some subjects act like hinges between two general topics. They serve both equally well. When a directory cross-references these hinge subjects, all is well, because the topics appear under two or more topics and all their links are available to you whichever place you look. In other cases, it can be a flummoxing experience to search in vain for a topic that you think should fit in the category you've chosen. Table 1-1 shows some of these annoyingly flexible topics, with suggestions as to where they may be lurking. Remember, the names of the broad categories that you see here only approximate the actual words that appear in various Web directory menus.

Table 1-1	Tips for Searching Web Pages for Elusive Topics	
If You're Looking for . . .	*And It Isn't Here . . .*	*Try Here*
Cyberculture	Society & Culture	Computers
History	Society	Science
Computer Science	Computers	Science
Information Technology	Science	Computers
Medicine (all kinds)	Science	Health
Fitness	Health	Society & Culture
Sexuality	Society & Culture	Health & Medicine
Law	Government	Social Sciences
Politics	Social Sciences	Government or News
Humor	Entertainment	Society & Culture
Multimedia	Computers	Entertainment
Online Courses	Education	Computers-Internet
Teaching	Education	Social Sciences
Economics	Business	Social Sciences
Humanities	Social Sciences	Arts
Web Marketing	Business	Computers-Internet

Useful (maybe) comparisons

Web directories operate like telescopes: The more you extend a directory, the more magnified the detail. As you prowl more deeply into the directory levels of any particular search, you see the possibilities of your topic in greater detail. The Web often proves a great place for discovering more than you expected. (It's equally good for wasting more time than you thought possible.)

You also can think of directories as a series of combs. Imagine raking smooth a sand trap on a golf course. If you start with a gardener's rake with widely spaced prongs, you create a design of lines in the sand, and you get a very general, unrefined smoothing effect. Switching to a hand rake with smaller spaces between its prongs smoothes the sand more finely, affecting more of the actual grains. Finally, using a hair comb (pretty far-fetched for this task, of course) creates a very finely groomed effect, aligning almost every grain of sand. In the same way, descending to the most specific directory level for any topic reveals, along the way, the thousands of links to other sites. Drilling deeply into a directory is a great way to comb through the Internet.

Bookmarking directory levels

Don't lose track of your landmarks! Almost all Web browsers include a bookmark (or favorites) feature with which you can add any page to a list with a single mouse click. Then you can return to that page during any session just by clicking its place in the bookmark list.

If you were exploring a new forest, you'd want to make note of the major trees, boulders, and other prominent landmarks around which your wanderings hinge. When drilling down through a directory, you may find the temptation to wander through some miscellaneous links irresistible. If, for example, you're searching for suitable and entertaining Web sites to share with your children, you may be distracted by a <u>Magazines</u> link that's on the same directory page as children's entertainment. You follow that link. Before you know it, your kids' bedtime approaches and you're still browsing the cyberversion of your favorite newsmagazine. Not a problem, provided you bookmarked the page from which you went on your tangent (and provided you have patient kids).

Here's the rule: Every time you enter a Web directory page that has useful links, bookmark it immediately. Don't let yourself think, "I'll just follow one link and then come right back" — the famous last words of every Net surfer. Bookmark it first and then play.

And now we pause . . .

. . . for a commercial message? Yes, it's true. You encounter advertising in Web directories. After all, some of these directories are commercial enterprises; yet they offer their service to you for free. Advertising pays their bills, and these ads seem to assume a higher profile every day. They take the form of graphical hyperlinks. Often the hyperlink features a button that, when clicked, takes you to the sponsor's Web site. Follow these links as your curiosity dictates, and use the Back button to return to your search.

Retracing your steps with the Back button

All Web browsers have a Back button that enables you to retrace your hypersteps one link at a time. Clicking it returns you to the previous Web page of your session.

The Back button has a limit to how many steps backward it takes you, and that limit is defined by the size of the memory buffer (sometimes called a memory cache) that your browser has set up in your computer. Use the Options or Preferences menu of your browser to increase or decrease the buffer size. The buffer size determines the number of Web pages stored for backtracking.

Experienced users of Web directories make good use of the Back button as part of their searching style. As you drill down through the directory levels, you always leave a trail, as if you were unrolling a long piece of string. Because many directory searches are experimental, you can use the Back button often to follow that string back to the page from which you started so that you can try a different direction. This type of Web searching resembles a dog in the woods — dashing down each hyperlink path, sniffing out information, and then returning to the main path to try new links. Remembering to use the Back button gives you the freedom to experiment with new paths without worrying about getting lost or wasting time starting from scratch at each dead end.

Don't confuse advertising links with actual directory content. Advertising links aren't part of the informational lists you browse, though they are sometimes related to them — just as Saturday-morning cartoon ads on television are sometimes related to the cartoon characters. Their top position on the page, plus distinctive graphics presentation (often a company logo and tagline), give them away.

Chapter 2

Using Specific Internet Directories

- -

- -

*H*aving just one, big, all-inclusive Internet directory would make searching for things on the Web a lot easier. After all, you need only one phone book and one map for your town. But the Web is different from a physical location in two important ways:

> ✔ The Web grows and changes so rapidly that a single directory can't keep up with it comprehensively.

> ✔ The Web doesn't require users to register descriptions of their Web sites with one central agency the way they register their phone number and address, for example, with a local phone company. So each directory compiles its listing differently than other directories.

A directory can approach cataloging Web sites in various ways. Companies have formed to tackle this challenge, and the results differ from one directory to another. Confusing? When you search for information, the lack of a central authoritative directory may seem inconvenient, but the situation presents you with more opportunities to find what you're looking for.

Internet directories compete with each other, which is usually good news for the consumer. The result is a better online experience and the likelihood of finding things of interest with minimum hassle. The trick is to find your way around the biggest, most comprehensive Net directories and become familiar with their individual characteristics. This chapter introduces you to the most popular directories.

Choices, Choices

Having multiple directory services means you work a little harder to find things, but the variety offers the following advantages.

✔ Each Web directory uses different methods for gathering its contents, so the sites you can link to from each directory differ. You can sometimes find an unexpected link that reveals a location you never would have thought to look for, but are glad that you stumbled across. The more directories you try, the better chance you have for serendipitous findings.

✔ Web directories categorize their content differently. If you drill down through the Entertainment topic of three Web directories, you find not only links to different Web sites about entertainment subjects (no surprise, because many thousands exist) but also different subtopics of Entertainment.

✔ Directories, though similar in appearance, have unique ways of displaying their menus and pages, just as different newspapers format the news in individual ways. You may just feel at home in one directory, simply because of its appearance and page design.

✔ As Web directories evolve into more complete services, they add a variety of useful features. Some offer reviews of their linked sites. Others group new additions together for an easy overview of what's new. Directories may include editorial content in the form of articles and tutorials to give you a well-rounded searching experience.

Yahoo!

I'm not just being jubilant. Yahoo! (complete with exclamation point) is the name of a Web directory. In fact, Yahoo!, the most famous and widely used directory, was one of the first to gain a reputation as a good Internet searching site. Venerability has hardly diminished its value — quite the contrary. Yahoo! is a dynamic, frequently updated, constantly evolving tool for helping you find stuff on the Web. Its address is

```
www.yahoo.com
```

Directory features

When you arrive at the main Yahoo! site, you see the top page of the directory, below the keyword entry form (Chapters 3 and 4 explain keywords). A glance of this top-level page gives you an overview of how Yahoo! categorizes sites on the Web (see Figure 2-1).

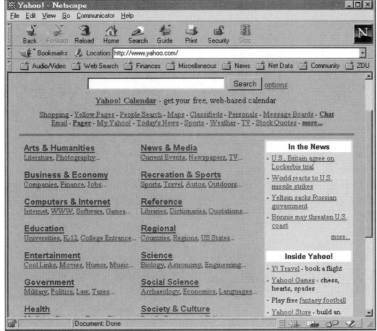

Yahoo! shortcuts

Like all the major Web directories, Yahoo! is a multilevel index of topics, with each level of each subject contained on an individual Web page. You drill through the levels by clicking hyperlinked menu items. Making your way through the levels isn't hard or particularly time-consuming, but if you do it a lot, you can feel the tedium of constantly shuffling up and down the levels. To save you from all this constant clicking, Yahoo! offers a shortcut from the top level to the third level in the largest categories.

A few subcategories immediately follow each of the main subject headings (you would find these same subcategories if you clicked your way to the second level in that heading). For example, the News & Media heading is followed by Current Events, Newspapers, and TV links, which are also found on the second level if you click the top-level News & Media heading. Clicking a subcategory directly from the top page carries you immediately to the content of its page, which you find on the third level.

Shortcuts exist only on the top Yahoo! page — but hey, you have to take what you can get.

An even faster way to search Web sites is using keywords. Yahoo!, and the other directories that I discuss in this chapter, provide keyword entry forms so that you can do a keyword search. I talk about using keywords and the entry forms in excruciating detail in Chapters 3 and 4.

Yahoo! indices

Taking the high road to arcane grammatical usage, Yahoo! spells this word *indices* instead of the more common *indexes*. Nevertheless, *indices* refers to collections of indexes that the Yahoo! staff has gathered under various subject headings as a reference service.

You can usually find a link for the Yahoo! indexes for a subject (sorry to be grammatically gauche, but *indices* sounds like a medical condition) on the second level of the directory. Click the <u>News & Media</u> subject heading and then look for the <u>Indices</u> link at the bottom of the subtopic list. After you click the <u>Indices</u> link, you see a page of reference links that lead to scads more links related to the category you've chosen. All these links may sound confusing, but the following steps outline how you would use one of these Indices. In this list, I start with the Government subject heading, but the procedure works the same no matter what subject you use as your starting point:

1. **On the top Yahoo! page, click the <u>Government</u> link.**

   A second-level page appears, listing subtopics for you to explore, plus the <u>Indices</u> link, which you find at the end of the subtopic list (see Figure 2-2).

2. **Click <u>Indices</u>, which is at the end of the subtopic list.**

   A third-level page appears, listing links to indexes outside the Yahoo! service (see Figure 2-3).

3. **Click any one of the links, such as <u>Government Resources on the Web</u>, to visit a Web site that lists *other* Web sites related to Government.**

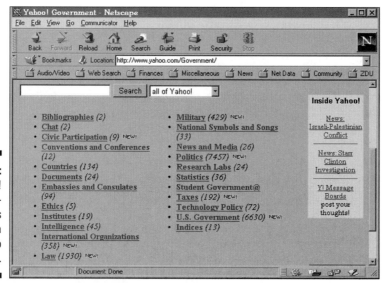

Figure 2-2:
All Yahoo!
second-
level pages
contain a
link to
indices.

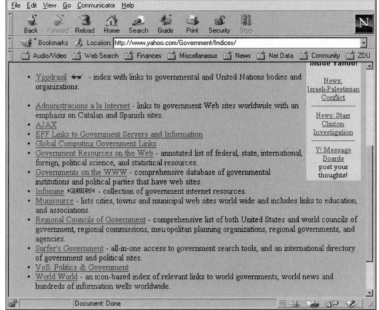

Figure 2-3:
The Yahoo!
Indices
pages list
Web sites
with more
links.

Added attractions

In the endless quest for excellence, popularity, and utter Web coolness, many Web directories offer extra services in addition to raw search potential. In fact, extra features often get more publicity than search features. Yahoo! is a leader in the extra features department, though its index and search tools remain the centerpiece. This section discusses the extras scattered around that main structure.

Yahooligans!

Yahooligans! is Yahoo! for kids. In an age when parents allow their children online with some trepidation, wondering what adult material they may stumble across, Yahoo! provides safe searching for children. Yahooligans! provides a risk-free kid zone in which every link has been reviewed and found acceptable for young surfers. Kids (and parents) can find their way to Yahooligans! with this address:

```
www.yahooligans.com
```

Yahooligans! obviously gears its top level for kids (see Figure 2-4). It shows broad directory topics aimed at a young audience. The content may differ, but the system works identically to the way the mother directory works, featuring shortcut links to the largest third-level topics.

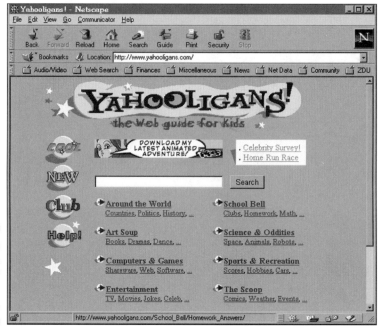

Figure 2-4:
The home
page of
Yahooligans!
for kids.

Yahooligans! sometimes uses games to turn directory searching into fun for kids, but the way you find things differs little from what you do in the adult directory. You find the multilevel directory structure in place here — just with different names and kid-appropriate links.

Yahooligans! and Yahoo! offer a text-only version (which you access by clicking a link at the bottom of either top-level directory page) for impatient kids of all ages who don't like waiting for graphics to appear.

If you're guiding your kids through the Internet experience, Club Yahooligans! is something worth leading them to. It's an area of Yahooligans! with games and special directory links, plus an e-mailed newsletter. Kids find out a lot about the Internet by joining Club Yahooligans!, including how to link to sites, register at a site, fill out on-screen forms, and receive an e-mail newsletter.

Yahoo! local directories

It has become clear over the last year or so: Yahoo! wants to dominate the world. It's not that Yahoo! wants to rule the world, but it apparently wants to map it on the Web, with directories geared to individual countries and United States cities. To date, Yahoo! has installed national directories for over a dozen countries. Regional U.S. directories include Atlanta, Austin, Boston, Chicago, Washington D.C., Dallas-Fort Worth, Los Angeles, New York, San Francisco, and Seattle.

The directory style for these regional directories remains the same as in the rest of Yahoo!, with a top-level selection of broad categories leading to lower levels of subtopics and specific sites. The difference is that everything relates to a region or a country. You can link to city maps, real estate information, local businesses, education resources, job listings, city (or national) sports and entertainment, and travel information.

A quick icon click takes you to the Regional news headlines, and the pages even have a collection of message boards for connecting with other Yahoo! visitors. Yahoo! divides these boards into the same topical groupings as the directory, so you can read (and post your own) messages on a city's best restaurants, the baseball teams in the area, or current issues. You can use the boards to look for a carpool, discuss stocks, or set your kids loose on the children's message area.

You can link to Yahoo! regional directories from the bottom of the Yahoo! home page. If you don't live in one of the preset cities, take advantage of the zip code entry form. Type in your zip code, press the Enter key, and watch a local directory appear on your screen. Although the range of content differs from one locale to another, in the best cases, these zip code directories are an outstanding blend of sports scores, local news, weather, yellow and white pages, and of course a Yahoo! directory of local Web sites.

Live Net Events

events.yahoo.com

Clicking the Live Net Events link on the bottom of the Yahoo! home page displays the Yahoo! Net Events page. Net Events are activities on the World Wide Web that happen live — that is, in real time. A regular, static Web page isn't an event. An event involves some kind of broadcast, conference, or chat experience in which many people can participate. The Yahoo! Net Events page provides a directory-style schedule of live happenings for the current day, with summaries, plus links to the sites that host the event (see Figure 2-5). Check Live Net Events when you're in the mood for a more participatory Web experience.

Some live events require Web browser plug-ins (utility programs that plug in to your browser program), so you can hear a broadcast or chat with other attendees. Many chat events require only a Java-capable browser, such as Microsoft Internet Explorer or Netscape Navigator (versions 3.0 or later).

Yahoo! Internet Life

Internet Life, an electronic magazine produced in cooperation with ZD-Net (the World Wide Web empire of Ziff-Davis Publishing), offers links to fresh, new, original Web sites. Yahoo! *Internet Life* is also a print magazine, and the two editions (print and Web) share lots of content. The content focuses on entertainment and fun on the Web. *Internet Life* offers zillions (that's an estimate) of links in broadly defined categories such as Health, Travel, Reference, and Nature, accompanied by editorial content from ZD-Net. *Internet Life* throws the sparse directory design out the window in favor of a lively, graphical approach complete with animated, moving icons.

You find the Internet Life link at the bottom of the top-level Yahoo! page, as well as on many other pages throughout the directory. If you're navigating your Web browser with the graphics turned off for speed, you'll need to turn them back on for this part of Yahoo! You can get to the magazine manually by using the following address:

```
www.zdnet.com/yil
```

Yahoo! Finances

One of Yahoo!'s major content areas corresponds with one of the most popular information topics on the Web: Money. Yahoo! Finance is covered in detail in Chapter 18, but if you would like an advance look, click the Stock Quotes link near the top of the home page, or go directly to this address:

```
quote.yahoo.com
```

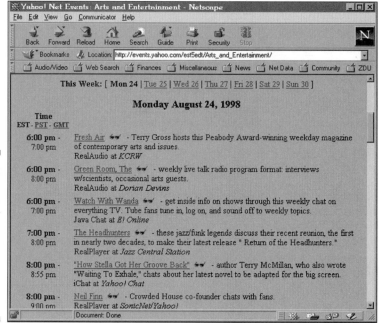

Figure 2-5:
The Yahoo!
Net Events
directory
page points
you to live
conferences
and
broadcasts
on the Web.

Yahoo! Shopping

If you enjoy buying products online, the Yahoo! Shopping area provides a good directory of Internet merchants, some of which you probably want to know about. If you're considering dipping your toe into online purchases, Yahoo! Shopping may tempt you to take the plunge. Click the Shopping link on the home page, or go directly to this address:

```
shopguide.yahoo.com
```

As you can see in Figure 2-6, the Shopping Guide is displayed in the usual directory format. Click any category to reach the second-level page, where a nifty feature called Comparison Shop resides. Comparison Shop invites you to type the name of a specific product that interests you (in the Books category, for example, you might type the title and author of a book), and a software robot presents a list of Web merchants that carry the product as well as a price list. This is computer database access for the empowered consumer! Take advantage of it.

Figure 2-6:
The Yahoo!
Shopping
Guide.
Lower
levels of the
directory
provide
comparison
shopping
features.

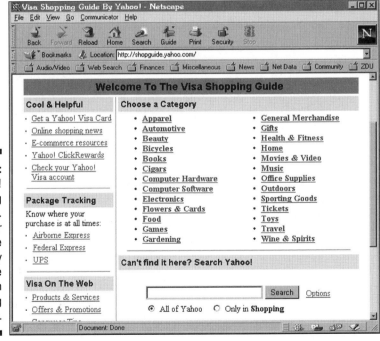

Lycos

Lycos is the most subjective of the major Internet directories. The well-known search site doesn't even try to offer a comprehensive directory of Web sites; instead, it attempts to evaluate sites in various ways and then presents high-quality sites in each subject category. Speaking of categories, Lycos organizes the Internet in some interesting ways. Get a look at the main subject heading of the Lycos directory at this address:

```
www.lycos.com
```

In its ranking of sites, the Lycos directory has a practical bent. It claims to offer links to the most popular ten percent of Web sites. (How it determines site popularity remains a company secret.) The directory's top level (see Figure 2-7) looks like a typical directory, but it holds a few category surprises:

- **Kids:** All the sites in this category are safe for young eyes.

- **Space/Sci-Fi:** From *Star Trek* to *X-Files,* this category pushes science fiction sites into the forefront.

- **Shopping:** Materialists rejoice! This topic gathers tons of money-draining links under categories such as Apparel, Flowers, Virtual Malls, Autos, Books, Sporting Goods, Entertainment, Gifts, and Travel.

- **Internet:** Although other directories bundle Internet information under the broader topic of Computers, Lycos puts the Net into sharp focus. Second-level subjects include Access Providers; Ethics, Netiquette & Legislation; Web Publishing & HTML; Browsers & Interfaces; and Internet News.

When you bore into the Lycos directory to the levels that list outside Web site links, you get more than a bare list of hyperlinks. Lycos includes a description of every listed site — not at great length, mind you, but even a short paragraph can persuade you to zip over to a site or dissuade you from wasting your time there. Determining the full nature of a site from a simple link name is, after all, impossible, and the descriptions make up for the space they take by delivering good information.

Beginning with the second-level pages of the directory and continuing throughout, Lycos assumes the style of an *ezine* (electronic magazine), furnishing a highly editorialized approach to selecting Web sites. As you can see in Figure 2-8, a Lycos second-level directory page offers featured topics, headlines, links to related chat rooms, message boards, and shopping sites.

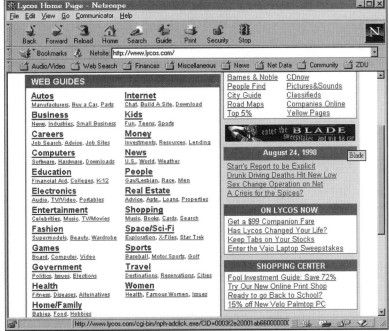

Figure 2-7:
The top-
level
directory
page in
Lycos.

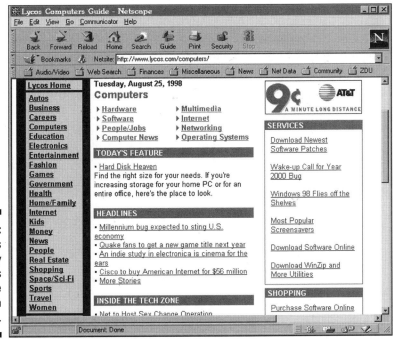

Figure 2-8:
The Lycos
directory
presents
sites in the
style of an
ezine.

Lycos offers more complete descriptions, called Top 5% Reviews, for selected Web sites. Lycos groups these reviews together under the Top 5% heading on each second-level directory page. From any second-level directory page, click the Top 5% button at the top of the page, and a separate directory appears, offering reviews by the Lycos staff. After perusing the review, click its title to visit the site or use the Back button of your browser to return to the directory page you left.

Lycos has pursued a directory tactic in which it chooses sites for you, rather than objectively presenting a large number of sites and letting you choose. This can be frustrating but is actually an advantage for busy people who don't want to spend a lot of time exploring and discarding useless sites.

I've watched Lycos since it began, and I think it reached the optimum level of subjectivity some time ago and then crossed over the line into bothersome distraction. Lycos has too many features for me, and too much editorializing. Its pages are so feature-rich that they are confusing, and the obnoxious little browser windows that pop open with display advertising are particularly unwelcome in a directory, where you visit the same pages over and over (suffering through those pop-ups each time). On top of all this, the site is infuriatingly slow. Remember, however, that this rant is just one person's opinion. The advantages of the Lycos system may outweigh the disadvantages for you.

Like Yahoo!, Lycos realizes the value of mapping the World Wide Web by geographic boundaries. Although cyberspace exists independently of political boundaries, you may find these regional guides to Web sites convenient and useful. The Lycos CityGuide offers a map-based directory in which you click increasingly specific locations until you reach a city. Start your directory travels at this address:

```
cityguide.lycos.com
```

As you can see in Figure 2-9, the main CityGuide page starts you off with a map of the world, inviting you to click your way into a continent (you can click either the map or the text links below it — scroll down to see them).

Follow these steps to get to the Paris directory:

1. **Click the European continent at the main CityGuide page.**

   The World City Guide page appears.

2. **In the map of Europe, click France.**

   You could also click the <u>France</u> link in the text section.

3. **On the France page, click the <u>Paris</u> link.**

Finally on the Paris, France, page, you see a description of the city on the left, and a list of links on the right (see Figure 2-10).

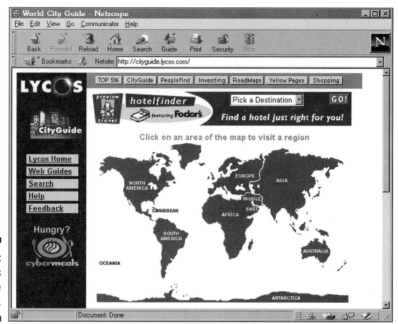

Figure 2-9:
The Lycos
CityGuide
main page.

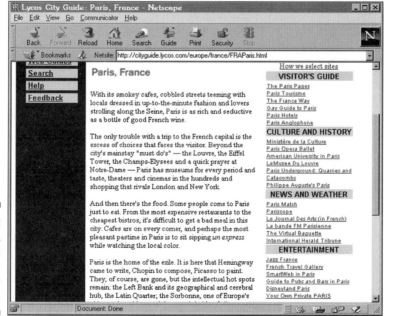

Figure 2-10:
A
description
and links in
the Lycos
CityGuide.

Excite

The top level of the Excite directory looks compact, which makes navigating through its uncluttered page easy (see Figure 2-11). See for youself at this address:

```
www.excite.com
```

A few surprises lurk among the top-level subjects:

- **Games:** Game-playing is a popular Web topic, but isn't normally represented at the top level of directories. Gamers attain heaven in Excite, which dedicates a whole subdirectory to all kinds of games, from the board variety to computer fantasies.

- **Relationships:** Sites about gender negotiations, marriage, divorce, and finding people on the Net are featured in this category.

- **Small Business:** Here you find all kinds of Internet sites about starting a business, office technology, legal issues, and marketing.

Excite places a premium on selection and description. As a result, the directory isn't the largest one on the Web. Excite reviews each site that links to it, however, providing a single paragraph that conveys the gist of the site before you spend time visiting it. Besides saving you time, the reviews give

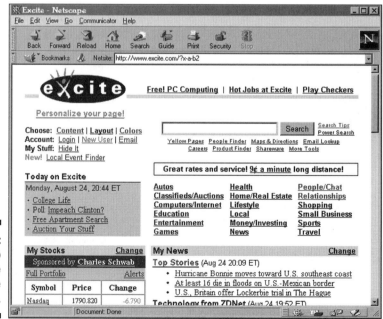

Figure 2-11:
The top
level of the
Excite
directory.

you a sense of high class, like a brand of coffee that uses only the finest beans. Perhaps most important, all the sites work and are of a reasonably high quality.

TIP

You may want to explore the Excite home page beyond the directory links. As with Lycos, Excite has evolved way beyond being a mere search tool, almost to the point of sweeping the directory under a carpet. Excite (and Lycos) used to be all about searching, with their directories and keyword entry forms, and now are more like on-screen magazines with some searching thrown in. Excite throws in news headlines, stock quotes, horoscopes, chat events, and a lot more to distract you from finding good Web sites *outside* Excite. A lot of Internet is out there. Don't let Excite lure you into spending all your time on its pages.

Infoseek

The Infoseek directory stakes a claim to an intermediate ground between the stark objectivity of Yahoo! and the flagrant subjectivity of Lycos and Excite. Check out the Infoseek home page (Figure 2-12) at this address:

```
www.infoseek.com
```

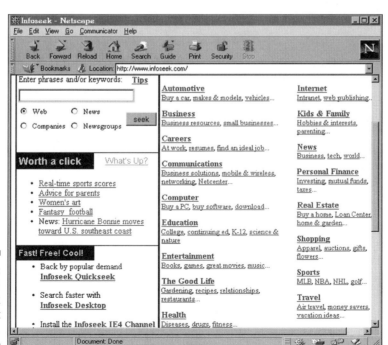

Figure 2-12: The Infoseek Internet directory.

In addition to all the regular subject headings you expect to see in an Internet directory, Infoseek includes a few unusual entries, including Women's and The Good Life.

Figure 2-13 illustrates the second level of the Infoseek directory in the Entertainment topic. The left-hand navigation bar lists subtopics; the center of the page highlights featured subtopics and a few featured sites. In this fashion, Infoseek takes you by the hand, leading you painlessly deeper into the directory.

Somewhat annoyingly, Infoseek keeps you locked into the directory for several pages — sometimes to the fifth directory level — before finally offering a link to an outside site. Too many mouse clicks are required to get anywhere, but on the other hand, you learn something about where you're going along the way. Short site descriptions help, and the one-step-at-a-time approach keeps you on track and makes it hard to get lost.

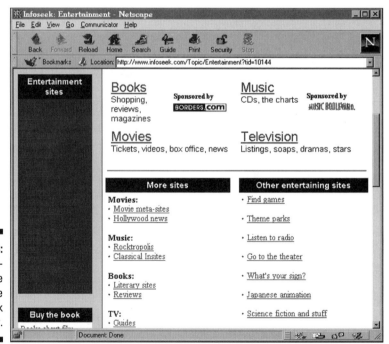

Figure 2-13:
A second-level page of the Infoseek directory.

Final Appraisal

Of the four Internet directories described in this chapter, Yahoo! clearly takes the prize for size and objectivity. It is a vast, sprawling, massive menu of Web sites in just about every conceivable topic. I devoted more space to describing Yahoo! simply because there is so much to describe. (And believe me, I left a lot out.)

However, size and comprehensiveness may not be what you want or need. If you'd like a little more subjectivity and hand-holding, try Infoseek. If you want a rich mix of newsy, magazine-style features with your directory, try Excite and Lycos.

When you have time, take a look at Chapter 22, which lists and describes what I think are the ten best portals. *Portals* are orientation sites that give you search tools plus a range of other features to help you get your bearings on the Net.

Chapter 3

Introducing Keywords

●●●

●●●

*S*earching through menu-based Web directories can turn up some great finds. Plus, it's fun. And informative. And time-consuming! Furthermore, you tend to discover lots of information that you *weren't* looking for and not enough of what you really need. It's a way to search when you're also interested in browsing.

When you know exactly what you're trying to find, *keywords* can deliver what you need quickly and precisely. You see this for yourself in this chapter. Web directories throw broad illumination on the Internet, like a floodlight, but keywords take the flashlight approach, quickly revealing bits and pieces of the Internet that relate to your immediate information need.

Using Keywords to Narrow Your Search

Keywords give the Internet hints about what you want to find. The Web (or any other gang of computers) is not very smart, and you can't count on having an intelligent discussion with it. You have to nurse it along by giving it clues. So, for example, if you're looking for information on the pitchers of the 1955 Cleveland Indians, some possible keywords may be *baseball, indians, cleveland, pitching,* and perhaps a few names of players. Being able to say, "Give me statistics on the pitching staff of the 1955 Cleveland Indians, including both starters and relievers," is more convenient, but alas, Internet technology, although progressing nicely, isn't quite at the *Star Trek* stage yet.

The searching smorgasbord

Yahoo! was the first keyword searcher to achieve widespread recognition, and it quickly became a household word in the homes of Internet users. Other tools, such as Lycos, Excite, and AltaVista, have attracted prominence due to new approaches to searching. Relative newcomers, such as HotBot, claim part of the stage for their unique indexes and the horsepower of their engines. You can even find niche searchers that cover certain subjects or geographical areas. (The chapters in Part III unearth dozens of topical searchers.) Most search services offer their wares free of charge.

New developments and emerging services change the Web searching landscape almost daily. You can keep up on the new services by following the Internet magazines. You can also search the Web (ironically) for information on Web searching. And the best way to get a feel for the different search options is simply to use them. Start by placing the Web search sites used in this book in your browser's bookmark list, and go to them often. After you start searching, you see how easy it is, and the Internet becomes a much more manageable place.

This chapter and the next help you discover how to make keyword clues as effective as possible, depending on which part of the Web you're giving them to. This chapter gives you the basics of keywords and keyword operators, and Chapter 4 offers tips and tricks for maximizing keywords.

Keyword sites

Some specific Web sites accept search keywords. They gobble them up, digest them for a few seconds, and then splash the results of their search on your screen. In Internet lingo, the following names apply to these specialized searching sites:

- ✔ **Web search sites:** Blindingly original, isn't it?

- ✔ **Web indexes:** They are called *indexes* because the sites search prebuilt indexes of the Web, not the Web itself.

- ✔ **Web crawlers, worms, or spiders:** These evocative names help you imagine an industrious multilegged (or no-legged) creature that burrows deep into the Internet's resources on your behalf.

- ✔ **Search engines:** Sounds industrial, doesn't it? These sites are called *engines* because of the built-in software that drives the automated search routines. Each engine differs. You don't need to understand the technical differences, but you should know that the results of searches by different engines (sites) vary, even if you use the same keywords — not unlike the different responses that different car models have to the same gasoline.

Whatever you call these sites, such indexes are distinguished by their capability to accept keywords and then search with them. That capability spells the main difference between a Web directory and a Web search site — though, as you have seen, some directories include keyword search forms. And some crawlers (with their inevitable keyword search forms) include directories.

Entering keywords

You type keywords into empty boxes on Web pages called *keyword search forms.* So what are keyword search forms, anyway?

You type keywords into Web pages called *forms* that have text entry spaces called *fields.* Forms on the Web look like the paper forms you've been filling out all your life when you've applied for a job or a driver's license.

At their simplest, keyword search forms include a Search button and a field for typing in one or more words, as shown in Figure 3-1. Most forms are *case-insensitive,* so you don't have to worry about putting uppercase letters in the right place. (In certain keyword entry forms and in certain search situations, you do want to type uppercase letters. I get into that later in this chapter and in Chapter 4.)

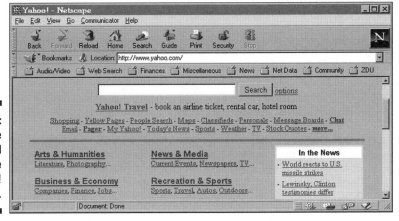

Figure 3-1:
A simple
keyword
form at the
Yahoo!
Search site.

To begin the search, you click the Search button with your mouse, although in some cases pressing Enter initiates the search. More complicated forms offer drop-down lists, additional slots for multiple keywords, and other helpful distractions (see Figure 3-2).

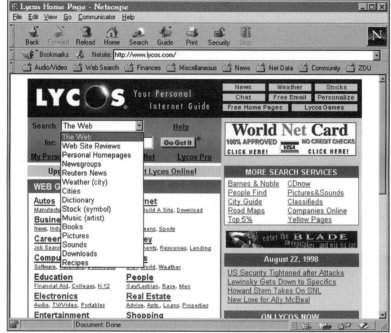

Figure 3-2:
Some
keyword
forms
include
options, but
you don't
have to use
them.

In the early days of the Web (way back in the archaic past — almost four years ago), forms weren't visible in all Web browsers. Browsers that could read forms were called *forms-enabled browsers.* (Another inventive piece of terminology.) These days, virtually all modern browsers can view forms.

When you're ready to venture into the unknown by beginning a keyword search, just follow these steps for entering a keyword:

1. Enter the address for a keyword search site in your Web browser.

You find these addresses sprinkled throughout this book, and I discuss the sites themselves extensively in separate chapters. But to get started with keywords, use any of the following addresses. They, along with all the other addresses in this book, are included on the CD-ROM for easy clicking.

```
www.yahoo.com
www.lycos.com
www.excite.com
www.altavista.digital.com
www.infoseek.com
www.hotbot.com
```

The top page of the search engine appears. It includes a form that looks similar to what you see in Figure 3-1 for the keyword search. You can safely disregard any other slots and options.

2. **Position the cursor in the input box and click it.**

3. **Type a word that relates to your search.**

   Almost any thing, place, or organization does the job, even if you aren't looking for something specific right now. Try *potato, ireland,* or *NASA.* (You can type *nasa* in lowercase letters.)

4. **Click the Search or Begin button or press the Enter key.**

   Some search engines enable you to begin the search process, after typing in the keywords, by pressing the Enter key on your keyboard. Others, though, require you to click an on-screen button, usually called Search.

The sparkplugs of the search engine

Entering a keyword is like starting a motor — Web search sites are called *search engines* for good reason. The search engine shows its horsepower by comparing your keywords to its entire index of Web material, and then it gives you the results of the comparison. In other words, a search engine displays all the sites in its index that offer matches to your keywords. But the whole site isn't displayed, you'll be glad to know. You see only a summary of the site (the completeness of the summaries varies among search engines, some of which don't give summaries at all), with hyperlinks that can take you to the actual site if you think you've found something useful.

The largest, most famous search engines compare your keywords to indexes containing millions of sites and billions of words within those sites. (I'm not trying to sound like Carl Sagan.) So how long does displaying the results of such an awesome search require? Hours? No, not even minutes.

Assuming that your telephone line is in good working order and that you're not being stalled by prime-time Internet traffic, you get the results of any search that you try within seconds. Isn't technology grand? Shouldn't you give up your social life to explore the Internet? Well, don't get carried away. But the impressive return times make it easy to conduct multiple searches through several engines when you track down a difficult subject. (By the way, you can read an explanation of the various causes of Internet delay in Chapter 15 in the sidebar about downloading.)

A mechanic's guide to search engines

The search engine is only one of the components required for the search process. The main component is the vast, hidden index of sites to which your keywords are compared. The search engine compares your keywords to the index. How is this immense index database formed?

Search indexes are usually created automatically, with the help of automated software programs that constantly scour the Internet for new material. These programs are sometimes called robots, or bots; and because of the way bots operate, search sites are sometimes referred to as worms or crawlers. Like burrowing animals, these programs roam the Net continually and invisibly, following links, gathering new document and page titles, and in some cases, collecting every word of the sites they visit. The bots collect and store this raw data.

Next, the program compresses and sorts the data according to the guiding search principles of the site. If the program considers word proximity important, such proximities are indexed and stored. If the program attempts to gather concepts from word placements, these concepts are extrapolated and saved. The index is a gigantic, evolving data organism.

You can thank the compressed index for the quickness of Web searches. All the time-consuming work has been performed (and is still being performed) by the ever-industrious bots. The search engine merely compares your keywords to the current, presumably up-to-the-minute, index and returns the matches in seconds. The speed with which the search engine accomplishes this process remains impressive.

Getting Specific with Keyword Qualifiers

As you can imagine, using single-word clues to find information in the vastness of the World Wide Web is akin to fumbling through the proverbial haystack with boxing gloves on. Surprisingly, it works, but you often have to sort through mountains of undesirable search results before you find something useful. You need to narrow the search before you begin it by using the right keywords in the right combinations.

Special words assist in this enterprise by telling the search engines how to treat the terms you've entered. You can use these words to emphasize some keywords, de-emphasize others, link terms by proximity, and exclude matches that coincide with certain terms. Don't panic; it's easier than it sounds. These special words are called *qualifiers* or *operators*.

In the following examples, and elsewhere in the book, I use capital letters (LIKE THIS!) to indicate keyword operators. Although search engines don't usually care whether you type keywords in uppercase or lowercase (caps or noncaps), they do care with keyword operators because using caps distinguishes them from regular words. As you see in the examples that follow, some search engines also let you use symbols in place of the keyword operators, which makes searching easier.

Using *AND* between two keywords links them as a pair, so any matches must include both words. (Some search sites enable you to use the plus (+) sign instead of the word *AND*.) The result list excludes documents and sites that contain only one of the words. An example is *cleveland AND indians*. This search, though simple, greatly narrows the field by eliminating most non-baseball information about the city of Cleveland, as well as most information about Indians as an ethnic group (see Figure 3-3).

Figure 3-3:
Using the
AND
qualifier.

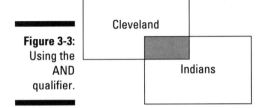

Cleveland

Indians

Using *OR* between two words opens wide the floodgates of information by allowing matches that correspond to either word. So to continue with the example, entering *cleveland OR indians* delivers the whole gamut of responses relating to the city of Cleveland, Cleveland Amory, Grover Cleveland Alexander, Indian gurus, Native American sweat lodges, and who knows what else. The *OR* operator has its moments, especially for broadening a search that isn't yielding enough results (see Figure 3-4).

Figure 3-4:
Using the
OR qualifier.

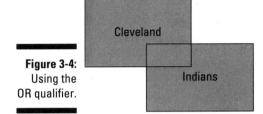

Cleveland

Indians

Using *NOT* between two keywords eliminates the second word from consideration as a match candidate. (Some search sites enable you to use the hyphen as an abbreviation for *NOT*.) You can use *NOT* when you anticipate that the frequent presence of the second word messes up your search. For example, if you need information on Cleveland but you don't want to include anything on its baseball team, you can use the NOT qualifier and type *cleveland NOT indians*. Using the NOT qualifier between *cleveland* and *indians* eliminates the baseball aspect of the search (see Figure 3-5).

Figure 3-5:
Using the
NOT
qualifier.

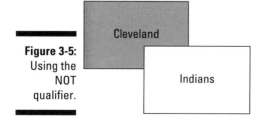

Using parentheses may bring back dreadful memories of high school math class, but it's not that complicated. You can use parentheses to surround words that you want to group with another operator. Imagine saying to yourself, "I want information on the Cleveland Indians as they fought the Yankees for the 1955 pennant." (And if that's as interesting as your private mutterings get, I'm not going to bother eavesdropping.) If you enter this keyword string, *cleveland AND (indians OR yankees),* you get references to sites that contain *cleveland AND indians,* as well as *cleveland AND yankees.*

Putting quotations around keywords makes the search engine treat them literally, exactly as you type them. (So watch your spelling!) It's a good way to look up famous quotations, personal names, and locations. For example, the keyword string, *"Big Bend National Park"* returns sites about the park in Texas, and won't burden you with sites about national parks in general or any of the millions of sites containing the word *national.*

The asterisk wildcard: As a search operator, the innocent asterisk (*) has a special meaning. As in a card game in which a specified card can have any value, placing an asterisk in a keyword string tells the search engine to match *anything* against the asterisk. What good is that? Doesn't it just open the floodgates to an infinite number of matches? Not really. You generally use the asterisk wildcard as part of a single keyword, not between keywords. Here's an example:

```
indian*
```

Typing that keyword instructs the search engine to find sites containing all words that begin with *indian.* Such words include indians, indiana, and indianapolis. Using the asterisk wildcard saves the time of typing multiple, similar keywords. It also saves the day when you're not sure how to spell a word. But you can't use the asterisk in the middle of a keyword — only at the beginning or the end.

Not all keyword operators work identically in all search engines. Some of them may not work at all in some keyword entry forms. Throughout the chapters in Part II, I spell out which operators work in which engines. Generally, most search engines recognize the AND, NOT, and quotation operators, and you can use them with confidence. Some engines, as you can see in Part II, provide search operators in the form of pull-down selection lists, which take the guesswork out of using them.

Combining Keyword Qualifiers

You don't have to select just one keyword operator to use in your search strings. The operators can be used in combination with each other, in many configurations. Here are some typical combinations.

- **AND and NOT:** Combining the AND and NOT operators makes a search very specific. When used liberally, you're basically giving the search engine some very precise instructions: *Search for this AND this AND this, but NOT this.* Here's a simple example:

  ```
  cleveland AND indians NOT american
  ```

  This example results in matches with sites about the Cleveland Indians baseball team, but not American Indians. However, the example also excludes sites about the American League, in which the baseball Indians compete. You could make things even more specific this way:

  ```
  cleveland AND indians AND american NOT native
  ```

  This example helps sift out undesirable sites, but as the search string gets longer, it's increasingly evident that using only the AND and NOT operators gets a bit clumsy.

- **AND, NOT, and ():** Adding parentheses to the mix makes your keyword string a more flexible tool. Now you can group keywords together in a way the search engine recognizes. Here's an example of what you can do:

  ```
  cleveland AND indians AND tribe NOT (native AND
        american)
  ```

  I include the word *tribe* in the preceding example because it's the nickname of the Cleveland Indians baseball team. By excluding both *native* and *american* from the search results, you get sites that match the word *tribe* in a baseball context, but not in a Native American context. Note, however, that the search engine excludes only sites that contain both *native* and *american*, not just one or the other. To be more precise, you need to add the OR operator.

✔ **AND, NOT, OR, and ():** Things can get quite complex when using several of the major operators at once. But it's fun to play with them, and sometimes the results can be very encouraging! Because getting the results of a search takes only a few seconds, it's worth experimenting until you feel comfortable with using search operators fluently. Here's an example of the possibilities:

```
cleveland AND (indians OR tribe) NOT (native or
        american)
```

This example delivers results that match with the Cleveland Indians baseball team, including references to its *tribe* nickname, but not sites that match with either *native* or *american*.

Here's another fun one:

```
cleveland AND (indians OR tribe) NOT "Grover Cleveland
        Alexander"
```

The preceding example returns sites about the Cleveland Indians baseball team, including references to its nickname, but excluding sites referring to Grover Cleveland Alexander.

Be careful not to confuse the search engine with conflicting instructions. These engines are smart, but not so smart that they can figure out a mistake on your part. So, for example, avoid keyword strings like this:

```
cleveland AND (american OR league) NOT (native OR american)
```

What's the problem with this string? Because the keyword *american* appears in both parentheses, one of them under the AND operator and the other under the NOT operator, the command conflicts with itself. The search engine doesn't know whether to give you matches including *american* or excluding it. Your computer won't explode or anything, but you'll get mixed results.

Not all search forms understand these keyword operators. If you type *ANDs, ORs,* and *NOTs* in a form that doesn't understand them, one of two things happens. The form considers them keywords, or it deems them insignificant and ignores them.

Search pages notify you when you can use keyword qualifiers. Some pages even offer a quick online tutorial on their use. (Needless to say, the tutorial is not nearly as lucid and invigorating as the explanation provided here.) Other pages build the qualifiers into drop-down lists between your keywords.

What Boolean is — and why you don't need to know

The common keyword qualifiers AND, NOT, and OR come from a kind of logic called Boolean, and you may run into that word in your searches. Don't be thrown. Boolean strings are a specific keyword order (sometimes called Boolean syntax) that help sift information from large databases.

This arcane syntax used to be very important, but now it is less so, thanks to the user-friendly features of most Web search pages. Most of them default to a certain assumed syntax that is sufficient for quick searches. (Usually the OR operator is assumed between words.) For more advanced projects, the search tools furnish drop-down lists that spell out how to link keywords effectively. Nonetheless, I provide details on how to use the AND, NOT, and OR Boolean operators for less hospitable Web situations.

Good keyword strategy takes into consideration other factors besides operators. Many times, a quick search with the right keywords can get you what you want without resorting to AND, OR, and NOT. Choosing effective keywords is part common sense and part practice. Chapter 4 covers all the keyword bases. In the next section "Making Sense of Keyword Results," you can see what happens after the keywords do their job.

Making Sense of Keyword Results

After you click the Search button, your keywords and the search engine work together to obtain a list of results. During this time, not much happens on your screen, though you may see an inconspicuous progress report at the bottom of the browser's window. You won't have long to wait. In less than a minute, if all goes well, you see a new Web page that contains matches to your query (see Figure 3-6).

Taming the numbers

You may often find that Web searching gives you too much information. Typical keyword results are overwhelmingly voluminous, sometimes returning many thousands of matches. Using crafty keyword selections to

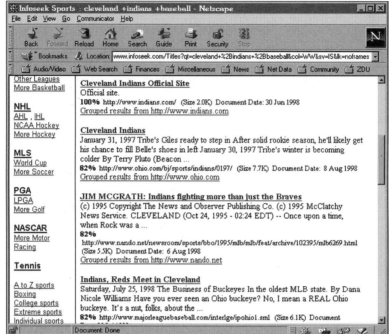

narrow the search before beginning can help you cope. But sometimes you want a truckload of matches for one reason or another. You may need to narrow your focus by reading material on a broad topic before knowing enough to search more specifically. Or you may just be in a browsing mood — after all, searching doesn't always need to be serious business.

Most search sites siphon large results to you in manageable amounts. There may be a default limit of 20 or 30 matches per page, in which case you see a hyperlink at the bottom of each page to bring up the next round of matches. Often the search engine sorts the results by grouping the best matches toward the top of the list, making it unnecessary to look beyond the first page of matches. Such a size limit per page prevents delays, but sometimes the limit proves undesirable. A few search engines enable you to choose the number of matches per page from a drop-down list.

Hits and glancing blows

In search-speak, a match is called a *hit*. If you enter *cleveland AND indians,* a hit is any result that contains both words. If you enter *cleveland OR indians,* a hit is any result that contains either word. (The latter entry generates many more hits.)

Not all hits are of equal significance or equally useful to you. If, for example, you enter *cleveland OR indians,* some hits contain one word or the other, and some results have both words. Most likely, those hits containing both words are more useful to you, and you'd want to see them first. Now if you enter *cleveland AND (indians OR yankees),* all the results contain either *indians* or *yankees*, along with *cleveland*, but only some hits contain all three words. Again, the greatest number of word coincidences is likely to be of greater value, and those hits are grouped at the top of the search results list. (Of course, you can always start a separate search on *cleveland AND indians AND yankees* to be sure of getting all three.)

What's in those matches?

Figure 3-7 shows part of a result page from the Lycos search site. Although each service presents its results differently, they all have common elements:

Hyperlink to the site   Document title   Document summary

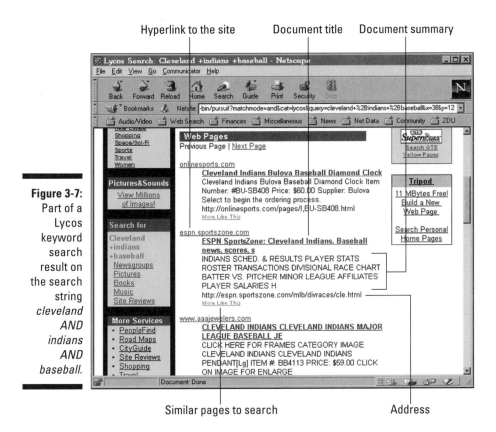

Figure 3-7: Part of a Lycos keyword search result on the search string *cleveland AND indians AND baseball.*

Similar pages to search   Address

✔ **Document title:** A *document* can be anything from a text file stored in an Internet library to a Web page. No matter what the document is, the search result is just a summary of it. The title sometimes corresponds to the document address (such as a Web address), or it may carry a separate name.

✔ **Document summary:** The summary can be an abstract associated with the document, the first few lines of the document itself, or a short review stored in the search engine's index.

✔ **Hyperlink:** The hit is worthless without some way of following up the lead. In the World Wide Web, that means one thing: a hyperlink that takes you directly to the site itself. The linked site can be a Web page, an FTP menu, or a newsgroup posting.

✔ **Address:** The Internet location, spelled out in case you want to make note of it without actually going there.

Most Web search engines focus primarily on matches to World Wide Web pages. Some search engines, however, also rummage through Usenet newsgroups and news wire services. In those cases, you may get a mixed bag in your search results. Or, as a search feature, you may be able to limit the search to one portion of the Internet (such as Web pages) or another (such as Usenet). Refer to the chapters in Part II for the features of each major search engine.

Chapter 4

Keyword Tangles and Tips

● ●

● ●

Keywords provide a terrific tool for searching the Web. Using them can save hours of fruitless searching through directories. Keywords also can spawn confusion (occasionally), frustration (fairly often), and a distinct sense of being overwhelmed by the Web's hugeness (all too frequently). Three basic problems can emerge in a keyword search:

✔ No results

✔ Not the right results

✔ Too many results

Now, you may think that getting too many results is a happy problem. It's better indeed than coming up empty with a keyword search. But after spending an hour rummaging through screen after screen of search results, following links and returning to follow more, you may want to find ways to narrow the search right from the beginning. Of course, a blank result screen presents the opposite problem, and in that case, you need to know how to broaden the search. You find out how to do both in this chaper.

Ideally, the perfect keyword selection delivers a handful of results (25 or fewer often proves a manageable number), each of which is interesting, useful, or at least fun. You rarely attain the ideal; but the closer you can get to it, the happier your trails are.

Narrowing the Search

Most people begin searching casually, without putting a lot of thought into choosing keywords. Nothing is wrong with a hit-or-miss approach — a search based on a quick, general keyword entry usually provides a wealth of links to explore, as if a certain Web topic had been roped off for exploration. In most cases, the defined subject area remains too big for precise searching.

As an example, performing a quick search on the keyword *animals* provides results that are either exhilarating or intimidating, depending on how much time you want to spend looking at animal sites. A recent test produced 3,182,066 links in the Infoseek service; AltaVista returned 2,616,090 hits (matched results). Those numbers would give even a Webaholic an overdose of surfing material.

By the way, a larger number of hits doesn't necessarily indicate a better service. Search results depend on how the service organizes its index. You may develop a preference for services that consistently deliver fewer hits, if those hits prove more useful.

At this point, having begun a casual search and having been most likely overwhelmed by the prospect of sorting through many thousands of results, the frazzled searcher needs to begin narrowing the field.

Choosing a more specific keyword

Choosing a more specific keyword is the obvious solution. Continuing with the present example and staying in the Infoseek service that provided a generous return of 3,182,066 hits, you then determine what kind of animal to use as the subject of the search. Entering *birds* in the keyword form begins the next round, and the results get narrower: only 1,314,796 hits. Anyone can check out all those links in a month, assuming no time out for meals. Getting still more specific, entering *cormorants* (a type of bird) brings 4,355 results. You're definitely moving in the right direction. Sometimes, though, you need to use other ways to narrow the search.

Adding a keyword

Generally, adding a second keyword reduces the number of hits in the search result. The second word is especially effective when the first keyword is ambiguous — that is, when it can have more than one meaning. If you first use a broad keyword, as with an example such as *animals,* simply replacing the keyword with a more specific single keyword may work just as well.

If a searcher wants to find Web information on state capitals in the United States and begins casually by using the keyword *state,* that poor soul is probably horrified to see over three million hits (in the Excite service). However, by simply adding *capitals* to the search terms (the entire keyword phrase is *state capitals*), the searcher gets a much shorter results list. Even more important, all the returned sites that match both *state* and *capitals* are grouped at the top.

Adding a keyword, by itself, does not always narrow search results as in the preceding example. It depends partly on the keywords and even more on how the search engine handles the keywords. Some engines, when fed two or more words, find sites that contain *any* of the words, and the result can be a hit list larger than you would get by using just one word. Other engines match multiple keywords to sites containing *all* the keywords, which definitely shortens the results list. To be sure of shortening the list, you can force the search engine to match *all* the keywords by using the AND search operator. Keep on reading to find out exactly how.

Using the AND operator

You often want to see only hits that contain *both* of your keywords. If sites containing only one keyword or the other don't matter to you, you may as well use the AND operator to eliminate them at the outset (see Figure 4-1).

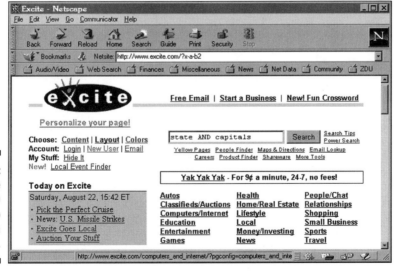

Figure 4-1: Using the AND operator to narrow a search.

Finding where the AND lives

To use search operators such as AND, OR, and NOT, you must be at a site that accepts these search parameters on its keyword page. Fortunately, the major search engines do support search operators, but in different ways:

✔ Lycos offers a Lycos Pro link beside its main keyword form. Click the link to go to an enhanced keyword page that accepts operators. Or navigate directly to that page by using this address:

```
lycospro.lycos.com/
lycospro-nojava.html
```

✔ Yahoo! provides an Options link to an enhanced keyword form. You find the Options link right next to the main keyword form on the Yahoo! home page. The enhanced page, alas, supports only some of the keyword operators. Either link your way to the enhanced keyword form or use this direct address:

```
search.yahoo.com/search/
options
```

✔ Excite gives you a link called Search Tips. This link takes you to a page of instructions that tell you how to use symbols for a few search operators. The direct address is

```
www.excite.com/Info/
searching.html?a-tip-t
```

✔ Infoseek has its own set of search operators and symbols that represent them. You can get a complete rundown of Infoseek's features in Chapter 9. In addition, look at the online tips provided by Infoseek itself. On the Infoseek home page (see the following address), click the Tips link.

```
www.infoseek.com
```

✔ HotBot uses an automatic AND operator. You can easily override it (see Chapter 10 for details about HotBot's operation), but you don't need to do anything to get AND between your keywords. For online tips about how to use keyword operators in simple HotBot searches, click the Advanced Search Features link from the HotBot home page, or go directly to this address:

```
www.hotbot.com/Help/
intro.html
```

Putting *AND* (or the symbol representing it, depending on the search service) between two words forces the results to match both words. All sites that match only one word are excluded from the results. Using the state capitals example, forming a keyword phrase of *state AND capitals* in Lycos (*state +capitals* in some services) reduces the number of hits from over three million (for *state* alone) to 5,260. Not bad!

After experiencing the relief of seeing the results page shrink by millions of hits, you may think that using even more keywords leads to cleaner, quicker searches. In some cases, using more keywords does improve your searches, but at some point, diminishing returns can reduce your search results to zero. Some search sites accept many keywords — Inktomi, for example, accepts up to ten keywords — but using more than four keywords rarely proves helpful, especially when you use the search-narrowing AND operator.

Forcing the service to find sites that contain four (or more) words doesn't produce many hits. Instead, having to match three keywords narrows your search into the ground.

NOT!

Using AND to specify matches that include two keywords tightens a search field effectively, but in one situation the NOT operator gets more to the point. You want to use NOT when you anticipate many matches that contain a word that relates to your keyword(s) and those matches don't help you. For example, if you're searching for travel sites in London, but don't want to confuse the results with sites about the author Jack London, you can use the keyword string *london NOT "jack london"* to solve the problem.

Don't overuse the NOT feature. If you see it more than twice in a search string, you're probably overlooking a simpler way to get good results. If, for example, you want to see sites about the NASA space shuttle, Voyager, you may also remember that the spaceship in the popular TV show, *Star Trek: Voyager,* has the same name. Trying to eliminate all overlapping sites, you can type *voyager NOT television NOT star NOT trek* . . . . You probably won't nip all those sites in the bud, and furthermore, you can accomplish your goal with one elegant use of the AND operator: *voyager AND nasa*.

Widening the Search

At some point, you'll stump the system. Blithely, confidently, you'll type a keyword or two, click the Search button, wait a few seconds, and receive the following curt reply: "There are no matches to your search criteria." (Or rude words to that effect.) Nothing. Zilch. Or perhaps a straggling two or three sites when you expected dozens. At that point, it's time to widen your search keywords.

Using fewer terms

Just as you add keywords to narrow a search, you can shorten your string to broaden the search. (Unless, of course, you start with just one keyword.) Reducing the number of keywords usually is not a question of simple elimination; you need to rethink your search strategy. If you started with a specific person, location, product, news item, or other topic, you may have to think backward to figure out a good place to start. As an example, you may be looking for information on *Macedonian folk dancing,* but *Yugoslavian culture* may be a better starting point for a search.

Shorten your keywords

Many keyword services have certain default capabilities. Some of them can extrapolate longer words from shorter ones, for example, making a plural from a singular. Therefore, if you use the keyword *cat,* the service also returns matches with *cats* (not to mention *cattle*). The reverse, however, is not true. You won't get *cat* from *cats* (or from a bunch of cows). If you want to widen your search to get more results, try shortening all your words to their roots.

Getting flexible with OR

The great widening search operator is OR, which also happens to be the standard default operator for most keyword indexes. What does that mean? Simply, if you type your keywords at the main home page without adding any operators, an OR is assumed between every pair of words. The results include any site that matches any *one* word, but not necessarily *all words.*

However, if you set up a different default or neutralize the assumed OR default and punch in keywords with AND between them, you may get sparse results by forcing the service to match every word. Throwing in an OR or two can change all that in a hurry by enabling the system to return sites that match only one word.

The OR operator also covers your bets when you don't know how to spell something or when a word has variant spellings. Simply type all your guesses separated by OR operators, and you get back all the links that match each of the words. Not only do you find what you want, but you get a spelling lesson! If you make wild spelling approximations, however, you won't get any matches for them (unless an equally bad speller put up a Web page).

Hints for Better Hits

In all search situations, some guidelines can smooth your way. The ultimate goal of keyword searching is to get the perfect results page in the fewest possible attempts. Searching can be a kind of sport, and the more tips you have at your disposal, the better.

How insensitive!

Keyword searching services are generally, to use the standard phrase, *case-insensitive,* which means that it doesn't matter whether you use uppercase or lowercase, even for proper nouns and names.

One search engine, Infoseek, treats capitalization in a particular way. If you don't capitalize keywords when typing them into Infoseek, Infoseek treats your keywords like any group of words even if they are proper nouns, such as names of people or places. However, if you capitalize a name — *Bill Gates,* for example — Infoseek treats the search string as a name, and does not separate the two words. Nor does Infoseek match the word *Gates* with sites about fence gates, because the capitalization establishes the keyword as a proper name. (See Chapter 9 for details about using Infoseek to the greatest advantage.)

In some cases, the capitalization of one or more keywords may be important to maintain, regardless of which search engine you're using. Using the quotation search operator, which most engines recognize, ensures that the engine takes your search string literally and doesn't break it up into its separate words. Using the preceding example, you can type *"Bill Gates"* in almost any search engine, and get back matches to only the president of Microsoft.

Getting fancy

If you're feeling adventurous and confident, you can fine-tune your results by using the parentheses operator (in the services that support it). Parentheses group several words that you want treated in the same way by the search engine. You usually see another operator between those grouped words. Take a look at the following example:

```
food AND (bread OR wheat OR bakeries)
```

This string returns food sites that also contain a reference to any, some, or all of the words in parentheses. But it eliminates all food sites that don't focus on either baking or grain.

Part II
Starting Up the Search Engines

The 5th Wave

In this part . . .

The Internet is a browser's paradise. You can easily get lost for hours among the Net's diverse and fascinating destinations, eagerly clicking your mouse to see what's around the next corner, and the next, and the next. . . .

But when you need to find something without spending half the night looking for it, keywords can save the day. If you're a poor online-addicted soul (like me), keywords can add years to your life. They enable you to have a life, instead of whiling it away in front of the computer, browsing endlessly for the proverbial needle in a hyperstack.

This part introduces you to several search engines, the online services that take your keywords, do the dirty work of comparing them to the engine's immense knowledge of Web sites and their contents, and display links to matching destinations right on your screen.

These services can get a little complicated, but that just adds to the fun. Honest! The trick is to start simple and gradually build up your expertise until you're a master (to whatever extent you want to be) of keyword searching. The chapters in this part start at the very beginning and walk you through all the possibilities at an easy pace. So decide what you want to search for and dive right in!

Chapter 5

Searching the Amazing Yahoo! Index

*W*hen Yahoo! burst upon the Web scene, this euphorically titled service lived up to its exciting name by providing the first popular way for Web surfers to get a grip on the vast, sprawling terrain of the Internet. Like a semi-intelligent weed-whacker, Yahoo! gave all surfers a way to cut through the Web's tropical growth and find what they really wanted. Its directory provided a smarter browsing system, and its capability to accept keywords saved time for people who knew what they were looking for.

Other services have developed in the meantime, as Web searching evolved into a promising commercial venture. But Yahoo! has not gone the way of other innovative companies that make their mark, only to fall behind the field as others pick up the idea and run farther and faster with it. To the contrary, Yahoo! remains one of the most original, dynamic, and useful Web search tools. This chapter explores the ins and outs of using keywords for searching the vast Yahoo! index.

Unlike some other search engines, Yahoo! doesn't search the full text of Web sites. Instead, it searches its own directory of the World Wide Web. The directory consists of Web page titles, sometimes with short descriptions provided by the page's designer. As such, Yahoo! doesn't qualify as a *full text* search engine. It matches keywords against all the words in its directory, but not against all the words in the Web sites that the directory represents.

A Quick Search

You can begin searching with Yahoo! with just three simple steps:

1. **Go to the main Yahoo! Web page (see Figure 5-1) by typing this address in your Web browser:**

   www.yahoo.com

2. **In the keyword entry form, type a keyword or more than one.**

3. **Click the Search button next to the keyword form.**

In a second or two, a new page (called Search Results) appears on your screen, displaying (surprise!) the search results (see Figure 5-2). If you use a general keyword, you get lots of matches. However, Yahoo! deluges you with only 20 results per page. At the bottom of the Search Results page, you find a link that, when clicked, displays the next 20 *hits* (keyword matches).

Using two kinds of search results

When you perform a simple search from the Yahoo! home page, a couple of things happen. First, Yahoo! matches your keyword(s) to pages of its own directory. Second, it matches your keywords to titles and descriptions of Web sites in the Yahoo! directory. What's the difference? Suppose you use the keyword *movies* (that's the example in Figure 5-2). At the top of the Search Results page, Yahoo! displays all pages in its directory that contain the word *movies* in the directory page title. Use <u>Business and Economy:</u> <u>Companies: Entertainment: Movies and Film</u> as an example. Clicking that link takes you to that directory page, where you can find links to Web sites in that category. Search results like these, to Yahoo! directory Web pages, are called Category Matches.

Category Matches appear in the top portion of the Search Results window. (Not every search results in Category Matches.) Beneath the Category Matches, Yahoo! displays the Site Matches, which link directly to Web sites outside the Yahoo! directory. Figure 5-3 shows Category and Site Matches in the same Search Results window. Category Matches provide a good way to navigate through the Yahoo! index — a vast, deep, complex, and detailed directory. In Figure 5-3, five category matches are found that match both keywords, *pets* and *collies,* because the keywords are fairly broad. You can expect to receive only Category Matches when you use a sufficiently broad keyword — very specific keywords (such as *engine block*) don't match with directory pages. (However, *engine block* does deliver Site Matches.)

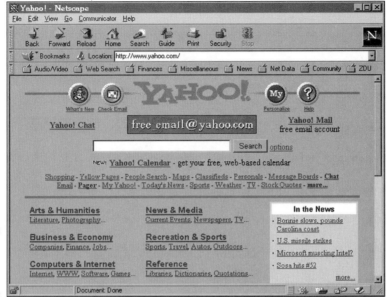

Figure 5-1:
The Yahoo!
home page.

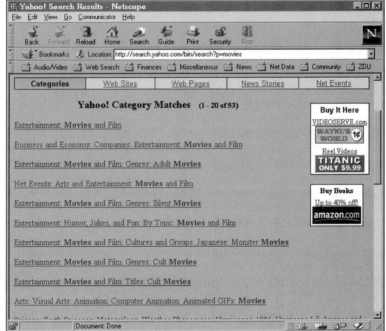

Figure 5-2:
The Yahoo!
Search
Results
page
displays
matched
keywords in
bold type.

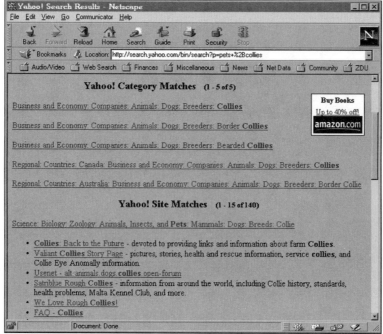

Figure 5-3:
Yahoo!
search
results
include
Category
Matches
and Site
Matches.

Working with category and site matches

The distinction between Category Matches and Site Matches has another quirk. When creating Category Matches, Yahoo! attempts to match *all* your keywords. Yahoo! isn't satisfied with only matching one out of two keywords or two out of three keywords. If Yahoo! doesn't find any matches to *all* your keywords, Yahoo! returns zero Category Matches. However, when matching keywords to Site Matches (linking to outside Web sites), Yahoo! becomes suddenly less demanding and delivers matches to any single keyword or combination of keywords. What does this mean for you? If you want Category Matches (links to directory pages), use one or two simple, basic keywords. If you're more interested in Site Matches, go to town with as many highly specific keywords as you want.

One important note: If your keyword generates a ton of Category Matches, seeing the Site Matches becomes very hard! Yahoo! gives you only 20 matches per screen. If your Search Results contain 400 Category Matches (yes, it can happen), you must trudge through 20 screens before seeing any Site Matches. You should click one of the Category Matches and then perform another search from within that category. Here's how it works:

1. **Perform a simple search from the Yahoo! home page.**

   As an example, use *movies* as the keyword.

2. **When the Search Results page appears, click the first Category Match.**

   Entertainment: Movies and Film is at the top of the Category Matches.

   The Search Results page tells you that Yahoo! has found 53 Category Matches (refer to Figure 5-2), and navigating through them all, 20 at a time, doesn't make sense.

3. **When the directory page appears, use the drop-down list next to the keyword entry field, and select just this category.**

4. **Type your new keywords and then click the Search button.**

Yahoo! Search Options

Clicking the options link on the home page takes you to the Yahoo! Search Options page (see Figure 5-4), where you can exercise more control over how Yahoo! treats your keywords, thus allowing you to conduct deeper searches. The searches work the same way as a quick search from the main home page: You type a keyword, or more than one, and click the Search button. But the Yahoo! Search page offers several additional ways to control your search.

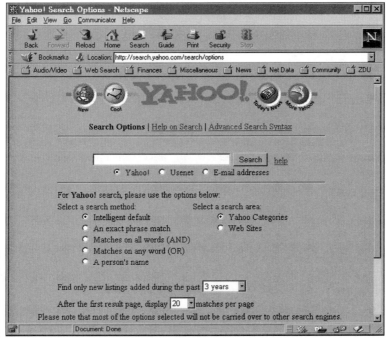

Figure 5-4:
Yahoo!
search
options.

Setting boundaries

Immediately below the keyword entry box appear three search choices, each representing areas of the Internet that Yahoo! can search for matches to your keywords:

- ✔ **Yahoo!:** This option includes the entire Yahoo! index of Web pages. Remember, Yahoo! searches only the titles of the Web pages, not the text content of the sites.

- ✔ **Usenet:** This area contains newsgroups — the bulletin boards of the Internet. Results of a Usenet search contain links to specific bulletin board messages that contain your keyword(s). This particular searching service comes to you courtesy of Deja News; in Chapter 11, you discover how to use the entire Deja News service. Yahoo! doesn't offer many Deja News features in its version.

- ✔ **E-mail addresses:** Checking this selection and then typing a name (first or last) as the keyword delivers a list of people with that name who have Internet e-mail addresses. Clicking any name in the list shows you the exact e-mail address of that person.

Choosing a keyword operator

Yahoo! is not as flexible with keyword operators as some of the other major services. Still, you do get a few choices. When you type more than one keyword, you can instruct the service to find matches that contain the following:

- ✔ **Intelligent default:** This is Yahoo! in its natural state, in which the search engine attempts to match *all* your keywords and groups those matches (if any) at the top of the search results list. Matches to fewer than all your keywords are listed lower in the list.

- ✔ **An exact phrase match:** Choosing this selection is like using the quotation keyword operator. An exact phrase match forces Yahoo! to evaluate your keywords literally, including capitalization and spelling.

- ✔ **Matches on all words (AND):** This selection requires the linked site to contain all your keywords. The Search Results page doesn't include any site that matches only one word.

- ✔ **Matches on any word (OR):** When you choose this option, the Search Results page shows any match that corresponds with any one of your keywords or with more than one keyword. The service requires only one keyword match to deliver a link to that site.

- ✔ **A person's name:** Similar to an exact phrase match, you use this option specifically with names. You can type a person's name without regard to capitalization — for example, *jodi foster*.

To select any of these choices, position your mouse cursor over the small circle next to your choice and click.

Selecting a search area

If you're tired of Category Matches getting in the way of your Site Matches, use the *Select a search area* portion of the Search Options page. Click the Web Sites radio button to limit your search results to Site Matches. Conversely, you can limit your results to Category Matches by selecting the Yahoo Categories radio button, but there isn't much sense in doing so. Because Category Matches appear first on the Search Results page by default, you don't need to use the Search Options page to isolate them.

Don't overwhelm me

The last two options on the Search Options page enable you to determine the time scope of your search and how many hits each Search Results page displays. Use the pull-down selection list (the default display is 3 years) to choose how far you want Yahoo! to look back in its index of Web sites.

If you have to hurry, nothing slows down your browser more than receiving an enormous list of links in response to your keywords. Yahoo! displays 20 hits as a default number, but you can order Yahoo! to reduce that number to 10 or increase it to 50 or 100. If you want big search results, you may as well get them in big chunks and save the trouble of linking from one small page of results to the next. But if you're on the run and want quick links to basically good Web sites, order up a small serving.

No matter how many links you command to appear on each search results page, Yahoo! tells you how many total matches it finds. So you always know what lies ahead and whether you should be searching with more (or less) precise keywords — or forgetting the whole thing and getting a cup of cappuccino.

To change the number of results that Yahoo! displays on a page, just click the downward-pointing arrow next to the number in the box (at the bottom of the page). A short list of options unfurls. Click your choice and you're set. When you perform a search, the Search Results page shows only that number of matched links — a <u>next page</u> link shows you the next set.

Final Notes on Yahoo! Searches

Yahoo! doesn't spend its resources on elaborate reviews as some search engines do. Neither does it muster any evaluation of how closely a site matches your keyword. Some services indicate how closely the keyword matches the site, how many times your keyword appears in the site, the degree to which all your words are matched, or how closely (shown as a percent) the site matches your search criteria. Because the Yahoo! index doesn't contain the full text of Web sites, all that evaluating is impossible. Hey, Yahoo! isn't fancy, but it is fast and useful.

Although Yahoo! lacks certain fine points that other services consider standard, Yahoo! has some strong features in its favor:

- ✔ Yahoo! is highly accessible. Stalled page displays are rare, even during prime Internet time.

- ✔ You may find the service's capability to restrict a search to only Usenet newsgroups or e-mail addresses terrifically handy. Although Deja News enables you to search Usenet newsgroups, and other sites enable you to search for e-mail addresses, Yahoo! provides a convenient feature by allowing you to access both newsgroups and e-mail searching from a common page. To access all the features of Deja News and various e-mail search services, however, you need to visit those sites.

- ✔ In a spirit of cooperation rather than competition, Yahoo! includes links for other search services at the bottom of its pages.

- ✔ The tight connection with its directory makes Yahoo! an integrated searching environment that enables you to browse and search from the same page. Because the Search Results page contains links back to the directory, as well as to pages outside Yahoo!, you can easily explore the Web and the directory in the same session.

Chapter 6

The Lycos Experience

● ●

In This Chapter

▶ Using keywords in the Lycos search service

▶ Simple and enhanced Lycos searches

▶ Fine-tuning a Lycos search

● ●

*T*he Lycos keyword searching service offers a well-rounded, review-enhanced, speed-enabled, operator-capable site for finding stuff on the Web. And if that sounds like Greek to you (like the Lycos name itself), this chapter gives you the rundown on how the search service works and the steps that you take to use it. Everything begins at the Lycos home page.

Doing a Quick Search

Even a child could begin a simple keyword search at the Lycos home page (see Figure 6-1). To begin using Lycos keyword searches right away, just follow a few basic steps:

1. **Direct your Web browser to the Lycos home page by typing** www.lycos.com/.

2. **In the keyword entry form, type a keyword, or more than one.**

3. **Click the Go Get It button.**

After you click the Go Get It button, Lycos searches the default database — the Lycos catalog of Web sites. (I describe how to change databases later in this chapter.) In a few seconds, you see the results page, which displays links to all the sites that match your keywords (see Figure 6-2).

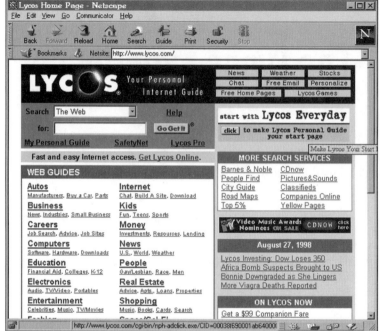

Each matched result has several parts:

- ✔ **The link itself**. The link is in bold typeface. Click the link to go to the Web site the link represents.

- ✔ **A brief description of the site**. Don't expect a ton of information from the descriptions because the Lycos staff doesn't write them. Sometimes they're about as informative as a sentence full of gibberish. Other descriptions prove more useful — and you can always get the story straight from the horse's mouth by clicking the link to visit the actual site.

- ✔ **The main site address.** This is located directly above the bold page address. You can click the main site address to visit the home page of the site that hosts the search results page.

On each Lycos search results page, you need to scroll down a bit to find your results. This little chore is necessary because Lycos fills up the top part of the page with a Matching Categories list, linking you to category pages in the Lycos directory that match your keyword. (Many more Matching Categories exist for broad keywords such as *movie* than for narrow keywords such as *travolta*.) Furthermore, Lycos stuffs in links to advertisers, such as Barnes & Noble's online bookstore and the CDNow online music store, which offer to sell you products related to your search. You may want to explore these Matching Category links and shopping opportunities, but if you just want to stay focused on your search, scroll past all that to the result links.

Main site of page   Link to page

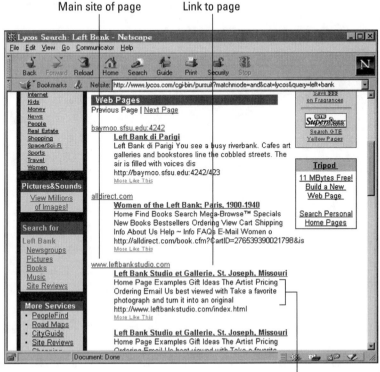

Figure 6-2:
Part of a
search
results
page in
Lycos.

Description of page

Choosing your source

Immediately above the keyword search form on the Lycos home page, you
can choose which search field the search engine explores by selecting from
a drop-down list (Figure 6-3). When you arrive at the Lycos site, the first of
these fields — The Web — is selected by default. But you can change the
selection at any time, according to what kind of results you want. Lycos
offers the following search fields:

✔ **The Web.** This default setting appears when you first enter Lycos, and
   searching the Web returns matches of Web pages from the entire Lycos
   database of World Wide Web content. The Web is the broadest possible
   setting.

✔ **Web Site Reviews.** This selections restricts the search to sites reviewed
   by Lycos.

✔ **Personal Homepages.** Searching with this option doesn't scour for *all*
   personal home pages, just those located in the Tripod and GeoCities
   community sites. Lycos may add other communities as time goes on.

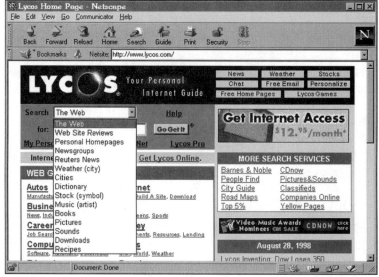

Figure 6-3:
Where to
search?
Lycos gives
you several
choices.

✔ **Newsgroups.** Search the bulletin board messages in the Usenet
newsgroups. (Chapter 11 describes Deja News, a search engine devoted
to Usenet newsgroups.)

✔ **Reuters News.** This selection prowls through the posted stories of the
Reuters wire service.

✔ **Weather (city).** This slightly dysfunctional setting purports to deliver
weather forecasts by city, and it does for major metropolises. If your
environment isn't highly urban, don't bother — get your weather from
another source.

✔ **Cities.** This option connects with the excellent Lycos CitySearch
database of information about cities around the world.

✔ **Dictionary.** Select this one, type any word, click the Go Get It button,
and wait for the definition from the American Heritage Dictionary. Click
the <u>Full Entry</u> link for a longer definition.

✔ **Stock (symbol).** You need to know the stock exchange symbol of a
stock to use this feature. Just enter the symbol (try MSFT or INTC). The
results page displays a stock quote and, as a bonus, headlines to
related news stories.

✔ **Music (artist).** Hype alert! This one's a good example of what many
people consider to be the pollution of search engines by commercial
interests. Type a musical artist with this selection activated and you're
sent to CDNow, the online music seller, to buy CDs of that artist. To get
Web page links for a certain musician, just use the default The Web
setting.

- ✔ **Books.** Same deal with Books as with Music (artist). This selection sends your search request to Barnesandnoble.com, the online bookstore.

- ✔ **Pictures.** The Pictures option does a great job of tracking down images stored in Web sites. Your keyword(s) are compared to the titles of GIF and JPG files (GIF and JPG are the two most common graphics formats on the Web).

- ✔ **Sounds.** This selection searches for any of various sound file formats, including MIDI files (MID), WAV and AIFF files, and RealAudio (RA) presentations.

- ✔ **Downloads.** When you use this option, Lycos matches your keywords to available downloads at the software library of ZDNet, a well-stocked shareware emporium.

- ✔ **Recipes.** Recipes? Recipes.

Using the drop-down list on the home page provides one way of selecting the search field. Lycos is extremely user-friendly; it displays the search fields on almost every page during your search. If the drop-down list does not appear on a search results page, Lycos assumes that if you enter new keywords on that search results page, you want to search the same area you chose with the drop-down list. If you want to change search options, retreat to the home page and start over.

Trying, trying, and trying again

To familiarize yourself with the search fields, simply give each a try! Because a keyword search takes only a second or two, you can get a feel for each selection's pros and cons quickly. Use the same keyword for all the search field searches so that comparing the results has more meaning.

Enhancing Your Lycos Search

Performing a quick search from the Lycos home page scratches only the surface of the available options. To dig below the surface, you need to familiarize yourself with the Advanced Options page. Here's how:

1. **Go to the Lycos home page at this address:**

   ```
   www.lycos.com
   ```

2. **Click the Lycos Pro link.**

When you get to the Advanced Options page, you see an enhanced keyword search form just bristling with options. These options enable you to tailor the results of your keyword searches.

The Advanced Options keyword entry form

The Advanced Options page has a keyword entry form similar to the Lycos home page, but with a new set of Search for options. Click the drop-down list above the keyword form to select them, as shown in Figure 6-4.

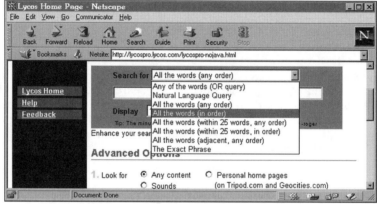

Figure 6-4:
The Advanced Options drop-down list offers new search choices.

The Advanced Options drop-down list provides options that determine how Lycos interprets and matches your keywords. These options let you fine-tune how multiple keywords relate to *each other:*

- **Any of the words (OR query):** Basically, this sets the OR search operator in place (see Chapters 3 and 4).

- **Natural Language Query:** Choosing this option lets you type a phrase of keywords as if you were naturally asking a question. Lycos uses its logic formulas to match your query to Web sites more or less accurately. Experiment with this option to see how it works for you.

- **All the words (any order):** This choice forces Lycos to match all your keywords, but they may occur anywhere in the Web site, even out of order.

- **All the words (in order):** Lycos must find all your keywords in any search result, and they must occur in the same order you typed them, but not necessarily right next to each other.

- **All the words (within 25 words, any order):** When using this option, Lycos must find all your keywords, and they must be within 25 words *of each other.* However, they can be in a different order than you typed them.

✔ **All the words (within 25 words, in order):** With this choice, Lycos finds all your keywords, within 25 words of each other, found in the same order you typed them.

✔ **All the words (adjacent, any order):** Use this option if you want Lycos to find all your words, next to each other, but not necessarily in the same order you typed them.

✔ **The Exact Phrase:** No compromises. Lycos must find all your keywords, exactly as you typed them.

Getting a grip on your options

As you can see in Figure 6-5, the Advanced Options page presents you with four groups of options.

✔ **Look for:** The Look for options enable you to select how the keywords are interpreted by the Lycos system. You may notice that they are identical to some of the options found on the drop-down list at the home page, described previously. The value of using them on *this* page is in combination with the other options described next.

✔ **Search the:** These options determine whether Lycos will search entire Web sites for your keywords or just titles or URLs (Web addresses). You can even select an individual Web site (if you know the URL), and Lycos will search that single site for your keywords.

Figure 6-5:
The
Advanced
Options
page
displays
several
search
options.

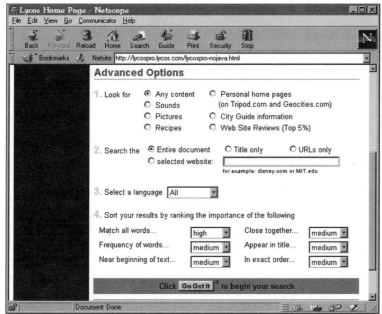

When using the Selected Website option, remember to click the radio button after you enter the Web site you want to search.

✔ **Select a language:** Lycos searches for Web sites containing text in approximately 15 different languages. Select one from the drop-down list.

✔ **Sort your results:** This option determines how your search results are listed. By selecting high, medium, or low from each of the drop-down lists, you choose the importance of your keyword matchups. If you want search hits whose page titles contain your keywords, select high from the Appear in Title drop-down list. Likewise, if you want the top of your search results list to contain sites that match your keywords many times, select high from the Frequency of Words drop-down list.

The important thing to remember about this option is that it doesn't affect how Lycos interprets your keywords — that's what all the previous options are for. The Sort your results option determines in what order your results are listed.

Hmmm . . .

With all these search and display options at your command, you need some keyword strategies. Lots of experimenting, plus some basic tools, places you on easygoing terms with the Lycos enhanced search page in short order.

Starting big

You can just dive in and swim around in the massive number of sites the Web offers in your subject area. Sometimes you should start big and then narrow down. Follow these guidelines for the first stage of a wide search. (Figure 6-6 shows what these settings look like on your screen.)

✔ Use fewer keywords, rather than more. Don't try to narrow your search until you know what you're narrowing down from. Start with one or two keywords.

✔ Use the Any of the words (OR query) option from the drop-down list. This option provides the widest possible setting.

✔ In the Display field, select 40 results per page. This selection gives you the quickest overview of how overwhelmed you may be.

✔ In the Look for field, select Any content.

✔ In the Search the field, select Entire document.

✔ From the Select a language drop-down list, select All.

✔ In the Sort your results drop-down lists, select Low in each menu.

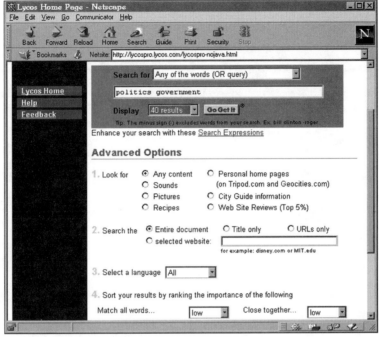

Figure 6-6:
These
Lycos
settings
cast the
widest
possible
searching
net.

Narrowing down

Okay, you're overwhelmed! Unless you have a great deal of time for surfing huge lists of matches, you need to narrow your keyword commands. Figure 6-7 shows these settings:

- ✔ Use more keywords. If you're looking for sites about cars, add the names of automobile models, manufacturers, and years.

- ✔ Use the Exact Phrase search option. Combined with more keywords, this option narrows the results drastically.

- ✔ Change the Display field to read 10 results per page. You should get more information about fewer sites per page, which is an appropriate selection now that you're honing in on better matches.

- ✔ In the Search the field, select Title only.

- ✔ In the Select a language drop-down list, select English (or any language).

- ✔ In the Sort your results drop-down lists, select High for all choices.

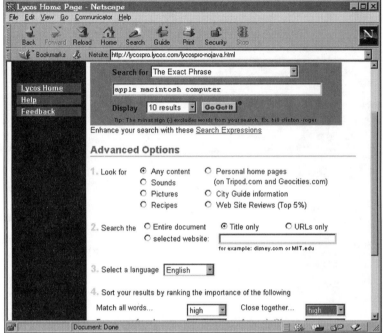

Figure 6-7:
Set the
Lycos
search
options like
this to
narrow
down the
results.

Fine-tuning

If you narrow your search too much, you won't get any results. That's no fun. Widen cautiously and back out using a combination of these tools:

- ✔ Take off a keyword or two from your string. Usually, three to five keywords will zero in on a good number of hits.

- ✔ Select one of the All the Words options from the drop-down list, but not The Exact Phrase option.

Chapter 7
The Excite Concept

· ·

In This Chapter

▶ Searching by concept in Excite

▶ Doing quick keyword searches in Excite

▶ What a concept! Concept searching

▶ Becoming a power searcher

▶ Trying keyword operators with Excite

· ·

*T*he Excite search service introduced a novel idea to the World Wide Web: searching by concept. (Other search engines have copied the idea, but Excite was the first and has the most experience with concept-based searching.) Anyone who has spent some time entering keywords into a search engine and examining the results knows how literal the process is. It takes some effort to think of the best keywords — the ones that lead the way to the best Web sites. Then the situation is compounded by keyword operators, the AND, NOT, and OR words that fit between your keywords and help the search engine know exactly what you're looking for. (I describe keyword operators in Chapter 3.)

Enter the Excite search engine, offering a blissful promise: Just tell Excite in plain English what you want, and Excite finds it for you. No need to tangle yourself in keyword phraseology and operator syntax — a simple English phrase will do. Excite purports to deal in concepts every bit as fluently as it deals with literal keywords. Does it work? Yes. How well? You have to decide for yourself because it depends on your needs. While you're finding out, Excite offers regular keyword functions, too, as well as a variety of surprising features that place Excite squarely in the forefront of Web searching.

Starting Quickly

Use the Excite home page as your starting point for concept-based Web searches. You get there by entering this address into your Web browser:

```
www.excite.com
```

The concept concept

How does the Excite search engine, which after all, is just a computer, understand concepts? Can computer software really stop being literal-minded long enough to be that smart?

The Excite search engine has a kind of learned intelligence that it bases on how words work together. If certain words often appear in close proximity — such as *ice* and *cream* — they tend to imply a concept that differs from the meaning of either word separately. Furthermore, you can get the gist of that concept from the consistent proximity of words such as *eat, mouth, soft, dessert,* and *frozen.* Excite can recognize many different word groupings and the concepts implied by those groupings. The search engine can recognize that the keywords *ice cream* match a Web site with the words *frozen dessert.*

In typical keyword searches, synonyms (words that mean the same thing) and homonyms (words that sound the same but have different meanings) can cause confusion. For example, the keyword *play* can have essentially the same meaning as drama, but the two words do not match when you search for drama sites. The keyword does match, however, with uses of the word *play* that mean frolic, an irrelevant match.

Excite gets around this problem by understanding words in context, according to a formula that takes word proximity into consideration. For example, if you type the phrase *plays by william shakespeare,* the Excite software may know enough to also link up pages that include the word *drama* close to the words *william shakespeare,* even if the word *play* isn't there. In this way, it strives to deliver search results based on concepts rather than on literal keyword meanings. Of course, in the competitive world of Web searching, each search engine's secrets are closely guarded, and this general explanation does not fully describe the complex Excite search formula.

Here's a concept for you: When searching by concept, don't think too hard. (Not thinking at all is my preference.) Type in what you're looking for as if you are telling a friend. Are you looking for pictures of the Star Trek Voyager crew? Type *pictures of the star trek voyager crew* into the keyword entry box. How about state senators in California? Just type the phrase in. You can be as conversational as you want, within the limits of a single phrase. If the results aren't satisfactory, you can always resort to more disciplined keyword searching.

The Excite home page sports a handy keyword form (see Figure 7-1).

You can test the waters in Excite immediately by following these steps:

1. **Place your cursor in the keyword form and click.**

2. **Type a single keyword, more than one keyword, or a simple phrase describing what you want to find.**

   You can be informal and relaxed about keywords you use in Excite. Just type in any short phrase describing what you want, such as *how to create Web pages.*

3. **Click the Search button, which you find next to the keyword form.**

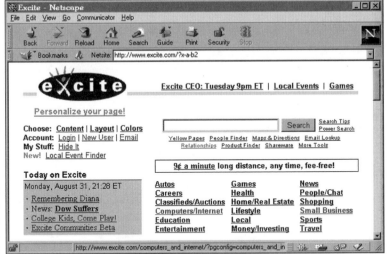

Figure 7-1:
The
keyword
entry form
on the
Excite home
page.

A few seconds after you click the Search button, you see the Search Results page, which lists your hits (see Figure 7-2). At this point, Excite has found Web sites that match any one (or more) of your keywords. Excite presents the sites that match your keywords in the order that the Excite search engine deems most useful. Excite clusters the matches that correspond to more than one of your concept words at the top, as it does those that match your words many times within the Web site.

Each link also offers a one-paragraph summary of the site and a percentage evaluation of the accuracy of the match. (Excite does not divulge the formula for determining hit accuracy, which it calls *confidence.* Just as well, because probably very few people would understand it.)

Excite can sort the search results page in three ways:

✔ **Default:** As shown in Figure 7-2, the default search results page displays the site link and a brief description and is ordered by the closeness of the match to your keywords.

✔ **Show Titles only:** This setting gets rid of the brief descriptions. The advantage is that you can see all your results on the screen without scrolling, because showing only titles takes much less room.

✔ **List by Web site:** When you choose this option, Excite scraps the confidence rating scheme in favor of listing the matched Web sites in a directory style. Excite groups individual Web page links under the home page to which they belong (see Figure 7-3). In this fashion, you can see at a glance when multiple links all belong to a single, inclusive site.

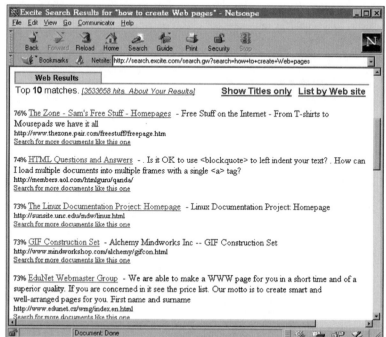

Figure 7-2:
A Search
Results
page in
Excite.

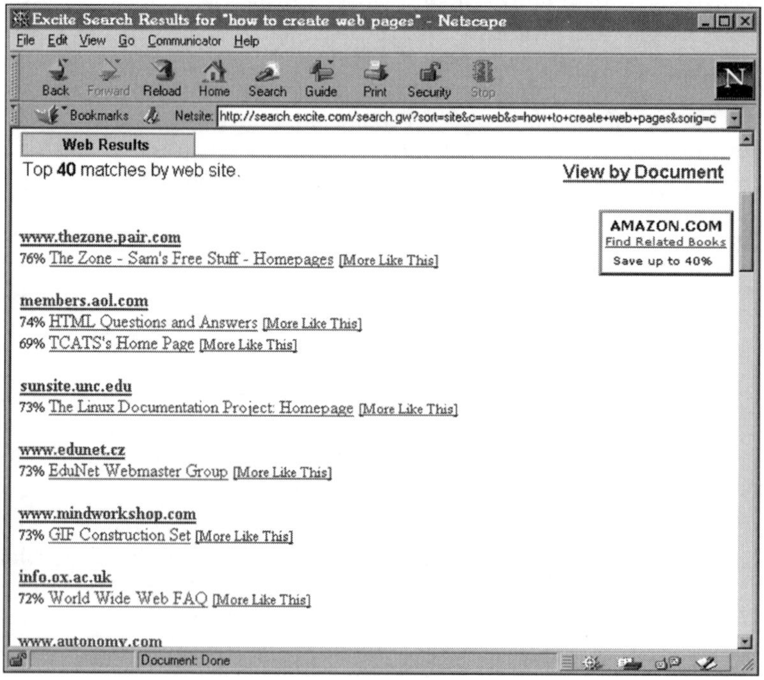

Figure 7-3:
The Query
Results
page
displayed
with the List
by Web site
option.

You can switch between the three ways of sorting results by using the links near the top of the Search Results page (see Figure 7-2). Click the links to switch from one setting to another.

Mastering the Excite System

The Excite search engine is unique. All search engines have individual strengths and weaknesses, but Excite is — if this makes any sense — more unique than others. Excite goes against current conventions among search engines, but not just for the sake of being contrary. The system is successful in a way that benefits the user. In my opinion, Excite manages to deliver more of what a beginner wants than other search engines while hiding from the user the sophistication of its concept searching.

Excite's magic trick is to deliver several different *types* of search results and further, to know which type is appropriate to your keyword(s). Because the system is so transparent, no explicit features control it. Other search engines, for example, offer drop-down lists for determining the type of search result you get. It may seem that Excite is committing a sin of omission by not providing such selection menus. The beauty is, Excite takes control of your search by providing the type of results you benefit most from receiving, based on your keywords. Such presumption must be executed well or it will be merely annoying. Excite is not annoying.

 Although I'm praising Excite quite a bit in these paragraphs, I recognize that its unique system may not be for everyone. It definitely takes some getting used to. You may prefer the strong search control options provided by other search engines. You may not like the way Excite chooses the type of search results it thinks your keywords deserve. The Excite search results page requires a bit of navigation, and that effort can be distracting during a focused search. The purpose of this section is to give you the understanding necessary to test Excite fully and see how (and if) it meets your needs.

The Excite game plan

Excite always assumes that your search is asking a question, and its search results attempt to answer that question. This doesn't mean that you must phrase your keywords in the form of a question — I'm just describing the built-in attitude of the search engine, which explains why it delivers more than one type of result. Excite never assumes you're looking *only* for a Web site. It assumes that you can use information contained *within* Web sites, and attempts to deliver that information directly to the search results page.

An example of how each search could be a question is seen in the keyword string: *new york yankees record baseball season.* (A likely keyword string in 1998, when the Yankees baseball team broke team winning records.) Many search engines would dutifully list every Web site that contains at least one of those keywords, beginning with the sites that contain all the keywords. You'd have rich pickings, sorting through many thousands of sites. Excite, on the other hand, assumes that you're really asking a few questions, such as: What is the Yankees' record right now? Did they win last night? Where is the official Yankees home page? How can I read news reports of the team published in today's papers? To all these questions, Excite has explicit answers and delivers them directly to the search results page, which can save a lot of time and hassle.

Types of search results

Excite solves the ambitious goal of answering your search question by dividing search results into different types. You may browse among the types of results provided to your keywords, but you can't predetermine them. Excite just does its thing, and if the results are useful to you, you'll keep coming back for more.

Following are the types of search result you're likely to see in Excite:

- **Company information:** If you type the name of a company as a keyword, Excite delivers an assortment of information about that company before it even shows you related Web sites. Depending on the company, you're likely to see a stock quote; the company address; a product search if that company is a manufacturer; links to a company profile, analyst ratings, and financial information; and a link to the company home page. (See Figure 7-4.)

- **Team information:** If you use the name of a sports team as your keyword, Excite displays information about the team before listing Web sites about the team. Included information can cover these points: team playing schedule; recent results (win or lose) and scores; link to the official team home page; calendar of upcoming games; statistics and team rosters; and league standings, schedules, and statistics. (See Figure 7-5.)

- **Regional information:** If you type a locale (such as a city name) as a keyword, Excite pushes current regional information to the front of the search results. This information can include the weather; links to maps and travel guides; links to travel reservations services; and links to regional classifieds and Yellow Pages. (See Figure 7-6.)

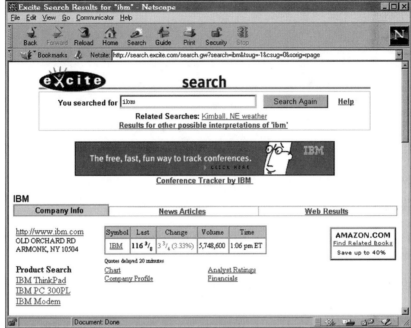

Figure 7-4:
Company
information
displayed
by Excite
for the
keyword
ibm.

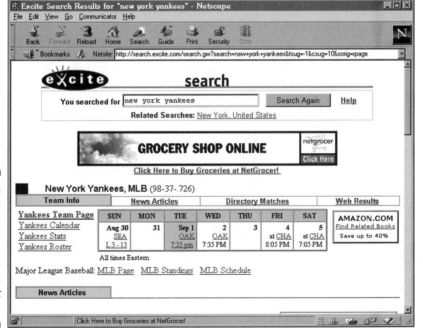

Figure 7-5:
Team
information
displayed
by Excite
for the
keywords
*new york
yankees.*

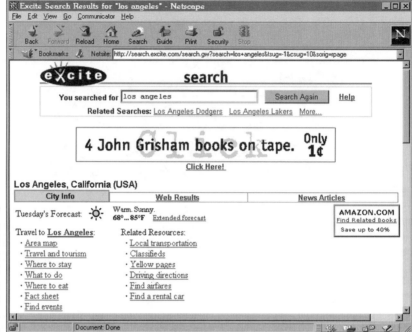

Figure 7-6:
Regional
information
displayed
for the
keywords
los angeles.

✔ **News articles:** Excite apparently believes everyone wants some news. That may be true. The News Articles heading of a search results page (Figure 7-7) signals links to current stories related to your keyword(s). The articles are from a variety of Web-based news sources. (See Chapter 16 for a search expedition for news on the Internet.)

✔ **Directory matches:** It's sometimes useful to abandon a keyword search in favor of the search engine's directory menu. Excite makes it easy by linking you directly to the directory pages that best match your keywords.

✔ **Web results:** This heading rounds up the links to related Web sites that make up the traditional search results. Web results are usually placed at the bottom of the search results page.

Excite is not infallible. It sometimes misinterprets your keyword "question," and delivers the wrong answer. For example, I recently typed the keywords *stock market*. Excite thought I was searching for a company, and displayed information about Market Guide, Inc. It also delivered links to Web sites about the stock market, further down the page, but it was an obvious misunderstanding. I guess that's what we get when we rely on the intelligence of computers.

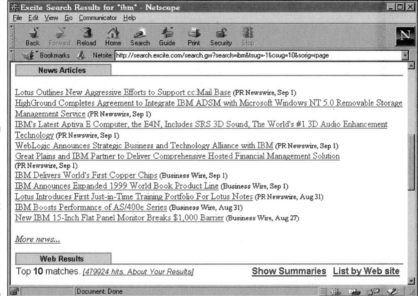

Figure 7-7:
Excite
includes
links to
current
news
articles on
the search
results
page.

Excite sometimes gets confused by long keyword strings. If you'd like a variety of Excite-style information about a sports team or company, it's best to type the team or company name, and no other words. If you use *role of apple macintosh in the personal computer revolution,* you won't see the company information you get by typing *apple.*

Power Searching in Excite

Simple, concept-based searching may get you where you're going by itself. If you need something more specific or if you're a glutton for keyword punishment, Excite can give you a run for your money. (Just a figure of speech; Excite offers its services for free.)

You can find the Excite Power Search link next to the keyword entry form on the home page. (Refer to Figure 7-1.) Clicking it displays the Excite Search Options page, which contains an array of keyword entry fields and drop-down lists (see Figure 7-8).

Where to search

Your first choice when power searching is deciding what portion of the Excite database to search in. You have a few alternatives:

✔ **The Web:** This is the default setting when you first enter Excite. Excite matches your keywords against its entire index of Web sites.

✔ **Selected Web sites:** When you choose this setting, Excite limits the search to its collected reviews of Web sites. The review database is smaller than the total search index, but you get more critical information about matching sites.

✔ **Current news:** Excite keeps a running database of news stories from about 300 publications and news services. Choose NewsTracker to limit your search to current news items.

✔ **International searching:** Excite has country-specific indexes of Web sites, and you may limit your search to Germany, France, United Kingdom, or Sweden. (Excite may expand the list of countries.)

Keyword options

The Excite Search Options page provides no fewer than three keyword entry fields, each accompanied by a drop-down list that helps Excite interpret your keywords correctly.

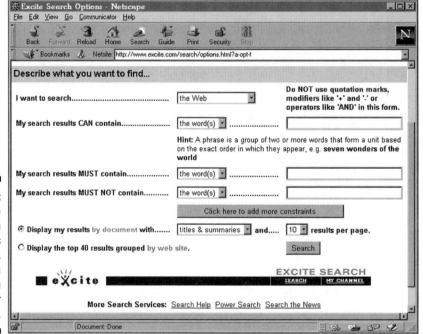

Figure 7-8:
The Excite
Search
Options
page,
where you
perform
power
searches.

Use the drop-down lists to indicate whether or not your keywords represent a literal phrase. For example, *yankees record baseball* is a keyword string, but is not a literal phrase. You don't want Excite searching for those three words in that order, because you won't get any results. However, *new york yankees* can be treated as a literal phrase, and it matches sites that have "New York Yankees" somewhere in their text.

This is what the keyword options mean:

- ✔ **My search results CAN contain:** Use this option to type words (or a phrase) that *may* exist in matches sites, but are not necessarily found in those sites (the OR search operator).

- ✔ **My search results MUST contain:** Use this option to type words (or a phrase) that *must* exist in matched sites (the AND search operator).

- ✔ **My search results MUST NOT contain:** Use this option to specify words (or a phrase) that *must not* exist in matched sites. If the words or phrase do exist in a site, it will not appear on your search results (the NOT search operator).

Keyword Operators in Excite

Although Excite features its capability to understand and search on phrase concepts, it also accepts run-of-the-mill keywords. At any time, you can type keywords in the traditional, literal fashion and type standard keyword operators. (See Chapters 3 and 4 for detailed hints about using keyword operators.) Excite uses symbols as an alternative to spelling out the operators. You have the following options:

- ✔ **Using AND (+):** When you enter more than one keyword, you can require the system to match all your words, not just one or some of them. Use the word AND between the keywords, or substitute a plus (+) sign:

```
stephen AND king AND movies
stephen +king +movies
```

- ✔ **Using NOT (-):** Sometimes you may want to eliminate a word occurrence from your search, especially when you use a keyword that may often bring up irrelevant results. When you anticipate such a word and want to eliminate results that contain it, place a NOT before the second keyword or type a minus (-) sign with the hyphen key:

```
jazz NOT ragtime = jazz -ragtime
```

> ✔ **Using OR and parentheses:** Use the OR operator when you want Excite to send back results on *any* of your keywords. Using OR gives you the most results of any of the operators. Using parentheses to group words — even when you separate the words by other operators — narrows your search and gives you fewer results.

When you use the plus and minus symbols (+ and -) in place of AND and NOT, don't leave a space between the symbol and the following word (which is the word the symbol refers to). The string may look a little weird, but what could be stranger than launching into cyberspace from your living room in the first place?

You can get complex and technical with search operators. Sound like fun? I didn't think so. If you slip into an existential malaise, however, look in Chapter 3 for a complete tutorial on using search operators. It'll snap you right back to reality.

Chapter 8
AltaVista in Any Language

*1*s AltaVista a has-been search engine? It still enjoys a well-earned reputation for sophisticated Internet search tools. AltaVista has long been the choice of Net-savvy folks on the prowl for specific information. But as many search engines have succumbed to portal fever — trading a sleek, search-first interface for magazine-style, newsy design — AltaVista has abandoned many of the features that once distinguished it. The company's advanced searching tools were unparalleled; now its search options are marginally useful or, in some cases, outright hindrances. At least one feature is simply broken as of this writing.

AltaVista is still considered a major search engine, and I include this chapter out of respect for its lineage and because its search results may still legitimately appeal to many people. Furthermore, AltaVista is the most international of search engines, letting you search exclusively in any one of 25 (as of this writing) languages.

AltaVista cannot be eliminated from a definitive book about Internet searching . . . yet. If the site continues to reduce its research value, it will probably lose its status as a productive engine. It has recently been purchased by Compaq, the computer manufacturer, so perhaps better days lie ahead. In the meantime, this chapter describes the procedures and features of AltaVista.

Performing Simple Searches

Immediate gratification being a good thing, you can experiment with simple searches on the AltaVista search engine right away. Later, I show you how to accomplish more complex requests of the search engine. For now, just follow these steps:

1. **Type the following address in your Web browser:**

   ```
   altavista.digital.com
   ```

2. **When the AltaVista Main Page appears, type one or more keywords in the keyword entry form (see Figure 8-1).**

3. **Click the Search button to begin the search.**

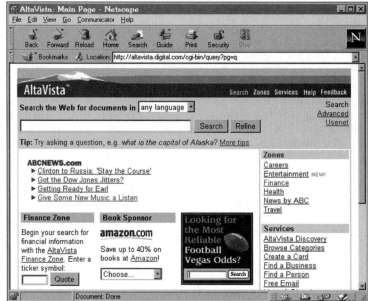

Figure 8-1:
The Main Page of the AltaVista search engine.

The search results page

Within a second or two of clicking the Search button, you see a results page that shows Web links that match your keyword(s). AltaVista searches entire Web sites, so the keyword match may occur in any part of the matched site's text. (The search may also match words that don't appear visibly on a page, such as keywords inserted invisibly by the page creator. Those hidden keywords push sites toward the top of search results lists.) You could find the match in the page title or in a footnote way down at the bottom of the page. The search engine automatically places the best matches at the top of the list.

How does AltaVista determine a best match or even a mediocre one? First, it recognizes whether all or only some of your keywords match in the Web site. (AltaVista groups sites that match all your keywords at the top of the list.) Also, AltaVista counts how many times the search engine finds the keyword in the Web site and then looks to see where the keyword appears in the site. When the match appears in the site's title or closer to the beginning of the site's text, the match gets a better score.

After a quick search, you see a results page that has links to matched Web sites (see Figure 8-2).

You should know the following things about the results page:

✔ The results page contains only ten items, even if your search found more than ten matches. This limitation speeds the display process, and — just as importantly — prevents you from being overwhelmed by thousands of links all at once. You can link to other pages (each with only ten items) at the bottom of any results page.

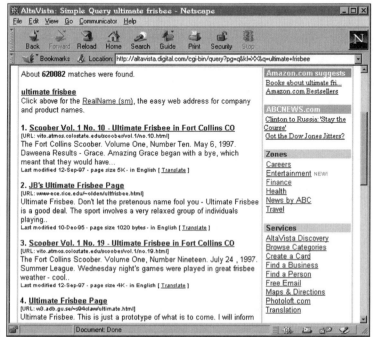

Figure 8-2: Part of the results page in an AltaVista simple query.

✔ The keyword entry form appears at the top of every search results page. In effect, it follows you — sort of like a puppy — from the Main Page, where you began, to the results page. Having the form on the results page comes in handy: You can refine your search by entering new keywords without backtracking to the Main Page. Handier still, all search options from the Main Page also follow along. And handiest of all, the keyword entry form is paper-trained.

✔ Each matched item contains a site title, a brief summary paragraph, and a link address (URL). You can hyperlink to the site by clicking the link title, not the URL. AltaVista lists the size and date of the page under the description.

AltaVista used to list how many times each of your keywords matched. This was sometimes useful, because it indicated which of your keywords worked the hardest and gave a clue about how to modify future searches. Alas, the listing no longer exists.

The Refine button

Near the top of every search results page in AltaVista lies a mysterious Refine button, right next to the keyword entry form and the Search button. Obviously, it refers to the highly refined nature of your character. Besides that, it initiates a feature designed to narrow your search.

Refine presents several keyword clusters, presumably related to your original keyword(s), which you may include or exclude from your search. Each cluster of keywords is fixed to a small drop-down list (see Figure 8-3). Select Require to add those keywords to your search string. Select Exclude to determine that matched sites must *not* include that cluster of keywords. Do not use the drop-down list (or select the ellipses — the three dots) for any cluster you don't care about or that seems irrelevant to the search.

AltaVista presents only additional keyword clusters that appear in potentially matched (to your original keywords) sites. Nevertheless, some of the clusters are bizarre and off-track. Just ignore them. Is Refine useful? It's good for bringing to the top of the results list sites that contain material you want, but didn't think to ask for in your keyword string. Refine is good to use after the first results page doesn't give you quite what you want. Also, you can Refine your Refine settings, which is a good way of narrowing the results to a manageable number.

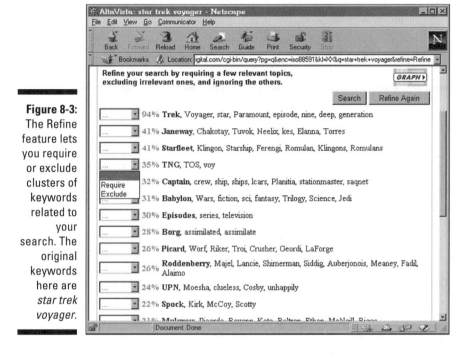

Figure 8-3:
The Refine feature lets you require or exclude clusters of keywords related to your search. The original keywords here are *star trek voyager*.

Setting Your AltaVista Preferences

At the bottom of each search page, including the search results pages, in very tiny print, is a link called Set your Preferences. On the Set Your Preference page, various options let you determine how AltaVista appears and operates on your computer.

The Preferences options that I describe next apply only to your current search session. If you bookmark the AltaVista Main Page, using that bookmark at any time resets the Preferences to their default settings. You can get around this: When you click the Set Preferences button, a new Main Page appears; bookmark that Main Page.

Following are the Preferences options for AltaVista:

✔ **Encoding.** AltaVista is great for searching in different languages. If you plan to search primarily in a non-English (and non-Western) language, you should set the correct encoding, and then bookmark the resulting Main Page. Encoding is what makes the transliterated language appear correctly in your browser. You probably need to refer to your browser's Help section for the correct setting in the language you choose.

✔ **Languages.** This is where you can select the language(s) in which AltaVista searches. Feel free to select more than one.

✔ **Text-only View.** With this option, AltaVista pages display much quicker and are free of advertisements. Text-only searching doesn't cause the search engine to operate more quickly, but your results are displayed more quickly. I think the text-only pages look pretty nice, myself, but that probably betrays my warped design sensibilities. (Confirm my bad taste by looking at Figure 8-4.)

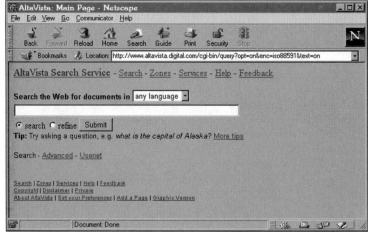

Figure 8-4:
The text-only view of AltaVista.

✔ **Advanced Search.** Use this option to get more search options, which I describe later in this chapter. A simpler way to get those options is to click the Advanced link on the Main Page at any time. Use the Set Your Preferences page to select the Advanced Search option in combination with another option, such as Text-only View, and package both options (and others, if you like) into a default set of choices.

✔ **Compact Format for Web Results.** This choice creates a more compact search results page by eliminating the descriptions of Web sites. You get the links and their posting dates, and that's about it. The type is really small, too, yet AltaVista still groups only ten per page. Go figure — as long as the type is conducive to microscope viewing, you might as well squeeze 50 on a page. Glance at Figure 8-5 to see a compacted search results page.

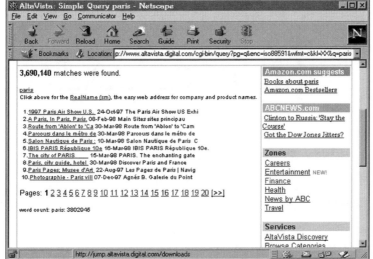

✔ **Detailed Format for Usenet Results.** When searching the Usenet newsgroups (as I describe in the next section), you may expand the search results list by using the detailed format — but the fact is, you don't get any useful added information this way, and the larger type just clogs up the page and makes it unreasonably long. I don't recommend this option, in case you didn't notice.

✔ **Graph View for Refine.** This option puts a new perspective on the Refine feature, which I describe in the preceding section. Instead of displaying the keyword clusters as a list with drop-down menus, the Graph View starts a Java applet that presents the keyword clusters as a subject tree. (See Figure 8-6.) Roll your mouse cursor over any main keyword to see the whole cluster, and then use the check boxes to select individual keywords for Required or Excluded status in your search.

The graph view of the Refine option takes a minute to load the first time you use it. Thereafter, as long as you don't shut down your Web browser, the view displays in a second or two.

The graph view brings the Refine feature to life and is highly recommended. You may find, as I have, that the sheer fun of using it makes you search for more topics. It certainly improves search results and is more flexible than the nongraph view.

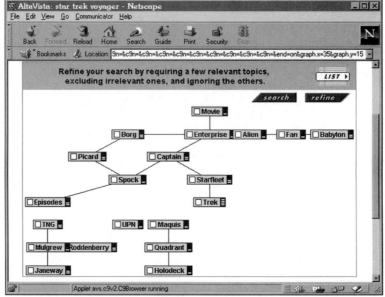

Figure 8-6:
The graph
view of the
Refine
feature. The
original
keyword
string is
*Star Trek
Voyager.*

Using the Usenet Option

AltaVista can perform searches of Usenet newsgroup messages just as easily as it can search for Web pages. (Usenet is the bulletin board system of the Internet.) Here's how to switch to a simple Usenet search:

1. **Click the <u>Usenet</u> link on the Main Page.**

2. **Enter one or more keywords.**

3. **Click the Search button.**

Searching Usenet newsgroups brings up a different search results page from the one you've seen previously (see Figure 8-7).

From this nifty page, you can do the following:

✔ Click the title of the Usenet message to display a copy of that message. Remember that seeing one message differs from reading a newsgroup from your news server: You see only the one message, out of the context of the rest of the newsgroup.

✔ You can view the message *in context* by clicking the L column for the message. You then see a copy of the message from your local news server, instead of from the AltaVista archives. When you use this feature, AltaVista embeds the message with other messages from the newsgroup, some of which may be responses to the message.

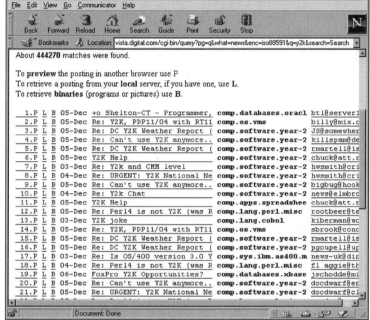

Figure 8-7:
The
AltaVista
results
page for a
Usenet
search.

✔ Click the e-mail name of the person who wrote the message if you want to send e-mail directly to that person, right from your Web browser.

✔ You can view binary files (such as pictures) associated with the message by clicking the B column for the message. Most newsgroups have no binary files to be seen. Usenet messages are mostly ASCII (a plain text format understood by all computers), not binary digitizations such as pictures. Therefore, clicking B usually displays just the message.

The Usenet search feature in AltaVista borrows technology from Deja News, another search engine I describe in Chapter 11. AltaVista borrows only part of the Deja News system, however, and the searching experience is compromised compared to searching in Deja News. In particular, when you view a Usenet message that matches your keyword(s), you cannot post a response to the message in a Usenet newsgroup from your Web browser. Furthermore, you can't reorganize the search results by date or subject, as you can in Deja News. So if you're bent on searching Usenet for a spell, it's best to flip to Chapter 11 and surf over to Deja News.

Advanced (So-Called) Searches

AltaVista no longer offers advanced searching that approaches its previous power. The most advanced feature in the present-day AltaVista is the Refine feature, which I describe earlier in this chapter. Still, an advanced search page exists, and this section describes it.

You can get to the advanced version of the keyword entry form by clicking the Advanced link on the Main Page. As you can see in Figure 8-8, you are still on the Main Page, but the keyword input boxes look different. The top field works exactly as the keyword entry field on the previous Main Page: Just type a keyword or two and click the Search button.

Figure 8-8:
The advanced searching page of AltaVista. Not much to rave about.

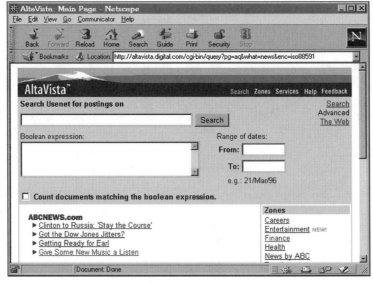

Using the Boolean expression form

Like other Web searching services, AltaVista enables you to incorporate keyword operators — the AND, OR, and NOT qualifiers that modify how the search engine interprets your keywords — into your search string. (Using search operators in the proper syntax is called Boolean searching, and those keyword strings are called *Boolean expressions*.) AltaVista also provides a few uncommon options that enable you to narrow your search in unusual and potentially useful ways. (Chapter 3 sheds light on keyword operators in a general way.)

The following list shows you how the operators work in AltaVista:

- **Using AND (&):** When you want to require the search engine to find matches to *all* your keywords, and not just one or two of a multiple-keyword string, place the AND operator between the words. The results page lists only links to Web sites that contain all your keywords. You also can use the & symbol:

  ```
  baseball AND cricket
  baseball & cricket
  ```

- **Using OR (|):** At other times, you may want to widen the search deliberately by allowing the results to match only one of your keywords. In that case, use the OR operator between your words. The results page contains links to Web sites that match at least one keyword; sites that match more than one keyword are grouped nearer the top. You also can use the | symbol (the one that looks like a broken vertical slash on your keyboard and is often the uppercase choice of the backslash key).

  ```
  broadcasting OR radio OR television
  broadcasting | radio | television
  ```

- **Using AND NOT (!):** To use the NOT operator, you need to type **AND NOT** when you perform an AltaVista search. If you just use NOT, the system bounces back a blank results page, whimpers in confusion, and asks for the correct syntax. Use this operator when you want to exclude a word that would generate a match in irrelevant Web sites. You can substitute the ! symbol:

  ```
  magic AND NOT marker
  magic ! marker
  ```

- **Using NEAR (~):** This very useful operator ensures that two words or phrases appear within ten words of each other in the target Web site. If the words appear farther than ten words apart, you don't get a match. Using NEAR provides a contextual aspect to your search. You also can use the ~ symbol:

  ```
  abbott NEAR costello
  abbott ~ costello
  ```

- **Using parentheses ((and)):** AltaVista groups keywords together with parentheses so that you can use other operators within the parenthetical group. This way, you can create a subset of keywords that AltaVista interprets differently than other words. AltaVista uses the parentheses search operator in a standard way, as I describe in Chapter 3.

  ```
  animals AND (barn OR farm)
  animals & (barn | farm)
  ```

Specifying dates

The advanced searching page contains two more fields besides the main keyword entry field and the Boolean expression field. Under Range of Dates, enter a beginning and an ending date that together define a time period within which to search. All Web pages are defined in time according to the last date they were modified, and AltaVista can use that information as part of the search.

On the results page, AltaVista lists your hits in the order you have determined: Matches to your ranking keyword appear at the beginning of the list.

Constrain yourself

AltaVista provides *constraining searches,* a specific type of searching. If you think that I'm getting too technical, suppress that reaction. You don't activate constraining searches with drop-down lists or button selections. Instead, you simply type certain tags into the Search Criteria field on the Advanced Query page. Then you follow the tag with a keyword. The tag determines how the search is constrained, and the keyword activates the search engine, as does any other keyword. Here's an example:

1. **You enter AltaVista bent on finding Web pages created by or created about the National Aeronautics and Space Administration, known as NASA.**

2. **On either keyword page (simple or advanced), enter the following keyword request:**

   ```
   title:NASA
   ```

   In this example, AltaVista searches only Web page titles, using the keyword *NASA.* The result is most likely constrained to official NASA pages, instead of a large search result of all pages containing *NASA* somewhere in their text. You can take the following step if the search results are too general and you want to narrow the field to Web pages by or about NASA that contain information about the Hale-Bopp comet.

3. **On a keyword entry page, enter the following keyword request:**

   ```
   hale-bopp title:NASA
   ```

Using constraining searches does require a learning curve, and AltaVista doesn't make it easy — we could use built-in selectors for the tags. But the learning curve is worth it! A constraining search tells the search engine to pay attention only to certain portions of the Web sites in its index. This feature can be very useful (upon occasion) if you remember to use it. The AltaVista search indexing software has catalogued every bit of millions of

Web pages — from their titles to their URLs, from their text content to the names of their downloadable graphics files. You can constrain your search to any of these areas. This nifty tool helps you find pages under a certain domain name or pictures that have a certain word in their filename.

Here are some of the specific possibilities, listed by the tag you use to activate them:

- **Finding pictures:** If you know the filename of a graphic and want to find it on the Web, you can constrain your search to image files by using the `image:` tag. Here's an example:

  ```
  image:simpsons.jpg
  ```

  In this example, AltaVista searches for all picture files in its database that have a `simpsons.jpg` filename. (JPG stands for a common type of online picture file.) Even if you don't know the exact filename, you can make an obvious guess that generally yields results. You can substitute `.gif` for the file extension or leave off the extension. (The latter option increases the size of your results dramatically and takes longer to display them.)

- **Finding links:** If you know a Web site and want to discover other Web pages that link to it, you can use the `link:` tag. Remember, you're not uncovering links *from* a particular site, you're searching for links that go *to* a particular Web site from other pages. The keyword following the `link:` tag indicates the Web page you want to find links *to*. This method offers an unusual and fresh way of finding related sites. You get some surprising results! Try this feature with the following example:

  ```
  link:whitehouse.com
  ```

  In this example, AltaVista finds pages that contain hyperlinks to any URL that includes `whitehouse.com`.

- **Finding titles:** Just about every Web page has a title — every self-respecting one, anyway. You can limit (constrain) your search to the words in World Wide Web titles with the `title:` tag. This method lets you obtain a smaller set of search results than normal, usually containing highly relevant links. Try it with this example:

  ```
  title:childcare
  ```

  This example finds sites containing the word *childcare* in the title bar.

AltaVista provides a complete list of allowable tags at the following address. You must use only an allowable tag — don't try making up your own!

```
www.altavista.digital.com/av/content/help.htm#simple
```

AltaVista touts one constraining search tag — the host tag — that displays a peculiar propensity: It doesn't work. At least, that's what I concluded in tests conducted right up to the publication deadline of this book. The host tag is supposed to deliver search results of a certain Web domain, such as nytimes.com, disney.com, or yahoo.com. If we are to believe AltaVista, none of those examples have any Web pages. I don't think that's the answer.

Here's a little tip for all you Webmasters out there. (*Webmaster* is a politically correct, cyber-hip term for a person of either gender who has a Web server or even a single page on someone else's Web server.) Use the link: tag to perform a constraining search on your own Web page. Keep in mind that this tag lists Web sites that link *to* the page represented by your keyword. Use this kind of search to find out which sites have a hyperlink to your page. Just type your URL after the tag. This example shows you how to do it:

```
link:www.yourpage.com
```

A Few Final Points, Finally

Just a few final words of wisdom to help you have a blast in AltaVista:

- ✔ **Don't capitalize unless you mean it:** Typing your keywords in all lowercase (noncapital) letters is safest. The search engine matches your keywords with any identically spelled word in a Web site, no matter how the site capitalizes the word. So *clinton* matches with *Clinton* or *CLINTON*. If you use a capital letter, however, the keyword matches only with identically capitalized words in Web sites. Therefore, *Clinton* matches with only *Clinton,* and not *clinton* or *CLINTON*.

- ✔ **Making phrases:** You can turn any sequence of keywords into a connected phrase, which avoids matching every occurrence of the individual words. For example, you could turn *former soviet union* into a phrase to eliminate every Web site that has *former* and *union* in it. You can make phrases in AltaVista in two ways: remove spaces or use quotation marks. Here is how *former soviet union* looks using both methods:

```
formersovietunion
"former soviet union"
```

- ✔ **Using the wild card:** Placing the wild card asterisk after a word fragment tells the AltaVista search engine that you want to match results with every occurrence of that root word, no matter what the actual word. For example, you could search Usenet for the following keyword:

```
legislat*
```

You get results that match all the extensions of that root word, including *legislature, legislative, legislator,* and *legislation.*

Chapter 9

Getting Practical with Infoseek

● ●

In This Chapter

▶ Searching in different Internet realms

▶ Using Infoseek search operators

▶ Performing advanced searches in Infoseek

● ●

*I*nfoseek, one of the most respected information services on the Web, gives you plenty of fancy search options. It also lets you perform a down-and-dirty quick keyword search. In other words, you can be as simple or as complicated as you want to be with Infoseek. One of Infoseek's distinguishing features is the capacity to search different portions of the Internet easily and switch among those portions at will. This chapter describes all the Infoseek features, and also spells out quantum physics. (Sorry, my editor cut the quantum physics part.)

One-Stop Searching

Infoseek makes getting what you want especially easy without a lot of rummaging through search pages. Although an <u>Advanced</u> search link leads to a distinct keyword page, Infoseek puts many of its search cards on the table right at the home page. Get a piece of the searching action by surfing to this address:

```
www.infoseek.com
```

Figure 9-1 shows the home page. You can dive right in by typing a keyword or two (or more) into the keyword entry form and clicking the seek button. Within a few seconds, your search results appear.

Infoseek enables you to define the area of the Internet in which your search takes place. I describe advanced search options later in this chapter, but a few simple choices pop up on the home page in the form of radio buttons, as shown in Figure 9-1. (Look right below the keyword entry form.) Here's what you need to do:

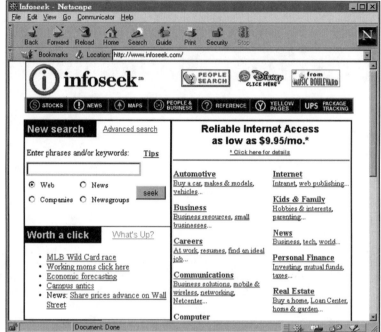

1. **Go to the Infoseek home page at the following address:**

   www.infoseek.com

2. **Select one of the four radio buttons or use the default Web selection.**

   At this point, you may not know what some of the choices mean. Good thing you're holding this book in your hands. Read on.

Infoseeking the Web

Infoseek uses the Web as the default search area; you see this option chosen as soon as you open Infoseek. You probably want to search the Web most of the time. You can use it to match your keywords against the Infoseek index of over 50 million Web pages.

When you start a search in the Web, Infoseek displays a search results page (see Figure 9-2) showing the first ten matches of your keywords, with the following information under each match:

Compress results   URL   Link to page

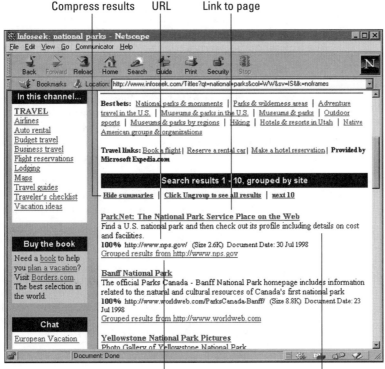

Figure 9-2:
Infoseek
gives you
great
results
when
searching
the Web.

Reveal all matched pages at the site   Page description

✔ **A brief summary of the Web site:** This lets you know a little of what
you're getting into before linking to the page itself. The Web sites
provide the summaries. The Infoseek staff doesn't write them, so a wide
range of intelligibility exists. If the summaries get too incoherent for
you, you can banish them by clicking the Hide summaries link above
the results list. A new page appears, sans silly summaries, with the
added benefit of squeezing 20, not 10, search results on the page with
the extra room.

✔ **A percentage ranking:** It's located just below the summary.
Supposedly, the higher the percentage, the closer the site matches your
search query. Many search engines use a percentage-ranking system,
using one formula or another to determine how suitable a Web site is to
your search. Infoseek bases the percentage on how frequently and how
close to the page title your keyword occurs. Take the results with a
grain or two of salt. I've always found that you can best assess
percentage rankings by ignoring them.

✔ **The site's URL:** This is right next to the percentage ranking. Although the URL isn't a hyperlink, you can still use it to see where you're going if you have a knack for reading URLs. Most Web browsers display the URL of a link when you move the mouse cursor over the link.

✔ **The size of the page:** Moving along, the page size appears next to the URL. This cool feature gives you an indication of whether the page loads quickly or slowly. The feature takes some of the guesswork out of a factor that can cause any Web veteran to hesitate about linking to a new site. Infoseek gives the size in kilobytes, abbreviated as K. However, graphics are not always included in the file size because they are separate files that may be called by the main page.

✔ **A Grouped results link:** This link appears below some of the matched sites, when the site contains multiple pages that match your keywords. Infoseek consolidates all page matches that exist in the same Web domain under a single search result. In Figure 9-2, you can see that the first site match comes from the National Park Service site, under the domain www.nps.gov. Clicking the Grouped results link reveals all the page matches in that site. A great feature! It saves space on the search results list, and helps you stay organized.

You may use the Click Ungroup to see all results link above the results list, but beware! Doing so expands your search results drastically. It's usually better to Ungroup only one Web site at a time.

Infoseeking Usenet

Newsgroups is another item with a radio button on the home page and represents Usenet newsgroups, the bulletin board system of the Internet. This selection limits your search to the texts of messages (called articles) posted to the Internet's Usenet bulletin boards. (See Chapter 11 for a more complete description of searching with Usenet.) When selected, your search results list links to the posted articles, which can be a few weeks old. Figure 9-3 shows a search results page of a Newsgroups search on the keywords *national parks*. Each match contains the following information:

✔ **Date:** This is the date on which the article was posted to the newsgroup.

✔ **A link to the Usenet message:** Click the link to read the article, but be aware that *article* is a high-falutin' term for what is usually a dashed-off message of a line or three. Usenet newsgroups provide informal discussion forms, and some articles are much more informative than others.

✔ **A listing of which newsgroup the article comes from:** This is not a link, but can be copied into your newsgroup reader to access the newsgroup directly.

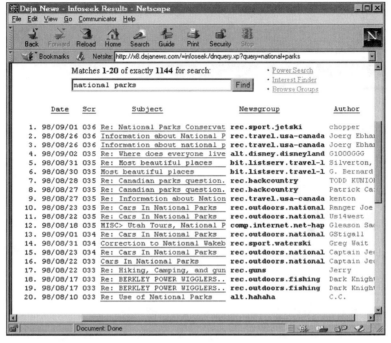

Figure 9-3:
Infoseek
search
results for a
Newsgroups
search.

| ✔ **Author:** Unfortunately, this column does not provide e-mail addresses, never mind links to the author's mailbox. The list merely provides the author's screen name. Not particularly helpful.

Infoseek borrows a Usenet search engine from Deja News, which I describe in Chapter 11. The Infoseek version is compromised in important ways, and if you want to seriously search Usenet newsgroups, it's best to head for Deja News.

Reading Usenet articles resulting from an Infoseek search differs from accessing Usenet newsgroups directly with a newsgroup reader, including the readers in Netscape Navigator or Internet Explorer. The Infoseek process is far more cumbersome, but the value lies in the accuracy of the search process.

Infoseeking the news

When you select the News radio button on the Infoseek home page, your keywords are compared to the texts of news stories from a variety of wire news services. The results look similar to results when searching for Web sites (see Figure 9-4). Each matched result consists of a link to a news story and the following information:

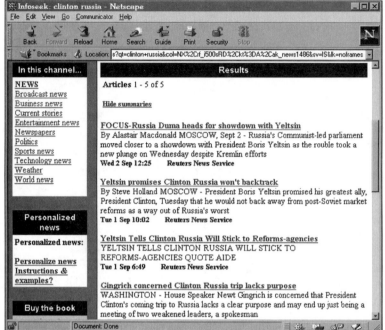

Figure 9-4:
An Infoseek
results
page when
searching
News
Wires
stories.

✔ **News story:** The first few lines of the news story appear directly below the story's link.

✔ **Date and time:** This is the date and time that the story was posted electronically. In most cases, the stories near the top of your Search Results page are no more than a few hours old. If you use obscure keywords, however, Infoseek may need to reach back into the news archives to find matches.

✔ **Source:** Next to the date and time is the wire service, newspaper, or other news source carrying the story.

When you click a news story in the Search Results page, Infoseek presents the full story, as written, without taking you outside the Infoseek service. Staying inside Infoseek is good news because the Infoseek site is very fast and almost never has delays.

Getting the company scoop

Infoseek provides a genuinely useful search option with its Companies search option. Choosing Companies provides an easy way to see a company's basic facts, a link to its Web site, news stories, stock quotes, and other miscellaneous information. If you know the company name you want to investigate, using this option is simple:

1. **On the Infoseek home page, select the Companies radio button.**

2. **In the keyword entry form, type the company name or part of the company name.**

    Infoseek is quite forgiving if you don't know the exact company name. In fact, even if you *do* know the company name, Infoseek delivers matches to individual words or parts of words in the company name, as well as companies whose descriptions refer to your keywords. For example, a recent search using *microsoft* as a keyword resulted in 39 matches, only one of which was the Microsoft Corporation.

The search results page of a Companies search shows a list of matches to your keywords. (See Figure 9-5.) If you type the exact company name, the only match that matters to you — the company itself — appears at the top of the list. Infoseek includes three items of information with each match:

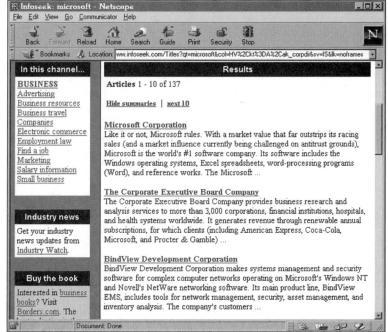

Figure 9-5:
A search results page of a Companies search for the Microsoft Corporation.

✔ **The name of the company:** This appears in hyperlink format, leading to the profile page.

✔ **A brief description of the company:** The company, not the Infoseek staff, writes this description.

Now click the company name you want to investigate. When you do so, the Company Capsule page appears (see Figure 9-6). The Company Capsule page provides a bunch of information:

✔ **Basic company information:** This includes a short description of the company's business activity, a link to its home page on the Web, phone and fax numbers, the address, and the status of its ownership (public or private).

✔ **A <u>Stock Quote</u> link:** When clicked, this link displays a current market price for publicly owned companies. During market hours, the quote lags behind real time by 20 minutes.

✔ **<u>Company News</u> and <u>Press Releases</u> links:** These display a list of headlines relating to the company, hyperlinked to the complete stories.

✔ **A <u>Job Listings</u> link:** This link divulges employment opportunities.

✔ **<u>Earnings</u> and <u>SEC Filings</u> links:** More financial information is provided by Hoovers (a financial information company) and the online database of the Securities and Exchange Commission, respectively.

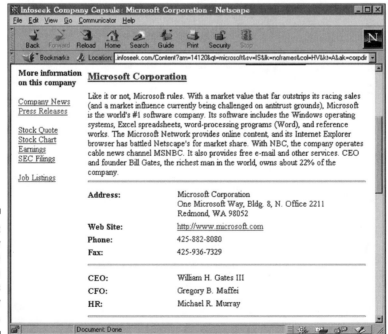

Figure 9-6:
A Company
Capsule
page in
Infoseek is
genuinely
useful.

Getting Infofancy

Conducting a simple search from the home page of Infoseek is easy and offers a wide range of options. Want more? Want fancier? Want greater control over your keywords? Infoseek can do that, too. Like any other search engine, Infoseek recognizes the standard keyword operators and provides a specialized set of symbols for using them. (See Chapters 3 and 4 to get the scoop on using keyword operators.)

Infoseek search operators

Infoseek enables you to use the standard AND, NOT, and Quotation search operators, in addition to a few special ones. Here's how they work:

- ✓ **AND.** Use a plus sign (+) in front of any keyword you want matched in your search results. Without a plus sign, Infoseek takes multiple keywords and delivers results that match any combination, including just one keyword. You can narrow your results by putting that plus sign (the AND search operator) in front of any word that must be included in a match.

- ✓ **NOT.** Use a minus sign (-) in front of any keyword you want excluded from your search results. Using the NOT operator proves more effective than simply omitting a keyword because it forces Infoseek to search for that word and then exclude any site containing it from your search results.

- ✓ **Quotation.** Use quotation marks (" and ") around any group of words you want Infoseek to treat literally. Placing the quotation mark operator forces the search engine to accept your keywords as an indivisible phrase, exactly as spelled, including capitalization. Watch your spelling!

- ✓ **Hyphen.** Infoseek enables you to use a hyphen (-) between words of a keyword string. Hyphens serve the same purpose as quotation marks by keeping the keyword sequence intact when searching. However, it takes the pressure off when it comes to capitalization.

You want to eliminate any spaces in your keyword string when using a hyphen; otherwise, the hyphen may be confused for a minus sign, the symbol for the NOT operator. In this example, I use a hyphen:

```
star-wars
```

The preceding example delivers results about the movie *Star Wars*. In the following example, I use a minus sign:

```
star -wars
```

Note that the space before the minus sign distinguishes it from a hyphen. The preceding example delivers results matching the keyword *star* to sites that do *not* contain the keyword *wars*.

✔ **Pipe.** Using the pipe symbol (│) tells Infoseek to perform a double search. First, it matches sites to a keyword, and then searches those results for a second keyword, all in one process. Here's an example:

```
movies | emma -thompson
```

In the preceding example, Infoseek finds movie sites, and then searches within those results for sites matching the keyword *emma*, but not including matches to the actress Emma Thompson (or any other mention of the name Thompson).

✔ **Name capitalization.** Infoseek has some smarts. If you enter first and last name as your keywords, capitalizing the first letter of each name, the search engine recognizes that it's dealing with a proper name and searches for examples of the name as a whole, refusing to treat the two words as individual keywords. If you enter *Jack London* as your keyword string, Infoseek finds sites about the author, refusing to return sites about the city of London.

✔ **Commas.** If you place commas between names that you type with capitalization, Infoseek recognizes them as separate names. Here's an example:

```
Jack London, Tom Paris
```

In the preceding example, Infoseek recognizes these words as names because of the capitalization, and it knows they are *two* names because of the comma. Without the comma, Infoseek regards *Jack London Tom Paris* as one long, inseparable name, and the probable search results are zero.

Infoseek field searches

Now you're getting into hyperfancy territory. Although you experience a slight learning curve when using field searches, you may find them worthwhile. Field searches enable you to restrict your search even more by using a certain keyword syntax that instructs Infoseek to limit searches to certain portions of Web documents — namely, the URL and title. Read on to see how to use field searches.

All Infoseek field searches use a single word followed by a colon, like this:

```
site:
```

The four field searches are as follows:

- site: The site: search instructs Infoseek to search within a certain site as defined by the domain portion of the URL. For example, if you're interested in search results from only the *New York Times* Web site, you can use this field search in your keyword string:

```
site:nytimes.com
```

  You can do this only when you know that nytimes.com is the domain name of the *New York Times* Web site. A completed keyword string using the site: field search may look like this:

```
albania +site:nytimes.com
```

  In the preceding example, Infoseek recognizes the plus sign (AND operator) and ensures that all results come from the nytimes.com Web site.

- url: The url: search instructs Infoseek to search only within the URLs of Web sites in the Infoseek index. Infoseek ignores the entire Web site content except for the URL address. Here's an example:

```
url:index
```

  The preceding example returns matches of the *index* keyword as it appears in the URL address of Web sites. Many home pages and site contents pages have *index* in the URL. Here's another example:

```
url:science
```

  In fact, try using any topical word in the url: field search and watch what turns up. This process gives you an experimental way of finding pages on certain subjects.

- title: The title: field search restricts your search to the titles of Web pages. You may find this field search terrifically useful when you don't know a site's URL, but you do know the site's organization. For example, if you're looking for the Village Voice Web site, use this field search:

```
title:"Village Voice"
```

  In the preceding example, I use quotation marks around the keywords to instruct Infoseek to search the exact phrase, and not the individual keywords *village* or *voice*.

- link: The link: search is sometimes called a *backwards search* because it delivers a peculiar type of result. Use this search when you want to see pages containing links to another, specified page. You place the other, specified page in the field search. Here's an example:

```
link:techstocks.com
```

In the preceding example, Infoseek finds sites that contain hyperlinks to Web pages with the `techstocks.com` domain. You must use a portion of the URL, such as the domain name, in the `link:` field search. You can't, for example, use a page title.

Infoseek Advanced Search

Using search operators is one way to tap into the underlying power of Infoseek. Another, more graphical way is to click the <u>Advanced search</u> link on the home page, which displays the Advanced Search page. Advanced Search provides a phalanx of drop-down lists for instructing Infoseek on how to interpret your keywords. The default settings present the following instruction: *Document must contain the phrase*. Using the drop-down lists, you can change three crucial elements of that instruction:

- **Document.** The default setting searches entire documents, which is to say, entire Web pages. You may change the setting to Title (titles of Web pages), URL (addresses of Web pages), or Hyperlink (hyperlinks found on Web pages).

- **must:** There are three selections here: *must, should,* and *should not.* The choices indicate how urgently you want to see your keyword(s) in the document, title, URL, or hyperlinks.

- **phrase:** Your keywords can be a phrase, exactly as typed; a person's name; or a sequence of words.

When you think about these selections, it becomes clear that you must make them work together sensibly. For example, arranging this instruction: *URL must contain the phrase* doesn't make sense, because URLs don't typically contain phrases. Furthermore, you have three instruction lines, which enables you to command an extraordinary amount of control over the Infoseek search engine. Remember that the instruction lines must work with each other, just as each command within an instruction line must work with the other commands.

Below the instruction lines is a Show only drop-down list, which lets you determine a specific domain within which to search. For example, you might search the *New York Times* Web site by typing **www.nytimes.com** in the form. The Show My Results drop-down list offers a choice between showing and hiding Web site summaries on the results page. The Number of Results drop-down list lets you increase how many search results appear at once.

Chapter 10
HotBot: Speed Rules

In This Chapter

▶ Getting to know HotBot
▶ Using HotBot search options
▶ Performing the SuperSearch

HotBot, a joint product of *Wired* and the Inktomi search engine, borrows a page from the design book of *Wired,* the magazine. If you've ever had your retinas scalded by the neon color stylings of *Wired,* you won't be surprised by the day-glo ambiance of the HotBot Web pages. Inktomi's contribution to the mix is a lightning fast, powerful search engine. The combination makes for state-of-the-art Web searching, especially when it comes to flexible and user-friendly search requests.

HotBot has the flexibility and power search tools to match its speed. Unlike many other search engines, HotBot has resisted (so far) jumping on the Web portal bandwagon, and its pages are blessedly free of customizing features, news headlines, weather reports, alluring links to message boards and chat rooms, and obnoxious display ads. You may not call the site pretty, but it is undeniably streamlined and not distracting. I hereby heap praises on HotBot's head for keeping searching — fast, accurate power searching — the centerpiece of the site. The combination makes for state-of-the-art Web searching, especially when it comes to flexible and user-friendly search requests, as you find out in this chapter.

Acquainting Yourself with HotBot

The first step in a HotBot search is to get there. Fire up your browser and surf to this address:

```
www.hotbot.com
```

HotBot's home page (see Figure 10-1) gives you a few choices right off the bat.

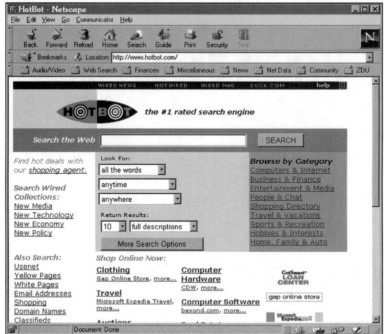

Figure 10-1:
The home
page of
HotBot.

A few drop-down lists spill beneath the keyword entry field, but you don't need to bother with them at first. Try out the search engine in two simple steps:

1. **Type one or more keywords into the keyword entry form.**

2. **Click the Search button or press the Enter key.**

Performing the preceding simple search displays a Results page that looks like Figure 10-2.

This page resembles the search results you see in other search engines. Each match on the Results page contains the following bits of information:

- ✔ **A link to the site:** This is the first line of information.

- ✔ **An abstract of the site:** As in most other search services, the text of the site itself provides the abstract (the HotBot staff does not compose these abstracts). Accordingly, the abstracts vary greatly in usefulness.

- ✔ **A percentage ranking:** Big deal. The percentage ranking measures how closely the site matches your search request, but such rankings are always superfluous. Closest matches are grouped at the top of the search results list.

- ✔ **The site's URL:** This appears next to the percentage and shows you the location of the link. The URL itself is not a live link.

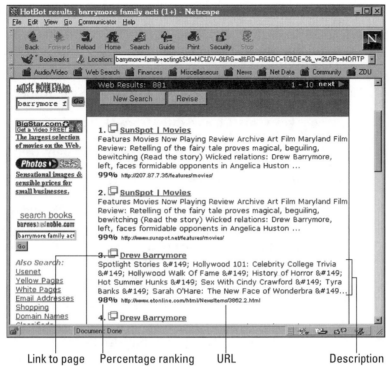

Figure 10-2:
A HotBot results page.

Link to page   Percentage ranking   URL   Description

At the top of every Results page is a keyword entry form that contains your current keywords. Likewise, a keyword entry form resides at the bottom of the search results page, with a drop-down option menu. (I'll get to it and other option menus a bit later.) These entry forms enable you to revise a search from any Results page. Just type new keywords or slightly adjust the current ones, and click the Search button.

Exploring the HotBot Search Options

HotBot doesn't make you go to another page to access a few advanced keyword features — it offers several main selectors right on the home page, buried in drop-down lists beneath the keyword entry text box. If you refer to Figure 10-1, you can see those menus, but they aren't dropped down in the figure. These menus enable you to control how HotBot interprets your keywords and how the search engine displays your results. Here is what those menus do:

✔ **Look For:** The Look For section provides three drop-down lists, as follows:

- **All the words:** The top menu tells HotBot how to regard your keywords. The default, *all the words*, forces the search engine to include only matches that contain all your words (the AND search operator). *Any of the words* is like the OR search operator, and broadens the results to include sites that contain all or any of your keywords. Choose *exact phrase* to tell HotBot to regard your keyword string as an unalterable phrase. *The page title* asks HotBot to find your keywords in page titles only. Use *the person* to indicate that your keywords represent a name. If you choose *links to this URL*, your keyword should be a URL, and HotBot will match sites that link to that URL. Finally, the *Boolean phrase* selection lets you use search operators such as AND, OR, and NOT.

- **Anytime:** HotBot can determine when a Web page was last revised, and use that date to determine whether the page falls within your time frame. This drop-down list is where you determine that time frame. The default setting, *anytime*, opens the doors to pages posted on all dates. Pull down the menu to select time frames ranging from one week to two years.

- **Anywhere:** The *anywhere* menu refers not only to the geographical location of the Web pages, but also their type as defined by the URL extension. You may search for .com and .net pages (general Web pages), educational sites (.edu), non-profit organizations (.org), or government and military sites (.gov and .mil). If you'd prefer to search geographically, select a continent from the list.

✔ **Return Results:** The last two drop-down lists let you customize how HotBot displays your search results. In the first menu, choose how many results per page you'd like to see. Then choose whether you'd like to see full descriptions of each matched Web site, partial descriptions, or only URLs. Figure 10-3 shows what the URL setting looks like on the search results page.

When selecting Return Results, you may want to choose partial descriptions or URLs only when choosing a large number of results per page. Use HotBot's brief descriptions option when you want to squeeze more search results onto your screen and don't care about the full abstracts describing each Web site in your results list. Using URLs only takes these priorities to an extreme, eliminating the abstracts and putting the squeeze on your results list even more.

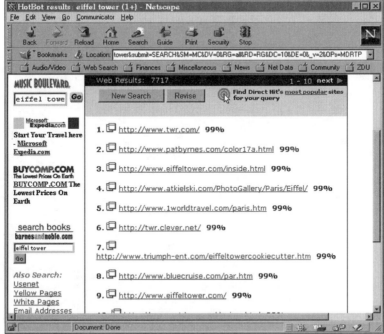

Figure 10-3:
The search
results
page with
the URLs
only setting
turned on.

The HotBot SuperSearch

If the HotBot home page doesn't thrill you with complex search options, the antidote to searching ennui is but a click away. See the More Search Options button? Click it to reach the SuperSearch page.

When HotBot says SuperSearch, it's not kidding. Take a glance at Figure 10-4, which illustrates only about half of the SuperSearch page of options. SuperSearch bristles with options and is a power searcher's dream come true. On this page you can fine-tune your keywords in several ways simultaneously, but it's best to acquaint yourself with the features one at a time.

The first menu, the Look For menu, operates exactly as the All the words menu, which I describe in the preceding section. You don't need SuperSearch to use only this menu; it should be used with other SuperSearch options. Likewise, the menus at the bottom of the SuperSearch page are duplicates of the Return Results menus that I describe in the preceding section and found on the HotBot home page. What happens between the Look For and Return Results menus is what's important on the SuperSearch page.

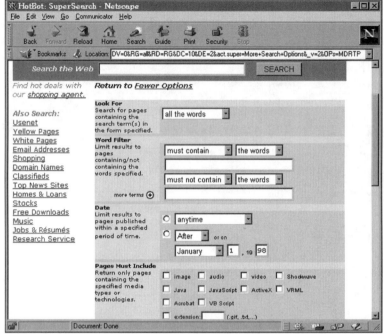

Figure 10-4:
The
SuperSearch
page
bristles with
advanced
features.

Each one of the advanced search options works *with* the keyword(s) you type into the keyword entry form at the top of the page. The options and their various menus and entry forms don't replace the keywords in the main keyword entry form. If you don't type any keywords into the main keyword entry form, your search isn't going anywhere.

Using the word filter

The HotBot word filter invites you to specify secondary keywords that are considered along with your main keywords. You can determine whether the secondary keywords must or must not be found in the search results. Furthermore, the secondary keyword string can be a phrase, a person, or just a bunch of words. To top it off, you can set up many secondary keyword strings, all of which are considered simultaneously by HotBot.

Figure 10-5 illustrates how a secondary keyword string might be used. Suppose you're searching on the main keyword *paris*. You want to know about all Web pages matching *paris*, but only if they contain the phrase *eiffel tower*.

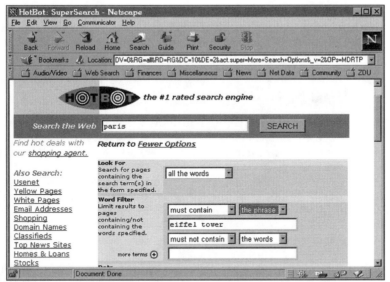

Figure 10-5:
Using a
secondary
keyword
phrase in
the word
filter.

Now, take it a step further to narrow the search results. You decide to
eliminate all search result pages that mention the Louvre (the famous
museum), the Champs-Elysees (the famous street), Notre-Dame (the famous
cathedral), and the Palace of Versailles (the famous bungalow). Accordingly,
you enter the keywords *louvre champs-elysees notre-dame versailles* into the
next line of secondary keywords. Figure 10-6 illustrates what the search
forms look like.

Figure 10-6:
Using two
secondary
keyword
strings
in the
word filter.

The result of these shenanigans is to gather Web pages that match the main keyword *paris*, contain the phrase *eiffel tower*, and don't contain any mention of the Louvre, the Champs-Elysees, Notre-Dame, or the Palace of Versailles.

Setting a date

The Web is hardly an ancient institution. It has been around for only a few years. Nevertheless, like the difference between dog years and people years, the Web's fast evolutionary track has packed a lot of development into a short time period. Web sites developed 18 months ago almost seem obsolete, and a topical Web site (such as a news or sports page) that hasn't been updated in 48 hours is definitely behind the times. Factoring in the date range in some searches makes sense sometimes.

When using the Date options, you have two choices:

- ✔ **Anytime:** The top radio button activates the same drop-down list you saw on the HotBot home page. Refer to the section above that describes how all the home page menus work. Basically, this is where you determine a time frame between one week and two years, within which HotBot searches.

- ✔ **Before or After:** The bottom radio button activates the other forms and a single drop-down list. These settings let you determine a date, and then tell HotBot whether to search before or after that date. Use the drop-down list to select Before or After, and then use the entry forms to specify the date.

You can select only one of the Date radio buttons, and you can't combine the two choices. It doesn't make much sense to anyway because the choices would conflict.

Mixing your media

What if you want to find pictures, sound files, or video clips, and you could care less about the text portions of Web sites? Scouring through entire sites looking for those multimedia files isn't much fun. Wouldn't it be great (so many a Web searcher has asked) to cut right to the chase with a search engine that can assemble a results list of multimedia files? HotBot is one such engine, and the Pages Must Include group of options can help you set up your search to do exactly that.

As you can see in Figure 10-7, HotBot confronts you with an array of checkboxes next to multimedia file types. Click image to find pictures of all file types; click audio to get sound and music; click video for matches to online video clips. Those are the three main types of multimedia, but HotBot goes the extra mile to offer other current multimedia types found on the Web, and the list changes as new multimedia types appear on the scene.

Unlike radio buttons, you can select more than one media type. Furthermore, you can use the entry field next to the extensions choice to type file extensions if you know them. For example, you may want to search for only RealAudio sound files, eliminating matches to .wav, .au, and other sound file formats. In that case, click the extension checkbox and type **.ra** (the file extension for RealAudio) in the entry form.

Where on earth?

The fourth group of options is the Location/Domain group, which enables you to limit the search to a cyber locale or a physical one. These options are similar to the Anywhere menu on the home page, which I describe in a previous section. The difference is that on the SuperSearch page, you may specify any domain:

- ✔ **Anywhere:** The top radio button opens the search to any cyber or physical location.

- ✔ **Domain:** The middle radio button provides an entry form for typing an Internet domain. Right next to the entry form, you see the example `hotwired.com`, the domain portion of the URL for the HotWired Web site. If you know the URL of a Web site within which you want to search, click the middle radio button and type the domain portion of the URL. (The domain portion lies after the `http://` and before the first single forward slash, if one exists.)

- ✔ **Continent:** The bottom radio button activates a drop-down list for specifying a continent.

Figure 10-7:
Searching
for
multimedia
gems in
SuperSearch.

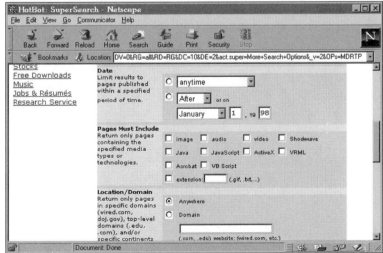

Going deep — or shallow

Most Web sites have many pages, which can be visualized in layers. The home page is the top level, containing links to many pages on the next level down, each of which has links for deeper levels . . . you see how it goes. HotBot, remarkably, provides a unique search option that determines how deeply the engine searches any site to match your keywords. Using the Page depth options, click the top radio button marked Any Page (it's the default) to disable this feature. Use the middle radio button marked Top Page to restrict your search to home pages only — no deeper. Use the third radio button and the entry form marked Page Depth to specify how deep HotBot goes in its search for matching pages.

Using all the options

You can use the SuperSearch HotBot options together in a wide variety of combinations to refine your search. With all the option fields on one page, you can craft a search in which the various options at your command work together.

Chapter 11
Deja News Gives Good Talk

● ●

In This Chapter

▶ Searching the Usenet newsgroups through your Web browser

▶ Performing a simple search in Deja News

▶ Using the Deja News power search

▶ Discovering how to use the Query Filter

▶ Making the most of the Query Results page

▶ Respecting privacy on the Usenet

● ●

*T*he site that offers one of the greatest resources for finding information through your Web browser is, in my opinion, Deja News. It specializes in searching Usenet newsgroups — the bulletin boards of the Internet, where anyone can post messages (called *articles*) on thousands of topics.

Such a search engine is only exciting if you like the Usenet newsgroups and their discussion-based article postings. If one of the following applies to you, you'll love Deja News:

✔ You're a participant in the Usenet yourself.

✔ You want to take advantage of Usenet information resources without subscribing to many newsgroups.

✔ You'd like to establish e-mail contact with experts in any number of fields.

✔ You want to track down e-mail addresses of friends who participate in Usenet newsgroups.

✔ You're bored and have picked up this book by mistake.

Not only is Deja News thorough and specialized, but it also provides all kinds of useful searching tools to get the right information quickly. Deja News has a clear interface, too, featuring easy-to-use keyword forms and menus for choosing search options. The options are numerous, but you can start with simple searches. By the time you're finished with this chapter, you'll be tracking down articles in no time. (Say good-bye to boredom and hello to geekish fascination.)

The First Search

You can get started right away, just to see how a basic search works. Here's how to begin using Deja News:

1. **Navigate to the Deja News home page (see Figure 11-1) by typing this address in your browser:**

   ```
   www.dejanews.com
   ```

2. **Type one or more keywords in the keyword form.**

   Leave the drop-down list on its default setting, standard.

3. **Click the Find button.**

When you get the Search Results page (see Figure 11-2) on your screen, you see a list (quite possibly a long list) of article titles, linked to the full article.

In the language of the Usenet newsgroups, *articles* are messages posted on bulletin boards. Don't expect to see articles resembling magazine articles. The newsgroups are more chatty than newsy. Some messages are nothing more than a line or two agreeing or disagreeing with a previous message.

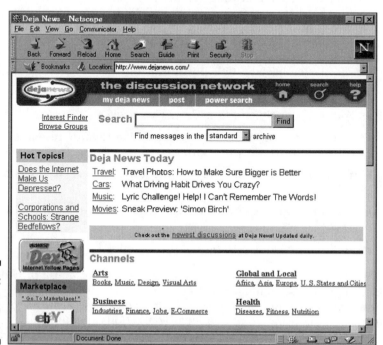

Figure 11-1:
The Deja
News home
page.

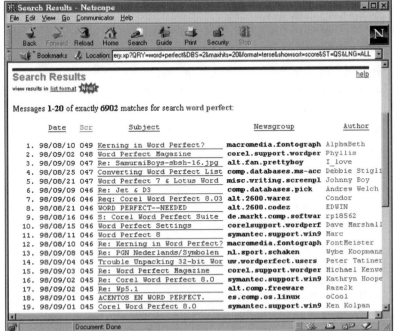

Figure 11-2:
The Search
Results
page in
Deja News.

For each article listed on the Search Results page, four other columns give
you information about that article, in unhyperlinked form.

- ✔ **Date:** This is the date when the article was posted to a Usenet
  newsgroup.

- ✔ **Score (Scr):** Deja News assigns a relevancy score to each result hit,
  based on how well it matches your keywords. Deja News raises the
  score for more matches, a high percentage of matches to the total word
  count of the article, and more recent posting dates.

- ✔ **Newsgroup:** This column identifies the newsgroup (bulletin board) in
  which the matched article was found.

- ✔ **Author:** The names in this column are the screen names of the people
  who wrote and posted the messages in your results list.

You can get more information about each column on the Search Results
page by clicking the hyperlinked column headings.

The Power Search

Deja News power searches give a bit of control over how your keywords are handled by the search engine. More than just keyword interpretive control, though, a power search lets you determine how the results are displayed and sorted. You can also limit the time period of the search. When you're ready for more detailed searching, the Power Search icon at the top of the Deja News home page sends you to the Power Search page (see Figure 11-3). You can get there directly by typing the following address:

```
www.dejanews.com/home_ps.shtml
```

On the Power Search form, you can type one or more keywords, just like a simple search from the home page. You get the same results, too, because the default settings on the Query Form match those of the home page form.

Directly under the keyword entry field, a drop-down list is set to the default of standard. The standard Deja News database conducts your search in all areas of Usenet except for the job, adult, and for sale groups. Select any one of those groups to limit your search to a single area, or choose complete to open the search to all areas of the database.

You get the real action farther down the page, under Search Options.

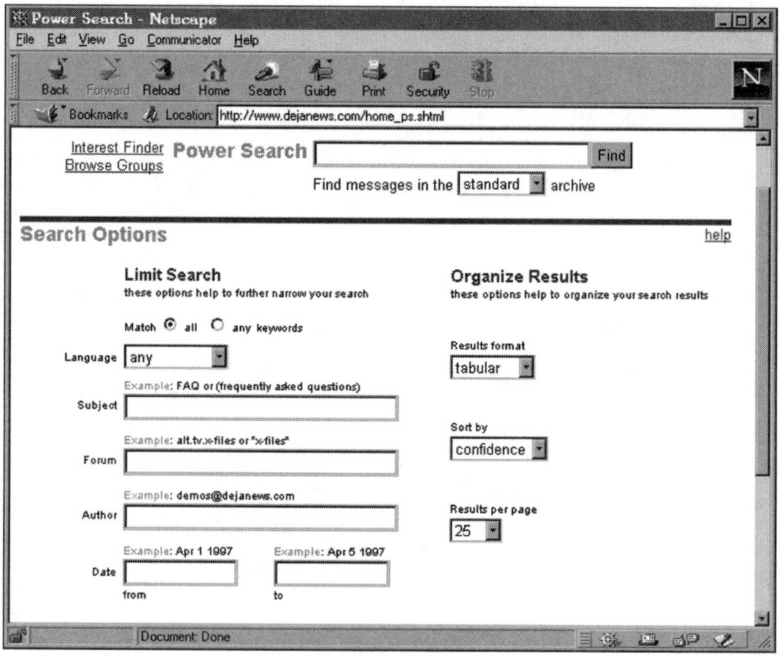

Figure 11-3: The Power Search page in Deja News.

The main function of the search options, of course, is to confuse the heck out of you. Besides that, they control how the search engine interprets your keywords and how the Search Results page displays your matches. The interface for controlling these options can hardly be simpler (thank goodness), and you can try it out before beginning a new search. The following sections explain the search options.

Keywords matched

Your first choice is between two radio buttons: all and any keywords. This matched option comes in handy when you use more than one keyword. Choosing to match *any* of your keywords searches out articles that contain a single keyword or multiple keywords but not necessarily all of them. If you want Deja News to match all your keywords and eliminate Usenet articles that contain only one or some of the keywords, select all.

Any and All are the equivalent of the standard search operators OR and AND. In fact, you can use those standard operators instead of clicking Any and All. Just type the operator between your keywords.

The Language option

Beneath the keyword match radio buttons is a Language drop-down list. It's pretty self-evident — just pull down the list and select any language to search for Web pages written in that language.

Search results format

The Results format menu is where you decide how Deja News formats the Query Results page. Don't let your design sensibilities get carried away, though, because you have only three choices: tabular, list, and threaded. The default tabular selection creates search results that look like Figure 11-2. The list setting takes up a little more room. Using the threaded option shows messages in the original order in which they were posted to the newsgroups, with response messages indented from the original messages. (See Figure 11-4.)

Take the time to experiment with this option. Try performing searches first in one format and then in the other. You must decide whether the extra bits of information are worth seeing, at the expense of a space-saving presentation. Certainly, the tabular view shows you more hits at one time, but it may look overcrowded to you.

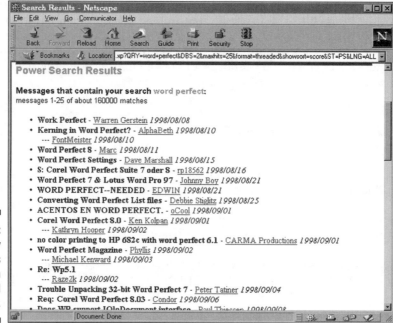

Figure 11-4:
The Query
Results
page in
threaded
format.

Sort by

The Sort by option is a complicated option offering five choices:

✔ **Confidence:** This choice, the default option, gives you results in the order of the Deja News evaluation score of each match. It's called confidence, presumably, because the search engine has confidence that the result matches your search needs.

✔ **Forum:** When you select this option, the Search Results page lists matched articles by newsgroup. Deja News clumps all the matches from one newsgroup together, and then all the hits from another newsgroup, and so on. The Deja News confidence score determines which newsgroup goes first.

✔ **Date:** Use the Date option to sort your results in chronological order, with the most recent postings first.

✔ **Author:** Here, the sorting priority groups different matching articles from the same author. The Deja News score sorts the list secondarily.

✔ **Subject:** The subject selection sorts results by subject line, but without threading them. Deja News groups messages under the same title on the Search Results page in chronological order.

Results per page

The number of matches (per page) option is a simple option that enables you to choose how many links appear on each Search Results page. Deja News uses 25 hits per page as the default setting, but you can change the default to 20, 50, or 100. When the total number of matches exceeds your limit for a page, you can click a link at the bottom of the page to see the next page. Each Search Results page adheres to your chosen limit.

The extra keyword forms

A few extra keyword entry fields let you narrow the search by determining keywords that must appear in the article subject, the Usenet newsgroup name, and the author name. You may use any of these fields, all of them, or leave them all blank.

Filtering by subject

Use the first extra keyword entry field to enter words that must be located in message subjects. You may want to use one of the same keywords you typed in the primary keyword entry field at the top of the page. Another idea is to use this field to search for FAQs (Frequently Asked Questions) files.

Filtering newsgroups

If you read individual Usenet newsgroups, use the Forum keyword field to define which individual newsgroups (or groups of them) to search. If you're not familiar with the Usenet structure, you can still use this feature to define by subject the newsgroups you want to search. In either case, you operate the filter by clicking the Forum keyword entry field and typing your filter command. Here are a few ways that you can type the command:

- ✔ **Specific newsgroup:** If you want to search the archives of a single newsgroup, type its full name in the form. Use all lowercase letters, include the periods, and don't put spaces between any letters. An example is

```
alt.invest
```

- ✔ **Specific newsgroup directory:** Newsgroup directories make up the first part of the newsgroup address, the part before the first period. The largest ones are `alt` and `rec`. If you want to see only articles from a certain newsgroup directory, such as `comp` for computer-related newsgroups, you can use the directory name followed by a period and a wildcard character, like this:

```
comp.*
```

This keyword and wildcard matches the entire `comp` directory of newsgroups.

✔ **Specific directory and topic:** To narrow the search, you can determine a newsgroup directory and a topic within that directory, even if you don't know the names of specific topical newsgroups. Here's an example:

```
alt.religion*
```

This entry finds matches on all kinds of religious subjects in a fairly broad selection of articles from several newsgroups.

✔ **Specific topic:** If you don't know your way around Usenet, you can simply specify a topic and place wildcard asterisks on both ends of it. This kind of entry opens up the search to all newsgroups that contain your word in their name:

```
*movies*
```

When you get the results, make note of the newsgroups represented in the matches. You can then narrow your search by inserting the name of a newsgroup in this filter.

Filtering authors

You can use the Author filter to search for a particular person's Usenet contributions. Knowing at least part of that person's e-mail address is helpful. John Edwards, for example, may have an e-mail name of jedwards, and you need to type that name to get matches on his articles. Using the wildcard asterisk gives you some leeway, however, and enables you to guess somewhat. You could try *john** at first, but that won't work. Persisting, you may then try **edwards**, and that does work.

When guessing a person's electronic name, remember that an e-mail address is longer than just the name. Usually, e-mail addresses adhere to this format:

```
name@domain.com
```

The domain name that follows the @ symbol is part of the address, but you don't need to know it. Just use the wildcard asterisk instead to cover all the bases.

If you don't want to bother with wildcards or with guessing a person's e-mail persona, does Deja News lock you out of searching for a Usenet author? Not at all! Deja News permits you to type simple names — without e-mail address elements or wildcards — and it does its best to find them. For example, to search for my newsgroup messages (though I can't guarantee you very interesting results), you can try this:

```
brad & hill
```

Because most of my e-mail addresses contain one of my two names, this search string gets results (assuming that I post any messages within the time frame you're searching). You can expand this type of search to more than one author by using parentheses and a vertical line to separate the authors. Here's an example:

```
(brad & hill) | (frederick & splatz)
```

In this example, *Frederick Splatz* is a fictional name, and the search probably doesn't yield any results. But if such a person does exist, you find messages from both him and me. (Last time I checked, I was still a nonfictional person.)

CompuServe e-mail addresses present a problem because they are numbers, not names. CompuServe is in the process of changing its system of e-mail identity, but until it achieves that goal, you need to know the CompuServe ID number of people who post newsgroup articles with their CompuServe accounts.

Setting dates

The two bottom keyword forms invite you to enter from and to dates, setting a time period within which to search. Using dates is more important when searching Usenet newsgroups than when searching Web sites because the content of the newsgroups changes drastically every day — every minute, for that matter. When searching for topical discussions, in particular, you can use those Date fields to good effect.

The Search Results Page

Unlike many results pages on other Web searching services, the Deja News Search Results page has several levels. The result of a Deja News search isn't a Web page, but a Usenet article posted by an individual on a newsgroup message board. As such, each item has three elements: the article itself, the newsgroup in which it appears, and the author. Deja News gives you ways of exploring all three parts.

Reading articles

When you conduct a newsgroup search, you don't want to only know about Usenet messages that are relevant to your keywords; you also want to read them. Here's how to do it:

1. **Perform a simple search or a Power Search as I describe previously in this chapter.**

2. **Wait a few seconds for the Search Results page (see Figure 11-5) to appear on your screen.**

   Deja News lists the matched newsgroup articles by title under the Subject column. Each item is hyperlinked.

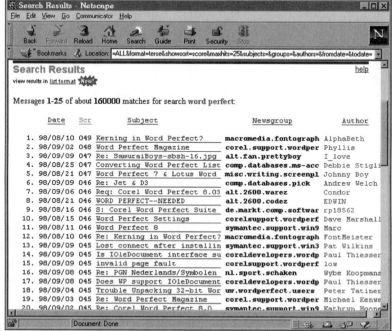

Figure 11-5:
The Search
Results
page shows
articles
under the
Subject
column.

3. Click any article title and wait a few seconds for a message page to appear.

The message page (see Figure 11-6) shows the newsgroup article, complete with the header as it appears in a newsgroup reader.

Some links near the top of the message give you a few choices:

✔ **Previous message** and **Next message:** Clicking either of these links moves you backward or forward through the articles on your hitlist (the Search Results page from which you linked here). Use this convenient feature to read all the articles on the list without darting back and forth between the page with the article on it and the Search Results page.

✔ **Author profile:** This feature offers an intriguing (and a bit controversial) feature of Deja News. (Why controversial? If you're interested, take a look at the sidebar, "Peeping cyber-Toms.") Clicking this link takes you to the Author Profile page, which lists a summary of all the Usenet postings of that individual, in every newsgroup he or she has participated in (see Figure 11-7). Deja News divides the list by newsgroup, and clicking any item sends you to a results page from which you can read any of those messages. This feature offers you a great way to read all the archived Usenet articles of an expert in any field.

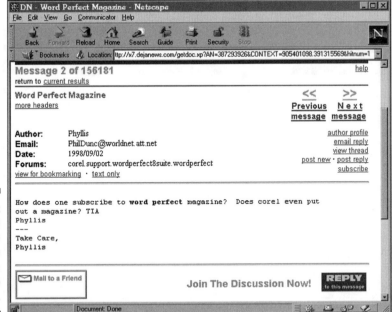

Figure 11-6:
The
message
page
showing a
newsgroup
posting.

- ✔ **Email reply:** This link pops open an e-mail response window in your Web browser, automatically addressed to the person who wrote the article you're reading. If you send this person a communication, it goes to his or her private e-mail box and isn't posted publicly in a newsgroup. But be nice anyway.

- ✔ **View thread:** Clicking this link delivers a list of messages connected to the matched article you're examining. If the matched article was posted recently — say, within the past three days — you may not see much of a thread. Usenet postings take a few days to make it into the Deja News archive. For older articles, however, using this feature gives you a nice way to see related discussion posts that may not match your exact keywords.

- ✔ **Post new and post reply:** Deja News allows you to post messages to newsgroups directly from your browser. Your message can be a reply to a post you're reading as a result of a Deja News search, or it can be a new message with a new message subject, posted to the newsgroup of the message you're viewing.

Deja News provides a convenient service by inviting you to post to newsgroups from your browser, but be aware that the process is tremendously more cumbersome and unsatisfying than using a newsgroup program for writing and posting messages. See Appendix A for a quick review of the newsgroup programs that come with two popular Web browsers.

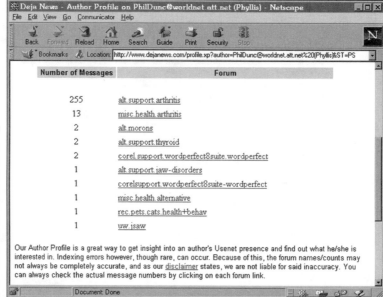

Figure 11-7:
The author profile link lists all Usenet postings for the author of the selected message.

✔ **Subscribe:** The subscribe link initiates a registration process at the Deja News site, after which you may set newsgroups as defaults within your browser when you visit Deja News. See the preceding Tip paragraph for a note about the difficulty of accessing newsgroups in this fashion, compared to using a dedicated newsgroup program.

Using the column headings

If you look on the Search Results page, you can see that the column headings are hyperlinks. You can click them to get instructions for using that column's contents. Of course, you don't need to do that because you have this book by your side. But getting onscreen help never hurts. Don't worry about my feelings. Really. I'll be fine.

The Deja News Directory

Deja News offers features around the edges of the keyword engine, and the most prominent of these new features is the directory. The directory topics, called Channels (see Figure 11-8) , let you browse for Usenet newsgroups the way other Internet directories let you browse for Web sites.

Peeping cyber-Toms

No question about it — the Author profile feature of Deja News is hip, cool, and useful. You can find people whose opinions you like and read all their messages without scouring several newsgroups to find them. You can track down experts in almost any subject and study what they have to say without drilling through endless discussion threads. So why are some people upset about it?

Deja News enables you to get a Usenet profile instantly on any individual who has posted a message in any public newsgroup. The profile doesn't tell you about that person's personal hygiene or political inclinations, of course, but it does tell you about the person's newsgroup habits. The profile shows where the person has posted messages and allows you to see them. You can then address e-mail directly to that person.

In most cases, this feature isn't a problem. But some people may be distressed to discover

that anyone can track their messaging activity across all newsgroup subjects. A doctor who provides valuable information to a public medical newsgroup and also posts comments in a sexually oriented newsgroup under a different screen name (but the same e-mail address) may be upset if people stumble across that connection.

This feature is yet another aspect of the privacy issues that inflame opinion in the online world. What to do? Privacy is a community ideal that we each must respect individually. Be discreet with what you find in the Author profile. Also, be aware that your Usenet activity can be tracked by anyone who comes across any single message that you author in a Deja News search. If you want some of that activity to be truly anonymous, use a separate e-mail address for it, and use it incognito.

The Deja News Channels work like any other directory. (See Chapters 1 and 2.) Click your way to lower levels by starting with any main subject header. Along the way, Deja News attempts to entice your interest in subtopics by displaying messages from relevant newsgroups and inviting you to respond right from your Web browser. When you get down to clicking a specific newsgroup, Deja News shows you a list of current topics in that newsgroup (see Figure 11-9). When you select any topic, you see the most recently posted message in that topic. Every newsgroup contains many topics, and most topics contain many messages.

Reading and posting to newsgroups through Deja News is awkward and not advisable. Using a dedicated newsgroup program streamlines the process tremendously. Both Netscape Navigator and Microsoft Internet Explorer (the two most popular Internet browsers, which I describe in Appendix A) contain newsgroup readers. Such programs let you subscribe to newsgroups (set them as defaults in your software), view discussion topics in threaded format, pull messages from newsgroups into your e-mail folder, easily post messages to newsgroups, and other smooth functions. Deja News excels at organizing the incredibly complex landscape of the newsgroups. I like to use the Deja News Channels to get newsgroup ideas, which I jot down; then I move into my newsgroup program to subscribe and read those groups.

Figure 11-8:
The Deja
News
directory
lets you
browse for
Usenet
newsgroups.

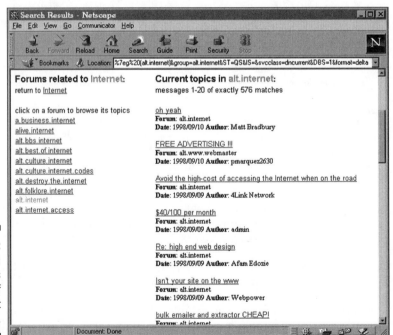

Figure 11-9:
The Deja
News
directory of
Usenet
newsgroups.

Chapter 12
Other Useful Search Engines

● ●

In This Chapter

▶ Seeing the Northern Light

▶ Using the unique Internet Sleuth

▶ Discovering how to run with WebCrawler

▶ Wandering with the World Wide Web Worm

▶ Going places with GoTo

▶ Taking the path of least resistance with EZ-Find

● ●

*T*he World Wide Web is crawling with search engines. The race is on to see who can create the best Web index, the most friendly user interface, and the most popular search site. The other chapters in Part II show you in detail how to work with the leading search engines. This chapter rounds up a few less well-known, but also helpful, search engines.

Northern Light

`www.northernlight.com`

Northern Light has attracted lots of attention to its uncluttered interface, fast search engine, and added features (see Figure 12-1). Among veterans of Internet searching, Northern Light has become a choice engine and the source of some excitement. A large part of the site's appeal lies in the innovative Custom Search Folders that organize search results.

Here's how to get started:

1. **Type a keyword or two into the keyword entry form on the home page.**

   To illustrate the Custom Search Folders, I am using *paris* as my keyword.

2. **Click the Search button.**

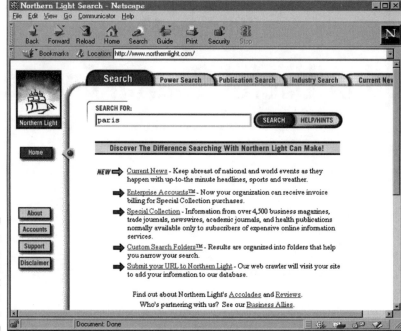

Figure 12-1:
The
Northern
Light
search
engine.

3. **Scroll down the search results page or click any of the Custom Search Folder links.**

    The Custom Search Folders are located to the left of the main list of search results. (See Figure 12-2.)

The Custom Search Folders are a marvel of organization and helpfulness. Northern Light can interpret your keyword (in this case, *paris*) in several ways, and sort out relevant links according to how they relate to that keyword. The search engine knows that Paris is in France, for example, so it sets up a Documents in French folder and places all French-language Web site links in there. Enough Yves Saint Laurent sites responded to the keyword to justify that folder. The search engine even knows that Paris is the name of a character in the *Star Trek: Voyager* television show, and sets up a folder for related pages.

In addition to keyword-specific folders, Northern Light sets up certain generic Custom Search Folders for most search results, including Current News, Personal pages, and Commercial sites.

As you begin exploring the Custom Search Folders, an interesting fact becomes apparent. The folders comprise a multilevel directory of search results, with folders within folders. When you click one of the folders on the first search results page, you're liable to see a list of secondary folders on

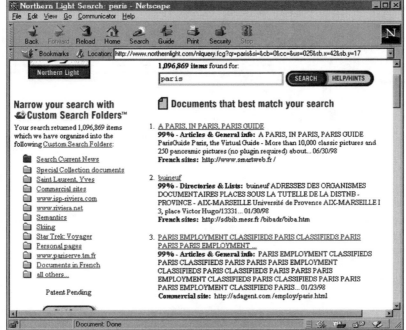

Figure 12-2:
Northern
Light
search
results
include
Custom
Search
Folders.

the next page, each folder a subset of search results related to the top folder. This excellent organizational feat puts a whole new light (a Northern Light?) on searching.

Northern Light provides a number of advanced searching features, but they are uneven in quality and clarity. They might be worth your time if you enjoy grappling with new systems, but Northern Light's real strength lies in simple searches and Custom Search Folders. Here are some of the advanced features you can try:

✔ **Power Search:** From the home page, click the Power Search tab to see the extravagant Power Search options. (See Figure 12-3.) On the Power Search page you can determine whether your keywords match against entire documents, titles only, or URLs only — furthermore, you can enter a different keyword for each of those fields. The radio buttons select between the entire Web, Northern Light's premium collection of information sources, or both. Most of the page contains checkboxes for choosing topics and sources for your search. You may use the date fields to determine a time frame for the search.

One keyword field, Select Special Collection Publication, is problematic. Northern Light is able to search any of thousands of periodicals, but doesn't provide an easy way to select among them. If you dive into the list of publications link, you're thrown into an extensive directory

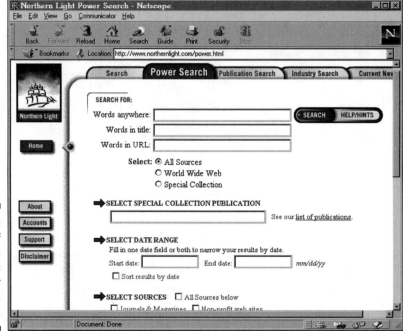

Figure 12-3:
Part of
Northern
Light's
Power
Search
page.

whose pages take forever to load. Then you must make notes of the publications you'd like to search, so you can enter them in the keyword form. Northern Light needs a simpler, point-and-click way of choosing publications — until then, I recommend skipping this feature unless you're highly motivated to engage in the process.

✔ **Publication Search:** This option is reached by clicking the Publication Search tab from any search page. The feature suffers from the same selection difficulty I describe in the preceding paragraph. I can't recommend the feature.

✔ **Industry Search:** Clicking this tab displays a search page with many checkboxes for selecting an industry, plus a basic keyword entry form. It's all self-explanatory, but not especially useful in typical searching situations.

✔ **News Search:** The News Search feature (see Figure 12-4) is designed well, but you have to be careful in how you use it. In particular, I suggest avoiding the Limit News Coverage To checkboxes below the keyword form. News searches tend to be self-limiting anyway — if your keyword string is *mark mcgwire,* for example, you don't need to further specify that you're looking for sports news. Using those checkboxes drastically limits your search results in many cases.

Northern Light uses the terrific Custom Search Folders in the News Search area, to very good effect. The folders separate news stories from various sources, such as wire service agencies.

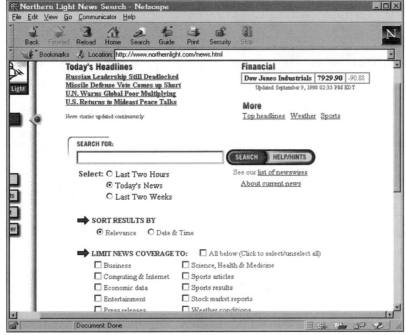

Figure 12-4:
News
Search at
Northern
Light.

Internet Sleuth

www.isleuth.com

Internet Sleuth is a unique search engine that everyone should know about. Internet Sleuth (or iSleuth as it is sometimes called) promotes keyword searching of specific databases, as opposed to the entire Internet. The site encourages such targeted searches by providing search engines for over 3,000 such databases, complete with keyword forms and even some advanced search tools.

Internet Sleuth's home page (see Figure 12-5) provides keyword forms for other search engines and a few selected shopping sites. From the home page alone, you might conclude that iSleuth is just another meta-search engine interface to Yahoo!, Lycos, Excite, and other big names. In fact, the home page is the very tip of an enormous iceberg, and nothing else is like it on the Internet.

The left-hand navigation bar is the place to begin. Select any topic there, and click it. (For this example, I chose Markets & Investments.) Figure 12-6 shows part of a typical topic page. Notice that you are suddenly empowered to search a number of specific information sources, all from a single interface.

Figure 12-5:
Internet
Sleuth, a
unique
search site.

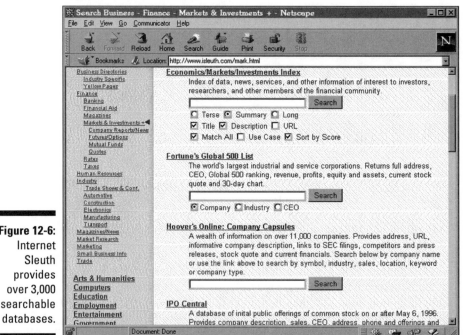

Figure 12-6:
Internet
Sleuth
provides
over 3,000
searchable
databases.

Internet Sleuth searches individual databases from the source site and sends you to that site to view the results. Unfortunately, iSleuth doesn't open a new browser window to show those results, so you are removed from iSleuth. There is no good way around this, and if you get absorbed in clicking results from the search results list, you could easily lose track of the iSleuth page you were on. To a certain extent, you can use your browser's Back button or history list to retrace your steps — as long as you haven't taken so many steps away from iSleuth that your browser has become lost. It's a good idea to remember, or even write down, the topical page at iSleuth where you started searching. Then you can start over again easily from the iSleuth home page.

WebCrawler

webcrawler.com

WebCrawler began as a student project in 1994 and was one of the first Web search engines to appear. Although other companies have advanced beyond its basic functionality and appearance, WebCrawler remains a solid search site, with a few especially useful features.

WebCrawler scores points for cuteness with its mascot, Spidey, who appears at the top of every page and is referred to in all the Help text. This cartoon spider presumably keeps you from being grossed out by a search service that's fashioned after a spider. To see the adorable arachnid in action, type its address into your Web browser.

WebCrawler is a service of GNN, a sprawling Web site and Internet service provider. The home page (see Figure 12-7) contains the keyword entry form. This entry form works in the usual manner: Just type one or more keywords in the form and click the Search button.

On the search results page, you can toggle between two views, one with site summaries and one without. The default setting includes summaries. When viewing summaries, click the <u>hide summaries</u> link; conversely, when viewing titles, click the <u>show summaries</u> link.

Like most other search engines, WebCrawler automatically uses an implied OR setting when you type multiple keywords. The implied OR means that the search engine finds matches to any one (or more) of your keywords. The results aren't limited to matches of all your keywords. (That is an implied AND.) Suppose you search with this keyword string:

michael keaton batman

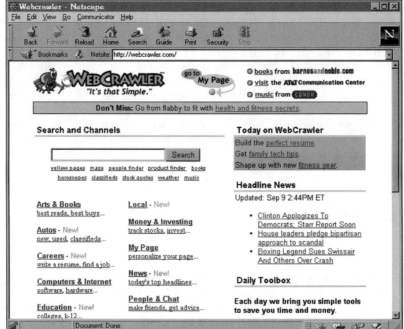

Figure 12-7:
The
WebCrawler
home page.

WebCrawler interprets this string as follows:

```
michael OR keaton OR batman
```

Accordingly, WebCrawler searches for Web sites that contain any of the words and displays a huge number of matches. It has the smarts, however, to group the best hits at the top of the list. What are the best hits? They are the ones that contain all your keywords, as if you had placed AND between them. Farther down the list, sites appear that match two of the three words; poor matches of only one word appear near the bottom. A little bar graph appears next to each link, indicating on a 1 to 5 scale the accuracy of the match.

This system allows you to rattle off a few keywords without worrying about proper keyword syntax or using search operators such as AND, OR, and NOT. However, WebCrawler does understand search operators. (I describe these in detail in Chapter 3.) The usual AND, OR, NOT (you don't have to capitalize them), and parentheses operators work well, in addition to the following specialized operators:

✔ **NEAR/xx:** The NEAR operator enables you to specify the proximity of two words by specifying the maximum number of intervening words. That is, the two words must appear within a certain number of words of each other in either direction. You specify the number of words after the slash. So, for example, the keyword string *salad NEAR/10 dressing* matches Web sites that contain phrases such as, "A salad should always be topped with dressing" and "Dressing often makes a salad better."

✔ **ADJ:** This Adjacent operator requires Web pages to contain two keywords right next to each other, in the same order that you type the keywords. For example, the search string *wall ADJ street* matches only sites in which those two words appear together (with no intervening text) and in the order written. It does not match with Web sites that contain simple instances of either word by itself.

✔ **Quotes:** Using quotation marks to surround a phrase keeps that phrase intact and literal for matching purposes. The quotes operator enables you to search for specific and complex combinations of words, such as *sexual harassment in the workplace,* without turning up miscellaneous hits on sites that contain the individual words. This operator limits your search results drastically, but you may find it helpful when you search for document titles and logos.

GoTo.com

```
www.goto.com
```

Getting tired of all the advanced searching tools described in this book? Is your head weary from sorting through options and trying to cope with too many choices? GoTo.com is designed for you. "Search made simple" is the motto at this site, which uses a bright, uncluttered interface to soothe frazzled nerves.

Absolutely nothing is complicated about GoTo.com. You arrive at the home page. You type a keyword. You click the Find It! button. You look at clearly displayed results. End of story.

EZ-Find

EZ-Find lives up to its name by giving you centralized access to several popular keyword searching services. It's not exactly simultaneous because you can use only one service at a time. But because you can access several services from a single page, the EZ-Find keyword page provides an ideal spot from which to make quick, simple requests of a number of search engines.

You can see how EZ-Find works by surfing to the EZ-Find home page (see Figure 12-8), which you can find at this address:

```
www.theriver.com/TheRiver/Explore/ezfind.html
```

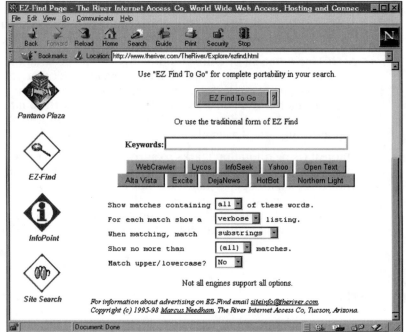

Figure 12-8:
The EZ-Find keyword entry form.

The keyword entry form on the home page appears along with ten buttons, one for each search service represented in EZ-Find. To use this array:

1. **Type one or more keywords in the Keywords form.**

2. **Click the button for the service you want to use.**

At this point, EZ-Find throws you unceremoniously into the site of whichever search service you choose. If you click on the Lycos button, for example, the search results page comes directly from the Lycos system, with all the same attributes as if you had started the search from the Lycos home page. Same deal with all the other buttons.

The EZ-Find To Go button on the home page opens up a little browser window with all the EZ-Find features in a compact format. You can leave this little window open while you continue to surf the Web, using it whenever you want. Searches initiated in the EZ-Find To Go window display their results in your main browser window. (You need to manually bring the main browser window to the forefront of your desktop — EZ-Find To Go stays on top by default.) It's a very handy little searching control panel that accompanies you on your Web travels.

Because so many great search engines are available from a central location, the question arises as to why anyone would go somewhere else to conduct a search. Each searching service has individual features, strengths, and design options. The big ones, such as Lycos, Excite, AltaVista, and Open Text, enable you to tailor the searching experience to your needs, at least to some degree. They all have specific keyword entry options. Many of the big search engines offer miscellaneous benefits that turn them into small online services — one-stop headquarters for a Web session.

EZ-Find is convenient for a quick, down-and-dirty search session, but it necessarily leaves out most of the features found in the individual services. EZ-Find does, however, offer a great way to compare the various search engines. Try typing the same keyword string, pressing each of the search buttons in turn. Do that a few times, and you begin to discover which services give you the best results. Then you can proceed to that service's home page to check out its full range of features.

Despite the built-in limitations of providing instant searching through different engines, EZ-Find does its best to provide some generic features that apply to most services. You can change five variables:

- **All/any:** Choose all to force the chosen service to match all your keywords. You get links to only sites that contain every one of your words. Choose any to allow matches to just one of several keywords. All and any are equivalent to the standard AND and OR keyword operators, respectively.

- **Verbose/terse:** This option determines what your search results page looks like. The verbose selection yields a full text rendition of the results, including any descriptions that your chosen service normally includes with its matches. The terse selection returns whatever brief version the service provides, which is usually a simple list of matched links.

- **Substrings/whole words:** When the search engine treats your keywords as substrings, they match against longer versions of the same root word. For example, plurals match with singular keywords, as do words with suffixes such as *-ing*. This feature varies among the search engines — some may not have it. Choosing whole words requires the search engine to find exact matches to your keywords as you type them.

- **Number of matches:** Use this drop-down list to select how many matches are displayed on each search result page. No matter which service you choose, a button or hyperlink at the bottom of each result page takes you to the next page unless you choose the all option, which is never recommended.

- **Match upper/lower case:** Some services may not understand if you choose Yes. Doing so forces the search engine to look at whether you type any capital letters and to match only with identical capital letters in Web pages. Leaving the default No setting on this option is usually best.

When push comes to shove

What is it that sets the Internet apart from other forms of recreation, such as movies, music, or television (besides the fact that it was built by geeks)? Consider that in a movie theater, you sit passively and watch a story unfold (or explode, in many cases). With television, it's the same thing, although you have more choices of stories. Listening to music is likewise fairly passive, air-guitar-playing notwithstanding. The Internet, on the other hand, requires a lot more effort, choices, and activity on your part. It won't do a thing until you do. It just stares back until you click a link. Surfing, browsing, and searching are all activities that demand constant decisions and selections on your part.

Something new has been happening on the World Wide Web during the past year. A new technology called push has shoved its way into a medium that until now has been defined by pull. Taking a cue from the television model, some Web sites have set themselves up as so-called channels, ready to send information and images to your computer screen without being asked. Actually, it's not so rebellious as all that — you must ask at the beginning, setting the ball in motion, and then these new channels continue streaming stuff at you unprompted.

The first well-known channel of this sort is the PointCast Network, a free Web-based service that delivers news and information directly to your computer through the Web. Notice the difference between the name *PointCast* and the term *broadcast*. PointCast does not broadcast like a TV station, from a single transmitter to a multitude of receivers. Adhering to the way the Internet works, PointCast delivers from a single point (the PointCast Web location) to another single point (your computer), with a different mix of information (programming, in TV parlance) going to each subscriber. So you certainly have more selectivity at your command than with a TV broadcast, but PointCast is pushing just like TV, not waiting to be pulled as with other Web content. Here is the address of the PointCast Web site:

```
www.pointcast.com
```

PointCast is still a leader in the push field, but no longer the only such Internet station. Other sources of pushed information have been created by IBM, Netscape, Yahoo!, AirMedia, and others, each delivering its own brand of information directly to your computer. News headlines, stock quotes, movie reviews, and all the other informational bits and pieces that you can pull from the Internet are now being pushed by the Internet. Push technology is fundamentally opposed to Web searching, which involves active and constant selection on your part. But it's still worth exploring, so here's a Yahoo! directory page that links to many Web push providers. Good luck!

```
www.yahoo.com/Business_and_
   Economy/Companies/ Media/
   Internet_Broadcasting
```

The Internet Searching For Dummies Directory

The 5th Wave   By Rich Tennant

"Now, that would show how important it is to distinguish 'massage therapist' from 'massage parlors' when downloading a video file from the Internet."

In this directory . . .

You can search for so much on the Internet — and with so many online tools — that a single book isn't enough to cover all the bases. The chapters in Part III provide search tools for major subject areas such as Health, News, and Education. This Directory is a review of the best search sites in many other topics. The descriptions are shorter than in the rest of the book, so more sites are covered in each category. Every site has passed my personal quality tests, and I hope that every reader finds some new, valuable information gems in this part.

The Internet Searching
For Dummies Directory

The Internet has so many directories and search engines, I couldn't possibly fit them all into a single book. This directory is a noble attempt to stuff as many as possible in. I cover major subjects of interest in the search expeditions of Part III. The purpose of this directory is to touch on other topics of interest and point you to search tools in those subjects.

 My intent is not to provide a comprehensive directory of Web sites in any of the following topics. My primary criterion for including a site in this directory has been the existence of some kind of search tool in that site. The search tool can be a directory, a search engine, or both. But if the site doesn't help you search, it's not in this directory.

About Those Micons (Mini Icons)

They're helpful. They're adorable. They dance. (Actually, they don't.) The small icons above each site description in this directory tell you something about the site. They are meant to give you at-a-glance impressions of the site's important characteristics. Following is a list of the micons and what they mean:

I use this micon to indicate a site that is graphics heavy and may take a long time to load into your browser. Such sites are sometimes great to look at, if you don't mind watching your fingernails grow while the images crawl onto your screen.

★★ I reward exceptional page design with this micon. It doesn't mean the site is more useful than others, just that it looks great and its elements are laid out in a way that makes them easy to use.

This micon indicates that the site has a keyword entry form for searching. The sophistication of such forms can vary drastically.

If a search site contains a directory, it gets this micon. Directories encourage browsing; keyword forms encourage targeted searching.

My highest honor, a fave rave means the site is a must-see search tool.

Computer Information Searching

This section supplements Chapter 15. In addition to finding software files, the sites in this section can locate articles in computer magazines, software reviews, definitions of computer terms, news headlines about the computer industry, and other technical information.

Benchin' Software Reviews

www.benchin.com/cgi-win/$br/search

Software is subjected to what are called *bench tests,* in case you were wondering about the title of this site. Benchin' is a top-flight archive of software reviews provided by both professionals and regular users. The keyword searching form enables you to search for specific software products or types of programs. The reviews are extensive summaries of all feedback received by Benchin' for that product.

CMP Technology Database

www.techweb.com/search/search.html

CMP is a publisher of computer magazines, including *Windows Magazine, Internet Week,* and trade publications for the computer and online industries. The search engine lets you define which magazine to search or do a broad search across the entire database. One nice feature lets you sort search results by date, so you see most recent articles first.

Computer Information Centre

www.compinfo.co.uk/search.htm

This British site has a decided business slant. The search engine, attractive and option-filled though it is, does not deliver good results (or any results in many cases). I suggest going straight for one of the directories. One of them? Yes, this site provides a number of topic-oriented directories, including directories of hardware manufacturers, software manufacturers, and computer news sites.

Computer News Daily

nytsyn.com/live/cndkey.html

This searchable archive lets you prowl around the stored articles of *Computer News Daily* and, as a bonus, the last three days of PR Newswire. PR Newswire posts press releases of companies and distributes them widely around the Internet. Using keywords here is a good way to angle into the database of company information. *Computer News Daily,* of course, carries stories related only to computer companies.

Dictionary of Computer Terms

www.currents.net/resources/dictionary/index.html

This site is produced by *Computer Currents Magazine* and is part of the larger magazine site. The dictionary is a keyword engine dedicated to computer terms, with an associated directory for browsing. The best use of this engine is when you have a term that you don't understand; simply type it into the keyword form and then click the Search button. Very usefully, the directory encourages browsing by setting up categories of computer terms, such as HTML Tags, File Types, Internet Domain Suffixes, Chat Stuff — categories that relate to Web page creation and Internet socializing. The search results are displayed in small type in the left-hand navigation bar — click a result to get a full definition. This system takes some getting used to, but pays off by keeping your choices visible at all times.

File Pile

filepile.com/nc/start

Search through over 1 million stored files at this famous archive. Keyword operators are allowed here, and the tutorial in how best to use them is helpful.

Media Central

www.mediacentral.com/cgi-bin/texis/webinator/search

Despite the broad title, this site is dedicated to tech news, with an emphasis on the Internet and online technologies. The search engine isn't without complications and takes some practice with all the radio buttons and drop-down lists. All the search results, from article summaries to full-length articles, are presented within the Media Central site — that's a plus.

Netly News

cgi.pathfinder.com/netly

This may seem too good to be true, but you can actually search for computer, Internet, and technical news from sources such as *Time, Money, Fortune,* and *CNN* — all from a single keyword entry form. Go

to the preceding address, squint, and find the form in the upper-right corner of the page. The search engine is part of Time Digital, but covers the other publications as well.

News.com

www.news.com

From the title and address, you'd think News.com would be the mother of all general news sites. In fact, it's produced by C-Net, a decidedly computer-oriented service site and one of the best places to search for computer news. The keyword form is inconspicuously located down the page a bit, on the right-hand navigation column. Articles are heavily slanted to the Internet but also include company news and hardware and software developments.

Search ZDNet

www.zdnet.com/findit/search.html

Ziff-Davis (ZD) is one of the largest publishers of computer-related magazines in the world, and this site lets you search for articles across almost all ZD publications. Using drop-down lists, you can narrow your search to reviews, commentary, tips, and news. Another list invites you to specify which magazines you want to search.

Snoopie

www.snoopie.com

Snoopie is a file finder specializing in FTP sites and Gopher archives. The search engine is useful in tracking down files that may not be accessible from the big, Web-based file supermarkets that I describe in Chapter 15. During my last visit to Snoopie before this book was printed, I noticed that the site was under construction, with most of its contents unavailable. It may be up and running again by the time you read this. If not, check back occasionally — Snoopie's incisive search tools are worth waiting for.

TechCalendar

www.techweb.com/calendar

Feel like attending a trade show or a computer expo, but don't know where or when they are being presented? This calendar rushes to the rescue with a database of such events throughout the world. Perform a keyword search or, perhaps more productively, use the directory links to browse by month, by category, or by location. The Advanced Search is an excellent method of pinpointing what you need, when, and where you need it.

Technology Encyclopedia

www.techweb.com/encyclopedia/defineterm.cgi

This outstanding resource is downright . . . well, encyclopedic in its range and depth of explanation. Enter any single word in the simple keyword entry form, and prepare to receive a treatise on the subject, links to related subjects, and links to partial matches of your keyword. Whew — somebody worked hard on this site, and we are the lucky beneficiaries. The only missing element is a directory for browsing alphabetically.

Wired News Search

www.wired.com/news/search.html

You have never seen a more stark, black, in-your-face page than this dungeon-like search form. At least it has no colorful distractions — this page is for searching and nothing but searching. Type a keyword or three. Use the pull-down menus to select whether to search for full text or headlines only and to select the time frame of your search (from one week to the millennium). The results are a little more colorful, in the neon *Wired* style.

ZDNet Software Library

www6.zdnet.com/cgi-bin/texis/swlib/hotfiles/pform.html

Although I mention this site in Chapter 15, I want to put it in here too, just to emphasize the utter coolness of this sophisticated keyword search tool. An armada of keyword fields and drop-down lists lets you narrow your search by type of software, file size, operating system, and several other defining characteristics. The <u>Power Search Tips</u> link helps make sense of it all.

ZDNet TipZone

www.zdnet.com/zdhelp/hpc

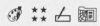

One of the most challenging aspects of computer ownership manifests when something goes wrong and you don't know how to correct it or even how to identify what the problem is. ZDNet TipZone rises to the challenge by providing a searchable database of computer tips and troubleshooting ideas. This search engine could replace many an owner's manual for hardware and software products. Users of Microsoft Windows products especially should take note because the site does an incredible job of helping you understand the operating system and explaining how to do things. Save that phone call to Microsoft technical support and come to this site first.

Entertainment Searching

The Internet has almost as many entertainment sites as Sean Connery has movies. Many entertainment sites, however, pride themselves on being up to the minute and don't archive their information. So searching for actors, movies, TV shows, and other showbiz stuff isn't easy. This section gathers the heaviest hitters in the field of entertainment searching.

All-Movie Guide

allmovie.com

The All-Movie Guide isn't as famous as the Internet Movie Database, but you might find it to be a better service. Search for movie information by movie title, actor, miscellaneous keyword, or plot line. Advanced searches provide more esoteric criteria. Search results are extraordinary. AMG doesn't link to other Web sites for its information — it is a complete database of exquisite depth. You get a summary, a list of cast members (hyperlinked to biography pages), production credits, awards, and a cross-referenced list of other movies with the same production personnel.

Cinemachine

www.cinemachine.com

If you want movie reviews, you can hardly do better than Cinemachine, which takes an interesting approach. Cinemachine itself doesn't review films. Instead, it collects reviews from everywhere else and gathers them together in response to your search query. Keyword entry is easy — just type the movie's name or partial name if you don't remember the whole thing. The search result is a page of links to reviews of that movie in newspapers and magazines all over the Web. A recent search for *The Truman Show*, for example, delivered 39 reviews, from publications as disparate as *A Feminist Perspective* and *USA Today*.

Ebert Movie Files

www.suntimes.com/ebert/ebertser.html

This site contains archives of Roger Ebert's movie reviews in the *Chicago Sun Times*. Use keywords and menus to search by movie title, actor name, director, date range, and rating.

Ha!

www.hardyharhar.com/ha/ha.cgi

Love that address. This site has enough jokes to keep you chuckling long past when you swore you'd turn off the computer. Three keyword boxes let you search by category, keyword, or phrase. Unfortunately and surrealistically, often little apparent connection exists between the search results and the query. Whatever strange search algorithm is governing this engine, the jokes remain funny. You can even add a joke.

Hollywood Online Video Guide

www.hollywood.com/videoguide/index.html

The directory for this search service is squeezed into a left-hand navigation bar, but at least there *is* a directory. Drop-down lists let you search for videos by genre or release date — and also alpha-betically — but the site has no keyword entry form.

Infoplease.com

www.infoplease.com

The renowned Infoplease Entertainment Almanac and Encyclopedia is opened to keyword searching at this site. Search results can be the briefest of brief. For example, when searching on the name of an actor, you're likely to be graced with the birthplace and birthday of that personality — nothing more. Your antidote to such brevity is to switch to the Encyclopedia setting, using the drop-down list next to the keyword field, and search again. Be aware, though, that many contemporary stars are not included yet in the encyclopedia.

Internet Movie Database

www.imdb.com/search

In its competition with the All-Movie Guide (a previous listing), Internet Movie Database has raised the stakes with some advanced searching tools. Naturally, you can search by movie title, actor, crew member, and character name. (Searches cover either movies or TV shows.) Furthermore, you can now search for two or more people working together on a movie or show; search multiple movie titles for common cast or crew members; and search for titles by genre and country of production. IMDb (as it's known) just keeps getting better.

Mega Media-Links

omnibus-eye.rtvf.nwu.edu/links/search.html

The search interface can hardly be simpler — just an unassuming keyword form and a Search button. The results, though, are hardly modest. This search engine is distinguished by breadth, if not particularly by depth. That is to say, almost any keyword having to do with television, movies, music, or other entertainment genres is likely to get results but probably not comprehensive results. Still, this is a good place to get linked around the Web to specifically targeted entertainment sites. Use key-words that aim for specific media prod-ucts, such as the names of TV shows or movies. Alternatively, browse the direc-tory for production companies, broad-casting schools, showbiz organizations, and other industry sites.

Mr. Showbiz

www.mrshowbiz.com/search.html

Three separate search engines grace the home page of the Mr. Showbiz mega-entertainment site. First, you're invited to search the entire Mr. Showbiz news archive, and the engine is gratifyingly flexible. Type a name, for example, or even a portion of a name, and receive a list of related article links. Second, scroll down to the Movie Guide, type either a movie title or a star name, and rummage through a database of 20,000 reviews. Finally, the celeb engine delivers star bios and fan sites for celeb keywords.

Playbill Online

www2.playbill.com/cgi-bin/plb/
news?cmd=search

Theater news from the magazine that knows all. A simple search interface combs archives for news stories, but don't expect to find links to Web sites. A small directory appears in the left-hand navigation bar.

Tag Lines Galore

www.mcs.brandonu.ca/~ennsnr/Tags/
search.html

The title is no overstatement — this site is stocked to the gills with one-liners. A start interface greets you with a single-keyword form; enter any word, and chances are the search engine will find something funny about it. From silly to sophomoric, from banal to brilliant, once you start reading these taglines it's the potato chip phenomenon all over again — you can't read only one.

Ticketmaster

events.ticketmaster.com

Being able to search the Ticketmaster database of concert and sports events is an excellent concept and is sometimes useful. But truthfully, this site has room for improvement. Although you can specify a type of event and a state along with your keyword, you can search according to only one parameter at a time! This means you can search for events in New York state, or you can search for orchestra concerts, but you can't search for orchestra concerts in New York state. Hmph. The lack of a comprehensive directory doesn't help

matters. Still, some great event information is to be had at this site, if you're willing to put in the legwork (or the mousework) to find it.

TV Guide Listings

www.tvguide.com/tv/listings/cgi-bin/login

Searching for information about TV shows is one thing, but how about searching for the shows themselves? That's where TV Guide Listings comes in. Only a tiny keyword form is necessary at this site — just big enough to fit your zip code in. That's all you need. Then TV Guide asks whether you want broadcast listings or cable listings, and gives you a choice of cable companies in your area. The listings have ads embedded in them, unfortunately, but are otherwise easy to navigate, in grid-style — much easier to deal with, in my opinion, than the *TV Guide* magazine listings.

Ultimate TV Show List

www.ultimatetv.com/UTVL

Ultimate is right. This awesome resource takes a simple keyword, such as the name of a TV show, and runs with it in five directions at once. Search results combine Web sites with Usenet newsgroups, mailing lists with episode guides, all available over the Net. The lists are extensive — exhausting, even. Topping it off, a few fine directories invite browsing, either alphabetically or by category.

Other Stuff to Check Out

www.earthcam.com

entertainmentnewsdaily.com/search1.html

pathfinder.com/ew

www.cinema.pgh.pa.us/movie/reviews

Cinemania.msn.com/Default/Home

http://newsfeed.hollywood.com/cgi-bin/newsmenu.pl

www.film.com/admin/search.htm

www.pbs.org/search

Fine Arts Searching

Refined culture is the subject of this directory section, with an emphasis on fine art.

Art AtoZ

www.booksatoz.com/artatoz/

A comprehensive index of museums, art galleries, art books, art history information, magazines, art supplies, and quite a bit more, Art AtoZ uses a directory system rather than a search engine. Actually, a keyword search service is buried in this site, but it costs money to use and I don't recommend using it. The directory is a good one, with descriptions of links and a clear layout.

Art Guide

www.finearte.com/search.html

The dark backgrounds that grace the pages of Art Guide may be artsy, but they sure make it hard on the eyes when trying to read the light-colored text. Nevertheless, Art Guide houses an extensive directory of art and museum sites and is searchable by keyword at the listed address. The directory is accessible from a link on the home page (click the Back to Homepage link on the search page) and

contains twenty categories that include art, music, poetry, dance, architecture, museums, art supplies, fashion design, and sculpture. Who knew the Web had so many artistic resources?

Art Planet

www.artplanet.com/

Art Planet is one of the few search tools outside the Yahoo! general index that encourages searching for individual artists. In fact, the Art Planet directory sports an Artists category that is by far the largest subject header, with over four thousand listings. Use the single keyword search form on the home page or click the options link for a more advanced keyword entry form that further solicits artist searches. If you're looking for information about a particular artist, this is the place to be — and the directory covers many other topics also. Check out the Medium categories, which let you browse, for example, by Etching, Photography, or Oil.

ArtsEdge

artsedge.kennedy-center.org/search

The Kennedy Center provides this search engine for arts and arts education. Very little help is offered, and much is needed — for that reason, you may have to experiment before getting the hang of this database. A drop-down list lets you select among several collections, and your choice is then searched according to your keywords. The For Students collection may be the most useful. Clicking the Guided Search button presents a Java search panel in a separate window — it's somewhat befuddling, but the site gets an A for effort.

ArtsResources: Museum Listings

artresources.com/guide/comp/indexes/museum.html-ssi

This museum-centric search tool gives basic information about museums in the United States (and a few abroad), many of them associated with colleges. Most results list the address, the number of collections, the director or curator, and in some cases, the operating hours. An alphabetical directory is supplemented by a keyword search engine.

CultureFinder

www.culturefinder.com/finder1.htm

Wow. CultureFinder contains season schedules for 1,500 performance organizations worldwide. The entire database is placed at your fingertips with a slick search engine that can narrow down exactly *when* you're searching for. Use the drop-down lists to establish date parameters, enter a city name as a keyword, and click the Search button. (Default dates are set to the current week! Very helpful.) The search results? Another wow. Separated by day, type of culture (art, theater, music, opera, and so on) and description, the results can be overwhelming, and may take a minute to load into your browser. It's worth the wait. Traveling to a city and looking to catch a concert or a gallery show? This is the only search engine you need. The site has too many other features to describe here, but again, wow.

Guide to Museums and Cultural Resources

www.lam.mus.ca.us/webmuseums/

Merging culture and science, this site can just as easily be placed in a Natural Science category. The page at the preceding address displays a geographical index of resources broken down by continent. Click the Search button, and be greeted by a surprisingly sophisticated search engine with advanced functions for finding resources all over the world. This site has a learning curve, but it's worth it.

International Directory of Art Libraries

iberia.vassar.edu/ifla-idal

This directory has the noble goal of tracking down specialized holdings in art, architecture, and archaeology all over the world. The keyword entry form invites you to enter the name of a library, a city, or a country, and the engine takes it from there. Search results link to informational pages but keep you in the site. You finally get museum contact information, but little about actual holdings. Where home pages for the museums are available, links are provided for in-depth information. I have just one question: Where is the directory that the engine is searching? It would be helpful if we could browse.

La Scala

lascala.milano.it/eng/db/form.html

Produced by the famous La Scala theater in Italy, this search engine accesses a broad database of over 9,500 artists, 2,500 authors, librettists, and choreographers, and thousands of different shows and performances at La Scala. The search engine uses a system of selectable radio buttons in combination with keywords. You must type a keyword that matches the selected radio button, but guidelines are provided.

National Gallery of Art

www.nga.gov/collection/srchart.htm

This is a beautiful site that allows you to search for artists, miscellaneous keywords, or images only. As you can imagine, the National Gallery has an impressive collection of images, ranging from the Middle Ages to the present. Try clicking the images checkbox, typing almost any word that might be found in a painting title (*summer* works), and clicking the Search button. Thumbnail versions of the images appear as search results — click any thumbnail to see a larger reproduction on your screen, with historical information. Click on *that* image to see a much larger version. How cool is this? Very.

Opera Schedule

www.fsz.bme.hu/opera/query.html

You might want to use this search tool with CultureFinder, listed previously in this section. Opera Schedule lets you zero in on a city and a date, and then provides a listing of performances. You may also search by composer and even specific opera title. Using radio buttons and keyword fields, you must make sure all the information jives so you're not, for example, searching for a composer with the city button selected (unless you're visiting the city of Puccini).

World Wide Arts Resources

wwar.com

This outstanding, search-intensive site sports an excellent directory and a good search engine right on the home page. The index covers crafts, art employment, art education, children, and off-center topics such as dance, opera, and theater. The search engine lets you select a category in which to search with keywords, and invites you to search the whole shebang if you prefer. It can hardly be easier to use, and the results are good. Hint: Maximize your browser window to see this site in the best light.

WWW Virtual Library: Museums

www.comlab.ox.ac.uk/archive/other/museums/search.html

An awesome directory with an uncountable number of categories starts you off on the right foot. The second level of each directory topic provides brief descriptions of the linked museums and an unexplained rating system that seems to highlight recommended links. A basic keyword form appears on every directory page, helpfully. This site isn't pretty, but it's a terrific resource.

Governmental Searching

The United States government is a pretty Net-savvy organization, and most Federal agencies have Web sites. Some have tools for searching through the sites. Even the White House allows a certain degree of rummaging.

Federal Web Locator

www.law.vill.edu/Fed-Agency

Like the title says, this site locates Federal (United States, that is) agency Web sites. The directory links directly to the sites of many agencies, and the keyword search box helps find others.

FedStats Search

www.fedstats.gov/search.html

Probe various Federal agencies for statistics of interest through keyword searching at this site. I don't know about you, but I'd have trouble getting started with such a search — what keywords should be used? — so I'm grateful for the helpful suggestions at this page. I'm also glad for the checkboxes that make it easy to restrict searches to specific agencies without knowing the exact name of the agency. Most search results are in PDF format, requiring the Adobe Acrobat reader to decode.

GovBot

www.business.gov/Search_Online.html

An awesome index of over 500,000 governmental Web pages (United States government only) is maintained at this site and is available to keyword searching. Follow the hints link for some starter information. Forget about using search operators such as AND or NOT — they are stripped from the search. A directory would be helpful, alas.

Inter-Parliamentary Union

www.ipu.org/english/parline/parline.htm

The IPU can tell you anything you need to know about the governmental structure of any country in the world. Just enter the country name in the keyword form, and you get back a page of data about the officials and bodies of that country's government. Lots of historical perspective and descriptive text make the search results a truly educational experience. Want to send an e-mail to the National Assembly of Bulgaria? Not a problem.

White House Searching

library.whitehouse.gov/Search/Query-All.html

Ever want to rummage through the White House? This site doesn't let you search for socks left on the floor by the President, but it does invite you to sift through a database of press releases, speech texts, photographs, and radio address transcriptions. (The four most recent radio speeches are available for your listening pleasure.)

Other Stuff to Check Out

www.fedworld.gov/search.htm

www.fedworld.gov/gils/docgils.htm

lib-www.ucr.edu/dbase/query_g.html

www.law.emory.edu/FEDERAL/usconser.html

www.access.gpo.gov/nara/nara003.html

library.whitehouse.gov/Search/Query-ExecutiveOrders.html

Job Searching

Job classifieds abound on the Internet, from highly organized employment sites to the disorganized listings of the Usenet newsgroups. This section is stocked with the best job-searching tools you can find online.

Best Jobs U.S.A.

www.bestjobsusa.com/jobframe.htm

A basic keyword form works with drop-down lists to specify a state and company category. The company category list is inadequate, but you can fill in the gaps by using keywords. Search results arrive as a long list of hyperlinks matching your query, each of which leads to a fairly detailed job description.

Boldface Jobs

www.boldfacejobs.com/help.htm

Boldface Jobs doesn't provide a keyword entry form on its home page, but displays two drop-down lists to facilitate searching. Use those lists to specify a job description and a state, and you're off and running. The job descriptions are nicely detailed but undated, which is a drawback.

Career Magazine Jobline Database

www.careermag.com/db/
cmag_postsearch_form

Searching the archives and postings of Career Magazine is enhanced by highly specific keyword entry options that let

you determine job titles, skills by keyword, and location. Search results are nicely detailed, complete with company logo and an automatic resume submitter.

Career Mosaic

www.careermosaic.com/cm/jobs.html

Career Mosaic is an international database of job listings as posted to Usenet newsgroups. Searching here is far more efficient than browsing the newsgroups themselves. An extensive set of keyword boxes lets you get very specific about where you want to work and for whom. Search results are in the form of Usenet newsgroup postings, which can sometimes be on the brief side. One of the big values of this database is its truly global nature.

Career Path

www.careerpath.com/cp/owa/cp_ads_ocs.
display_keyword_search?session_id=&status=

Nice address, huh? Sorry about that. Career Path has one of the fanciest search forms you'll ever see. You must scroll the page down to see it all. Dozens of checkboxes, pull-down menus, and a keyword entry field combine to create a detailed query of job listings that apply to you. Those listings are culled from classified newspaper listings across the United States.

CareerWeb

www.cweb.com/jobs

CareerWeb has a separate search category for international jobs, which distinguishes the search engine right off the bat. Search results are undated, but include an e-mail address for the recruiter or personnel manager, so checking job availability is simplified.

Espan's JobOptions

www.espan.com/focus/asp/default.asp

JobOptions offers a multiple approach of searching for job categories, searching for specific companies, and posting a resume so companies can find you. The Job Search form provides a typical range of selections, narrowing your search by state and job type. Job Alert is an e-mail service that notifies you of new job postings in your category.

Monster Job Search

www.monster.com/pf/search/jobserch.htm

A classy page design provides a nice environment for an online job search. Prowl through this database by job type, city and state, and keyword. The engine also allows you to specify part-time and temp work. International and company searches are available here, too.

Net-Temps

www.net-temps.com/links/job-search-national.html

Specializing in temporary and contract jobs, Net-Temps display a search interface using a pull-down state locator and radio buttons to signify the type of job you're looking for (full-time, part-time, contract, temp). This engine is for the United States only.

Overseas Jobs Web

www.overseasjobs.com/do/search.cgi

A small, growing database of overseas (from the United States perspective) jobs. Simple keyword searching is permitted, with the OR and AND operators.

Other Stuff to Check Out

www.summerjobs.com/do/jsearch

www.americanjobs.com/amerjobssearchwh.asp

Literature Searching

Here are a few sites with search tools for finding information about books or information in the field of literature.

Library of Congress

lcweb2.loc.gov/resdev/ess

The Library of Congress offers what it calls an experimental search engine — actually, two of them. The Basic Search lets you program such variables as title, subject, and author into your keyword exploration, as well as an English-only or All Languages switch. The Advanced Search contains those features plus a choice of collections. You may choose books, maps, music, software, and other categories in the Library of Congress collection. Furthermore, Advanced Search lets you get more specific with what language you're looking for; whether you want fiction or non-fiction; types of books; exact name of the author; and several other narrowing options. This search engine may be experimental, but I hereby declare the experiment a rousing success. This is quite a resource.

Literary Hyper Calendar

sparc1.yasuda-u.ac.jp/LitCalendar.html

This is a fun one. Using a slick calendar interface enlivened with literary quotes, this site lets you choose any day to find what literary events happened throughout history on that day. The site operates sluggishly for some reason, perhaps because it is served (located) overseas from the United States, where I am located. Still, it's fun and informative in an intellectually trivial sort of way.

Yahoo!: Arts/Humanities/ Literature

www.yahoo.com/Arts/Humanities/Literature/

This is the Yahoo! directory page for searching out literary interests. You may search within this category using the keyword form at the top of the page, as long as you set the drop-down list for Just this category. Or browse lower levels of the Yahoo! directory starting with this page.

Music Searching

A lot of music is on the Internet: from fan sites to record company promotions; from music directories to search engines for finding out everything about your favorite artist. This section just scratches the surface of music on the Net, from rock to classical.

All-Music Guide

www.allmusic.com

Like the All-Movie Guide from the same company, the All-Music Guide is an incredibly rich, comprehensive database, in this case of music artists and their discography. Search results include an extensive biography of the musician, a complete (and rated) discography, a list of albums the artist guest-appears on, and a list of so-called similar musicians. (That last category is debatable much of the time.) All-Music Guide keeps you within the site at all times and doesn't link to outside resources.

Classical Net

www.classical.net/music/search.html

A vast archive of information about composers and performers is available by keyword searching at Classical Net. Besides the formidable in-house pages, which respond to search requests, the site also points the way to outside Web pages related to your keywords. Nothing fancy here in the way of search options. You do well by typing just the name of a composer, a performer, or a performing group such as an orchestra or a string quartet. This site doesn't keep you waiting for results — it's lightning fast.

MusicSearch

musicsearch.com

MusicSearch gives you a choice of searching within the site or outside it. Both alternatives are impressive. The MusicSearch database is worth exploring in its own right. The outside search engine automatically puts your keywords through dozens of other music search engines and consolidates the results.

Rolling Stone: Artists A to Z

www.rollingstone.com/sections/artists/text/default.asp

This database from the famous music magazine puts too many mouse clicks between you and the information, but the information is worth working for. Besides biographies of musicians, the search results encompass photos, news headlines, discographies, and — this is unusual — audio samples of the artist (RealAudio needed). If only the site were streamlined, it would be world-class. As it is, the site is still a worthwhile search tool.

SonicNet

www.sonicnet.com

★★
★★

An unusual search interface here, and a few too many mouse clicks for my taste. Nevertheless, the site looks outstanding and delivers prime information if you're persistent. Click the Search icon in the left-hand navigation bar of the home page, and a little browser window opens with a keyword search form. That window stays present as you continue to search, so you can always enter a new keyword (even if you leave the site). Best results ensue when you type the name of a musician or a band. You get a bio, news, reviews, and discography, as well as a collection of links to other sites.

Ultimate Band List

www.ubl.com

Having earned its reputation as one of the great music searching sites on the Web for many years, the Ultimate Band List has dressed itself up with a fancy new look and much better navigation features than it had in the old days. You have two search avenues here: alphabetical directory (look for the little letter links beneath the main logo on the home page) and keyword entry form (type an artist or a band name). The search results list links to outside Web sites and breaks those links into coherent categories, such as official pages, fan pages, FAQ sheets, and MIDI pages. The Ultimate Band List was always well organized, and its new interface design makes it an absolute joy to navigate. When you want to know where on the Web your favorite band is, this is the place to go to find out.

Unfurled

www.unfurled.com

Unfurled made a big splash when it was launched in mid-1997, and it remains a groundbreaking music site in some ways. The keyword form is front and center of the home page, but you must scroll way down to see the Site Seeing directory. Above that feature is another directory called Categories, sporting unusual headers like Encyclomedia, Totally Wack, and Riffs Online — the last of which is a great listing of sites that offer streaming audio presentations. Rounding out the directory-intensive design is an alphabetical artist listing. I could do without the black backgrounds and faint typefaces on many of the directory pages, but aside from that complaint, Unfurled offers a deeply informed music site. It's a trip unto itself.

Other Stuff to Check Out

harmony-central.com/search.html

www.lyrics.ch/search.html

music.netsysinc.com/html/search_engine.html

www.jazznet.com/jz_searc.htm

jazzcentralstation.com/jcs/search

Reference Searching

Reference searching may seem like a dry way to use the Internet, but I've always found it to be kind of fun. Okay, so maybe I don't have a life. But anyone can get addicted to browsing through Encarta, one of the sites listed in this section. And I even included a reverse dictionary that's bound to give you a laugh.

Bartlett's Familiar Quotations

www.cc.columbia.edu/acis/bartleby/bartlett

The venerable dictionary of quotations has an Internet version that is both searchable and browsable. Enter any word into the keyword form and Bartlett's returns quotes containing that word. Alternatively, browse the complete list of quoted authors. True to the chronological scope of the book, the Bartlett's site goes way back in time, but doesn't come close to the present. Lots of ancient references are here, but you won't find the latest sage ruminations of Bill Gates.

Biographical Dictionary

www.s9.com/biography/search.html

The value of the Biographical Dictionary lies in its capability to search with keywords that are not necessarily names.

The main keyword entry form works best with single keywords; click the <u>Advanced Search</u> link for another keyword entry form that takes search operators. The problem here is that if your keywords are too broad and the search results number more than 25 hits, the site pouts and complains, "More than 25 matching records. Narrow your search request." Such fastidious behavior isn't welcome. Still, the search engine works quickly and delivers good, basic (nothing too deep) information.

Biography

www.biography.com/find/find.html

This site has nothing to do with the A&E series of television specials. It has everything to do with looking up capsule bios of famous people. The search engine accepts only names. You don't need to know the whole name, though; the search results give you choices whenever there is ambiguity. The biographies themselves are usually a single long paragraph divulging the essential career information of the person in question.

Electric Library

www.elibrary.com/search.cgi

The Electric Library searches through archives of thousands of newspapers, magazines, photo collections, and books to deliver search results on just about any type of query. Anyone can view the titles of the search results, but seeing the entire article (or photo) costs money. A 30-day trial subscription was being offered during a recent visit to the site.

Encarta Online

encarta.msn.com/EncartaHome.asp

The online version of the CD-ROM Encarta Encyclopedia is somewhat abridged but fully searchable. The radio buttons beneath the keyword form select whether you are searching the full text of articles or just the titles. Choose titles if you get too many search results. The site is beautifully designed, though the many graphics slow down the home page.

Infoplease.com

www.infoplease.com

The Infoplease database, mentioned previously in "Entertainment Searching," shines when it comes to reference searching. Use the pull-down menu to select Almanac, and then type a reference-oriented keyword such as *population* or *weather* or some other keyword that queries for the sort of information you'd expect to find in an almanac. The results are detailed and comprehensive.

Internet Dictionary Project

www.june29.com/IDP/IDPsearch.html

An innovative site that seeks to translate selected words into six languages, the Internet Dictionary Project knows only Italian, French, German, Latin, Portuguese, and Spanish. (English is the base language.) Type any word (in any of the languages), use the drop-down list to select which language you want, and go for the Search button. Be aware that the site stores a relatively small database of words. It's the flexibility that makes it stand out. A frame-based page design keeps the keyword entry form in sight at all times.

Internet Sleuth Dictionaries

www.isleuth.com/lang.html

The Internet Sleuth is a general-purpose search engine that collects databases and presents their keyword input fields. The Language page has the best collection of foreign-language, Web-based dictionaries all in one place. Best of all, you can search with the provided keyword form or link to the individual dictionary sites for more advanced search features (in some cases).

Reverse Dictionary

www.c3.lanl.gov:8064

A hilarious site that almost never works correctly, the Reverse Dictionary is designed to solve the tip-of-the-tongue feeling when you can't quite think of a word. Type a definition into the keyword form, and the search engine delivers a list of word possibilities as links; click any word to see a full definition. To the site's credit, it claims to be entertaining, and entertaining it certainly is. I recently typed *a set of bound printed pages for reading* as my definition, expecting to get back *book*. Well, *book* didn't make the list, but *horseflesh*, *bedroom*, *gastrointestinal*, and *playground* did. *Pamphlet* came closest. Visit this site when you'd just as soon not broaden your understanding of words.

Roget's Thesaurus

humanities.uchicago.edu/forms_unrest/ROGET.html

The 1911 edition of Roget's Thesaurus is online and searchable at this site. Enter any single word in the keyword form. The search results can be as dense as a brick, or even a pile of bricks. But the site is fast, and the results as complete as anybody could possibly want.

WWWebster Dictionary

www.m-w.com/dictionary.htm

Merriam Webster's online dictionary contains more than 160,000 words, and an effort is made to keep the lexicon up-to-date with new definitions. Fast and complete, this is far and away my favorite dictionary on the Internet. The site includes a thesaurus as well, and several features about words and their usage.

Other Stuff to Check Out

www.ojohaven.com/fun/crossword.html

Landau1.phys.Virginia.EDU/Education/Teaching/HowThingsWork/qsearch.html

www.forbes.com/tool/toolbox/rich97/index.asp

www.whoswho-online.com/search.html

www.speech.cs.cmu.edu/cgi-bin/cmudict

www.starlingtech.com/quotes/search.html

www.wordsofwomen.com/cgibin/var/women/index.html

Scores, articles, team histories, statistics — there's a lot of searching to do in the world of sports. This section assembles some of the heavy hitters in the field.

CBS SportsLine

search.sportsline.com/u/ATsearch/index.html

Holy smokes, this place is serious about searching. Even the Simple Search is imposing, with several menus and check-boxes to choose from when modifying

your keywords. If that's not enough, try the Power Search icon for a huge dose of options. You can tailor the search results to deliver just text or a variety of multimedia files. Unfortunately, the results aren't always intelligently sorted. Recently, I tried a search on the keywords *derek jeter*, the star Yankee shortstop, and received over 6,000 results. Nothing wrong with that, but the first match was for Derek Anderson, the basketball player. Such aberrations aside, this search engine is unique and excels at delivering colorful, multimedia results to any query. You must try it to believe it.

CNN/Sports Illustrated

search.cnnsi.com

A simple search engine helps you dig out sports articles from the combined resources of CNN and *Sports Illustrated*. The site is heavy on statistics and game updates, so searching on sports personalities won't give you the best results here. A sport-by-sport directory in the left-hand navigation bar offers another search path. The keyword form follows you to the search results page and accepts a few search operators.

Megasports

www.megasports.com

Megasports is broad but not deep. That is to say, its search results don't dig into the far corners of the Internet or deliver links that surprise you with originality. You don't find anything here that you can't find elsewhere. That said, however, I like this site for its design and coverage of major sports sites on the Web. Use the extremely thorough directory for browsing, or search by keyword. Names of athletes don't work well here, because few Web sites are devoted to individual sports stars. Names of teams provide better results.

The Sporting News

www.sportingnews.com/search

Any sports fan would appreciate the opportunity to search the article archives of the *Sporting News,* one of the great venerable sports publications. Keyword searching is a breeze, but the results are sometimes puzzling. A list of headlines is not sorted by date or by any other visible criterion, so you are forced to click among them randomly to find current material. That downfall is unfortunate, but it's the Sporting News, so give it a whirl.

SPORTQuest

www.SPORTquest.com

This British site provides an excellent directory to sports — just click the Pick a Sport link on the home page. Or use the down-down list to choose a sport. For keyword searching, you need to select the Advanced link, choose a sport, and then supplement the selection with keywords. Results are acceptable in some areas and surprisingly slim in others.

World Wide Web of Sports

www.tns.lcs.mit.edu/cgi-bin/sports-search

This is a most interesting search engine. Completely lacking in graphics, it moves fast — that's one advantage. If you enter keywords that attempt a narrowly defined search, you're sure to be disappointed — that's a disadvantage. Enter something ridiculously broad, however, such as *baseball* (go ahead, try it), and the World Wide Web of Sports charms you with

quirky, unusual search results. Where else can you find links to German, Swedish, Italian, Taiwanese, and Australian sites about baseball? Stick to broad topics here, and you won't leave disappointed.

Other Stuff to Check Out

www.onlysports.com

www.canoe.ca/Search/slamsearch.html

www.socceramerica.com/sa/search.cfm

search.usatoday.com

www.purebaseball.com

Part III
Embarking on Search Expeditions

The 5th Wave   By Rich Tennant

"The way the clown tells it, he was hired to deliver a balloon bouquet to the victim, who's this big computer nut—got all the equipment you can imagine. Well, it may have just been static electricity, but we're taking the clown in for questioning anyway."

In this part . . .

Ready for a field trip? The chapters in this part take you on expeditions to find topics of interest on the Internet. Here's where the book puts together everything described in previous chapters — but you don't have to read the earlier chapters first. This book isn't a detective novel, after all, and the butler had nothing to do with it, anyway.

This part gives you a handle on how to use many different Net-searching tools in the course of research. Whether you're looking for financial information, health sites, educational resources, software downloads, or e-mail addresses of long-lost friends, one of the chapters in this part tells you how to proceed and how to expand your searchlight to illuminate all corners of the Internet.

Chapter 13

Hunting for Health

. . . .

. . . .

*O*bviously, the computer offers no substitute for a doctor. Or even for taking your own temperature. But living in the information age can have healthy benefits, by helping you understand what in the world your doctor is talking about or research possible alternative therapies for a medical condition.

Recently, according to surveys, searching for health information has become one of the most popular uses of the Internet. Health and medicine are represented on the Internet in a couple of primary forms:

✔ **Web sites:** More medical Web sites appear every day. Some of them, I must admit, are on the far side of comprehensible if you haven't gone through your medical school internship. But others offer terrific resources for lay people who want to take responsibility for understanding their own medical conditions.

✔ **Usenet newsgroups:** The message boards of Usenet (where you can read and respond to messages pertaining to a certain topic) provide a rich vein of information and group support. Staying current with a certain medical or health newsgroup provides a great way to get pointers to the newest Web sites on that subject. You can also sometimes talk with experts at no charge.

Health Keywords

Coming up with productive keywords for general Web search engines requires a certain knack. If you're too general with keywords such as *nutrition, fitness,* or *alternative medicine,* you're simply replicating directory headings in the big general-purpose directories such as Yahoo! and Excite.

When using keywords to find health information, it's better to be specific. Following are some examples of the kinds of information you can find more quickly by using keywords than by browsing through directories:

- ✔ **Technical names of illnesses:** If you know the scientific name for a disease, searching with the technical name as the keyword gives you a shortcut to Web pages that deliver information you need about only that disease. Examples include *hypothyroid, scoliosis,* and *ischemic heart disease.*

- ✔ **Drug names:** Searching on drug names offers a good way to get information about side effects, protocols, and alternatives. You must know how to spell the drug's name, though, or you waste a lot of time guessing. If you already have the drug, just type the name as it appears on the container.

- ✔ **Body parts:** Using the names of body parts (especially the smaller ones) and other body elements, such as enzymes, hormones, glands, cell types, and so forth, generally gets good results. Searching on *pituitary,* for example, can lead you on a highly educational tour of the human endocrine system, just by following links that you encounter. If you or someone you know has been diagnosed with a medical condition (hypoglycemia, for example), searching on a relevant body part *(pancreas)* can shed light on the condition.

Technical medical terms are not the easiest words in the world to type accurately, and search engines don't cut you any slack in the spelling department. But remember, you can get some spelling leeway by using the wildcard keyword operator. You can use the asterisk symbol (*) after the first few letters of a word to indicate that anything following those first few letters is an acceptable match. Not only does the wildcard take care of some spelling difficulties, but it opens the door to more complete results. Say you're looking for information on autism. Using the keyword *autis** matches not only with *autism,* but also *autistic response.* Make sure that you include enough initial letters before the wildcard to eliminate extraneous matches. For example, using *aut** matches with *author* and *auteur.*

Health on Usenet

Casting into the Usenet newsgroups brings forth the community of the Internet. Here you can find all levels of helpfulness, from dialogs with professionals to sales pitches from cyber snake-oil salespeople. I've seen doctors post entire articles that they have authored for medical journals in response to a stranger's question. You can get quick, helpful suggestions in situations where you need to make treatment decisions quickly.

You should not rely too much on the Internet for guidance on health issues because personal diagnosis and real-time medical advice remain essential in any medical situation. Take the Usenet newsgroups as vitamins — they are strictly supplementary. As such, the newsgroups offer a great way to instantly meet many people from all over the globe who share an interest in a specific health subject.

The sci.med directory

The sci hierarchy offers the sci.med and sci.psychology directories, where you can find lots of helpful chats. The newsgroups of the sci.med directory are, as the directory name implies, rather scientific by nature. They are not restricted to doctors or scientists by any means, but many health experts frequent them. Shop talk abounds, as professionals bandy about such before-dinner questions as "Does thrombin cleave the fibrinogen, which is bound to the platelets or free fibrinogen?"

Amid such scintillating repartee you also can find regular folks asking about their conditions and taking advantage of a serious, professional environment. Ask a question in one of the sci.med groups (there were 32 such groups at my last count, ranging from sci.med.dentistry to sci.med.hepatitis), and you get an answer from other lay people who share your interest and quite often from doctors who offer advice, detailed information, personal experience, and recommendations. Of course, such dialog can't replace an actual consultation with a physician. But for gaining a better understanding of your health or a particular illness, the sci.med directory offers quite a resource.

The misc.health directory

A less technical environment reigns in the groups in the misc.health.* directory. Here, regular folks gather to share information and support. Misc.health.alternative is the most popular of these groups, and it offers a fine method of finding therapies off the beaten path. These newsgroups discuss exotic mushrooms and magnetic mattresses as seriously as calcium and nitrites.

The alt directory

Least technical of all are the newsgroups of the ever-popular alt directory:

```
alt.med.*
alt.health.*
alt.psychology.*
```

Testing the engines

In selecting health-specific search engines described in this chapter, I kept my keyword tests consistent to have a basis for comparison. I used one single-word string and one multi-word string. The single keyword is *hypothyroid*, a condition involving underactive functioning of the thyroid gland. The multiple-word string is *memory senility old age*, which I chose to see how effective the search engine is at delivering information about conditions such as Alzheimer's disease, without actually naming the disease. The multiple-word test is important in determining how helpful a search engine is when you don't know the exact name of a condition, but you do know its symptoms.

The asterisks in these examples indicate newsgroups within the respective directories. Exploring topics ranging from ayurveda (a traditional East Indian healing system) to oxygen therapy, and allergies to better vision (`alt.med.vision.improvement`), a wide range of folks congregate in the `alt` newsgroups to ask questions, seek support, and hold forth on personal agendas.

HealthAtoZ

`www.HealthAtoZ.com`

An extraordinary resource, presented with model clarity, HealthAtoZ earns a spot on the bookmark list of anyone in need of a health-oriented hub site. The site assumes that you want to get right down to business searching, and doesn't clutter the home page with eye-catching miscellaneous features, as you can see in Figure 13-1. A keyword entry form and directory occupy most of the home page real estate, and the quality of the search results is outstanding.

Using keywords in HealthAtoZ

HealthAtoZ's keyword entry form is stone-simple, lacking in fancy options. The tradeoff of simplicity for flexibility may not appeal to advanced searchers, but it's inviting to folks who need health information fast, without a complex interface getting in the way. (The <u>help</u> link beneath the keyword form doesn't cough up any advanced tips, either.)

I am impressed with the breadth of results to my single- and multiple-keyword tests. Results are listed in the order of relevancy, according to how many keywords are matched. In the case of *hypothyroid*, my single-word test, the hits ranged from articles of case studies to broad endocrinology sites and included sites devoted to thyroid problems, as you'd expect.

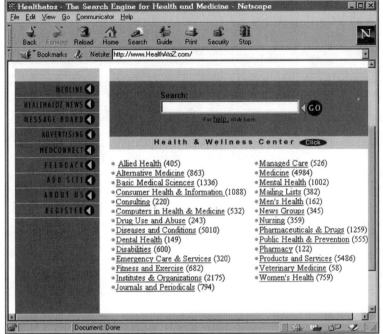

Search:

GO

For help, click here.

Health & Wellness Center Click

- Allied Health (405)
- Alternative Medicine (863)
- Basic Medical Sciences (1336)
- Consumer Health & Information (1088)
- Consulting (220)
- Computers in Health & Medicine (532)
- Drug Use and Abuse (243)
- Diseases and Conditions (5010)
- Dental Health (149)
- Disabilities (600)
- Emergency Care & Services (320)
- Fitness and Exercise (682)
- Institutes & Organizations (2175)
- Journals and Periodicals (794)

- Managed Care (526)
- Medicine (4984)
- Mental Health (1002)
- Mailing Lists (382)
- Men's Health (162)
- News Groups (345)
- Nursing (359)
- Pharmaceuticals & Drugs (1259)
- Public Health & Prevention (555)
- Pharmacy (122)
- Products and Services (5486)
- Veterinary Medicine (58)
- Women's Health (759)

MEDLINE
HEALTHATOZ NEWS
MESSAGE BOARD
ADVERTISING
MEDCONNECT
FEEDBACK
ADD SITE
ABOUT US
REGISTER

Document: Done

Figure 13-1:
The HealthAtoZ directory and search engine get right down to business.

The real beauties of the HealthAtoZ search results page are the clear layout, wealth of preliminary information, review depth, and innovative use of JavaScript to qualify each search result. (See Figure 13-2.) Here's how it works. Each hit is delivered with five bits of information:

✓ **Review.** Describes the site in no more than a few sentences.

✓ **Accuracy.** Ranks the hit according to its relevance to your keywords. One-keyword results have varying accuracy ratings, probably a result of counting the number of keyword matches in the result site.

✓ **Type.** Tells you whether the result site is geared to professionals, or consumers, or both. A very useful bit of information to have before surfing over to a page stuffed with unexplained medical terms.

✓ **Related Categories.** Links to the relevant category page in the HealthAtoZ directory.

✓ **URL.** Gives the Web address. You may simply link to the site by clicking its name, but the domain name of the URL (the portion just after the http://www) tells you something about what you're getting into. Medstudents.com, for example, is clearly a technical site, but thyroid.org is a nonprofit site aimed at consumers.

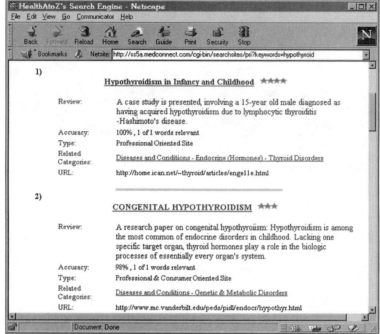

Figure 13-2:
Search
results at
HealthAtoZ
contain
reviews and
ratings.

Best of all are the red stars after each site name on the search results list. They represent a general rating of the result site, from one to five stars. (Inferior sites generally don't make the cut into HealthAtoZ, so you don't see many one-star ratings.) Roll your mouse cursor over any cluster of stars. A little browser window pops up over your main browser, with a ratings breakdown by HealthAtoZ's professional panel. It grades the site according to its ease of use, content, layout, and "Level of Appeal" (whatever that means), and gives it a final score. This little window disappears the moment you move the mouse cursor off the stars. Can you spell *c-o-o-l?*

The HealthAtoZ directory

Twenty-seven main health topics grace the home page of HealthAtoZ and comprise the top level of an excellent directory to health sites. (Figure 13-1 shows the directory topics.) Each main topic links to a list of individual Web sites or, in the case of broad topics, to a second directory level with subtopics. The individual site listings are presented in the same style as keyword search results, described previously. Each site has a brief review and a rating.

The directory is where you can quickly see the depth of the HealthAtoZ site. Some of the fat topics, such as the Pharmaceuticals & Drugs topic or the Diseases and Conditions topic, are almost overwhelming, and some of the directory pages are huge (and may take a bit of time to load).

Added features at HealthAtoZ

HealthAtoZ's added site features take a back seat to the excellence of its search engine and directory but are still worthwhile. The HealthAtoZ News link is the weakest part of the site, displaying capsule news items with no indication of date or links for more detailed information. Don't depend on this site for news. The message boards, however, are detailed, respectful, helpful, and operate smoothly. Some doctors participate in the discussion threads. A few dozen topics were posted during a recent visit, and anyone can start a new discussion on any health subject.

MedExplorer

`www.medexplorer.com`

A flashing, ad-saturated home page greets you when you visit MedExplorer (see Figure 13-3) — not exactly the atmosphere best suited to conducting serious medical research, but try to ignore it. MedExplorer doesn't offer the deepest information resource in the world, but it has worthwhile features. I've found good sites by using this search engine and directory.

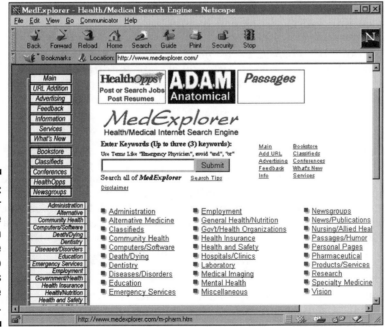

Figure 13-3: MedExplorer has more flash than substance but also includes worthwhile features.

Using keywords in MedExplorer

The search engine embedded in MedExplorer isn't flexible in some ways. For example, it doesn't understand quotation marks as search operators, so don't use them. Another example is that it assumes the AND search operator when you use multiple keywords, and returns only sites that match *all* your words. This means that my *memory senility old age* test fails miserably, returning no matches at my last visit. The simple *hypothyroid* test divulged a few good sites but revealed that MedExplorer's index isn't a profound resource.

Oddly, the best feature of MedExplorer's search engine is buried almost out of site. It's a drop-down list that lets you define what part of the index your search explores. To find this feature, click the Search Tips link on the home page. Another keyword entry form awaits you on the Search Tips page, beneath which is the magical drop-down list. Using the menu lets you constrain your search to include only alternative medicine sites, for example, or only health insurance sites, or only home pages.

The MedExplorer directory

Thirty top-level topics fill out the MedExplorer directory, some of which you should note. The Passages/Humor category can lighten the load if you're pursuing grim research, and Specialty Medicine may give you some new ideas (that one is surprisingly deep).

The directory's layout leaves much to be desired, with an annoying repetition of the entire subject cluster on each page. Furthermore, the site listings are confusing and so modestly presented as to be hard to find in some cases. Design is the weak link of the entire MedExplorer site.

The MedExplorer bookstore

Surprise! Another hidden feature turns out to be a MedExplorer gem. The bookstore (click the Bookstore link on the home page) contains its own search engine and delivers spectacular results for the serious researcher. Emphasize the word *serious,* because the search results tend toward text-books, some of them advanced and technical, and many of them expensive as all get-out. Nevertheless, a search on *thyroid* yields a wealth of reference books and even a CD-ROM.

You can search by title, a portion of the title, author, the first name of the author, dozens of categories, over a hundred publishers, publication date, ISBN number, and keyword. Then, when you've decided to become an expert on some obscure medical condition, you can buy the book(s) right from the MedExplorer site.

MEDguide

www.medguide.net

The shiny, metallic site design of MEDguide reminds me of scrubbed, antiseptic hospital corridors. (See Figure 13-4.) The keyword entry form is prominently displayed, and a quick scroll down the page reveals that the site has no directory. MEDguide embodies a peculiar set of features, making it more worthwhile in some areas than in others.

Keyword searching in MEDguide

Notice that immediately beneath the keyword entry field on the home page are radio buttons giving you a choice of search operators. Click OR to match sites with *any* (but not necessarily all) of your keywords, or click AND to force a match with all of them. A third radio button, URL, lets you limit the search to http:// Web addresses. A test of these options yielded peculiar search results. Trying my *memory senility old age* test, the OR selection turned up 1,397 results, while the AND selection divulged the same number, leading me to believe that the radio buttons are purely decorative. Further, the instructions beneath the buttons invite users to select the Phrase option, which doesn't exist.

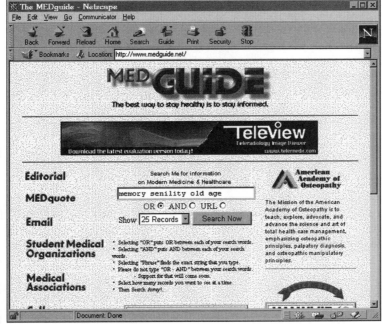

Figure 13-4: MEDguide has a strange search engine, no directory, and unusual added features.

Well, never mind the idiosyncratic radio buttons and concentrate on the quality of search results. The *hypothyroid* test ferreted out only four site hits, one of which was a case study of thyroid conditions in dogs! Another discussed estrogen patches and proved very interesting. Examining the results of *memory senility old age* is like taking a field trip through a medical school course, with considerable duplication among the results. Two lessons are to be learned when using keywords with MEDguide:

✔ Use multiple keywords, not just a single word

✔ Sift through the results as if combing a haystack for a needle

Added features at MEDguide

Skip the Editorial link on the MEDguide home page. Or read it, but don't bother checking it again for several months, because it is slow to update.

More interesting than the editorial is the MEDquote link. It's a page for finding stock quotes. What in the world is that doing in a medical site, you may ask? (I did.) Well, the site is slanted toward medical companies, health insurance companies, biotech firms, and other companies related to health and medicine. The right-hand frame links to stock quotes for many such companies. The main quote search engine lets you get any stock quote. It's a surprising and bizarre feature in the context of a health site, but why not?

The Student Medical Organizations and Medical Associations links display lists of such organizations, in link format. This is the shining point of the MEDguide site. The lists appear comprehensive and provide a great way to quickly find the official Web site for organizations as broad as the American Cancer Society or as narrow as the International Society of Nephrology Commission on Acute Renal Failure. The student organizations are described briefly beneath their links; the medical societies are not.

Wellness Interactive Network

`www.stayhealthy.com`

A bright and friendly home page greets you when entering the Wellness Interactive Network. (See Figure 13-5.) You must click your way to the search engine and directory pages, plus a selection of added features and articles.

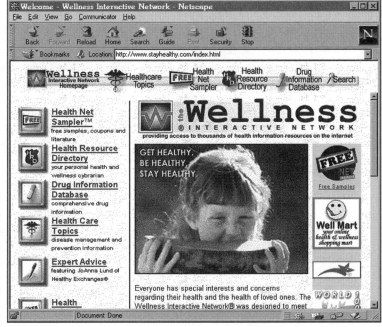

Figure 13-5:
Wellness
Interactive
Network is
a bright,
feature-rich
Web site.

Keyword searching in Wellness Interactive Network

Click the Search icon atop the home page to display the keyword entry form. You are immediately faced with a choice, presented by three radio buttons. You may perform a Category Search, a Links Search, or both. My experience is that the Category Search — which simply matches your keywords against categories in the site directory — is pointless. Go for both, which is the default selection. Enter your keywords and click the PERFORM SEARCH button.

Search results at this site tend to provide well-chosen, fundamentally useful sites, but not many of them. In some cases, you may have trouble getting any results. The *hypothyroid* test yields the Thyroid Home Page at www.thyroid.com — rather a no-brainer, but useful nonetheless. The *memory senility old age* string was a complete bust, with no results. Using the site's own example, *bladder cancer,* produces five high-quality results. This is not a search engine for plumbing the depths of detailed research into medical conditions.

The Wellness Interactive Network directory

The Wellness Interactive Network directory is actually called the Health Resource Directory, and it has the same scope and depth as the search engine. Click the <u>Health Resource Directory</u> link atop any page to see the somewhat awkward layout that forces you to scroll down, revealing topic categories. Thirteen main subjects are presented, including Geriatrics & Aging, which makes you wonder why the *memory senility old age* keyword string is such a failure. The reason is that the search engine matches your keywords only to the site title, not the body of text in the site. The upshot of this? The directory of this site is more useful than the search engine.

Each main topic drills down to a subtopic list, and from there you can proceed to actual site links. The quality of selected sites is outstanding. You can even report "dead" links, so users can participate in keeping the directory up-to-date.

Added features at the Wellness Interactive Network

One of the best added features of the Wellness Interactive Network is the Drug Information Database, in which you can search for information about specific prescription drugs. The database is searchable by keyword or through a directory format. If you know the spelling of the drug name, it's quicker to enter it as a keyword. If not, browse through the alphabetical directory. After you find the listing you're after, you get a rundown of how to take the drug, symptoms of overdose, side effects, and indications. If you've forgotten to take your medicine for a day, this information gives good advice. (Calling your doctor's office is a good idea, too.)

The Medical Tribune

`www.medtrib.com`

The *Medical Tribune* site is for doctors but open to anybody. As such, it provides a way to eavesdrop on professional medical literature. The *Medical Tribune* is a trade journal for the medical profession, and a selection of its articles is presented at this site. Be forewarned that nothing is explained here. If you don't understand the language of an article, you must puzzle it out on your own. Articles are archived — see the <u>Archives</u> link at the bottom of the page.

Also at page bottom is a <u>Search</u> link, but I suggest that you ignore it. It bombed out in my single-word and multi-word tests. Thinking I wasn't offering keywords that were technical enough, I tried *gioblastoma,* a type of tumor, but the search engine remained tight as a clam. If you have a specific condition, drug, or body part you'd like to try, it doesn't hurt. But don't have your expectations set on high.

With a recalcitrant search engine and no directory, the *Medical Tribune* site is hit-or-miss if you're trying to find something specific. But the articles do represent current medical thinking and research on many topics.

Reuters Health Information Services

`www.reutershealth.com`

A beautiful and professional site (see Figure 13-6), ReutersHealth looks like a site to get lost in all day until you realize that it is a subscription service. Most of the goodies are hidden until you join up, which, at a recent visit, was priced at $99 per year. Before you shrug your shoulders and walk away, however, this is a subscription that you may want to consider *if* you are engaged in ongoing, serious research about a medical condition (or if you are a medical professional). For example, if a family member has an ongoing, chronic, intractable medical condition and you are cooperating in the treatment plan by educating yourself as much as possible about the condition from every angle, ReutersHealth can be your most valuable online resource.

The subscription gives you these features:

✔ A professional medical news service, geared to doctors but available to every subscriber

✔ A consumer-oriented medical news service

✔ The vast Reuters archive of medical news

✔ A clinical pharmacology drug database, fully cross-linked to the news service stories

✔ Access to the National Library of Medicine's MEDLINE bibliographic database

A trial subscription is not available (grrr), but the <u>Site Demo</u> link shows you around the essential features of a subscription. If you don't care to subscribe, the home page delivers a selection of health-related stories free. You also get Health eLine, a free collection of consumer-level news connected to a search engine. Here's how to access the search engine:

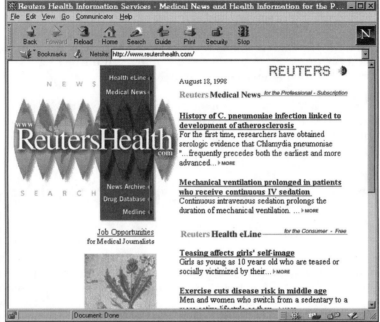

Figure 13-6:
Reuters-
Health is a
subscription
service with
a few free
features.

1. **On the home page, click the <u>Health eLine</u> link.**

2. **On the Health eLine page, click the <u>advanced searching capabilities</u> link.**

3. **When the keyword entry form appears, type your keywords and click the Search button.**

The results of a Reuters search are not sites, but news stories. As such, keyword hits are all professional and all informative.

Chapter 14

Exploring Education

- -

In This Chapter

▶ Keying into education with keywords

▶ Finding Usenet newsgroups about learning

▶ Exploring selected education search sites

- -

*I*nformation retrieval may seem like a technical enterprise that's only for professionals, but most parents of high-school seniors (as well as their college-bound students) have dabbled in the field. Choosing a college requires searching through one heck of a lot of information! Guidance counselors, being education professionals, have used information-age tools to help parents and students ever since personal computers became prevalent. Now that the information resources of the Web are equally available to students, parents, and their counselors, anyone who has Internet access can explore many aspects of educational searching, as you discover in this chapter. A student may learn more about research methods by selecting a college with the help of the family computer than by going to college.

Distance learning is especially well represented on the Web. *Distance learning* involves telecommuting to school — matriculating through a curriculum without showing up someplace. Correspondence courses provide one example of distance learning. Because opportunities for computer-based distance learning are available through the World Wide Web and e-mail, it makes sense that you can search for such opportunities in Web directories and through Web search engines.

Education Keywords

Searching for education Web sites in the big, generic search engines presents a different challenge from searching for sites for most other topics. The generic directories do such a thorough job of cataloging many types of educational subjects and institutions that searching with keywords plays a smaller role. These keyword searches, like others, however, give you a way to get to specific sites quickly.

If you know the name of an organization, an association, a guild, or a school and are looking for a Web page representing that name, try typing it as a keyword string in Yahoo!, Lycos, Excite, AltaVista, Open Text, or any of the services in this chapter that enable you to do keyword searches. Also, you can generally get good results from using the following clusters of keywords in different combinations — just remove the commas from between the words when you use them. See Figure 14-1 for a results page for the third keyword cluster in this list:

- *homework, help, assignment*
- *college, admissions, requirements*
- *financial, aid, tuition, scholarship*
- *distance, learning, online, courses, programs*
- *testing, SAT, entrance, examination, college*

Education on Usenet

The Internet bulletin boards known as *Usenet newsgroups* don't contain as much talk about education subjects as they do on more conversational topics such as sports or money. I can summarize the pertinent newsgroups quickly.

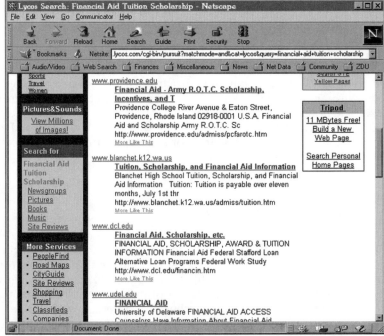

Figure 14-1: Searching on keyword clusters related to financial aid delivers several good leads in Lycos and other search engines.

The alt directory

The alt newsgroup directory seems to have a little bit of everything, and you can find most of the education newsgroups there. The first directory folder to look at is

```
alt.college.*
```

Six newsgroups lurk in this folder, including a few devoted to fraternities. The alt.college.us newsgroup provides an interesting hodgepodge of postings, some having nothing to do with education.

Moving down the list, another alt newsgroup directory to try is

```
alt.education.*
```

Here you have 11 groups to explore, including alternative education, distance learning, education for the disabled, research, and Christian education.

The soc directory

Try scrolling down the list of groups and folders in the soc directory. It includes a subdirectory called

```
soc.college.*
```

This subdirectory contains six bulletin boards, and although they are not the most popular, most trafficked areas of the Usenet, they are particularly focused, serious, interesting, and helpful. The soc.college.admissions group is a gathering place for trading information and support when applying to colleges; soc.college.financial-aid is a valuable repository of grass-roots tips about affording the high cost of college.

The k12.* directory

One main newsgroup directory focuses entirely on education:

```
k12.*
```

The k12.* directory (kindergarten through the 12th grade) has 34 groups, all focused on precollege issues. It offers an especially good resource for teachers but also proves interesting reading for anyone who is concerned with educational issues. A recent discussion in k12.ed.math, for example, went to great lengths in analyzing concrete and abstract reasoning skills and the development of intuition. The newsgroup also offers many less cerebral conversations. The `k12.chat.teacher` board, the largest in the directory, provides a nice meeting place for elementary school teachers.

Education World

www.education-world.com

Using a magazine-style format, Education World is geared to a precollege readership, plus teachers who are accustomed to the bright colors, cheery graphics, and nearly condescending attitudes of youth literature. (See Figure 14-2.) The site motto is "Where educators go to learn." Despite the cutesy design, Education World is packed with resources.

Using keywords in Education World

Education World's search engine boasts 50,000 sites, and I believe it. (I'd rather take it on faith than count them.) Search results tend to be both voluminous and of a high quality — the perfect combination. Most linked

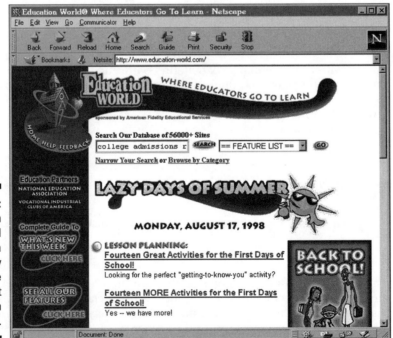

Figure 14-2: Education World combines a too-cheery interface with great search tools.

sites are described in a few sentences, so you're not surfing around blindly. Using the single keyword *SAT,* Education World returned 23 hits, including several recent and valuable sites such as Up Your Score and 500 SAT Words. Using the keyword string *financial aid tuition scholarship,* Education World delivered 167 sites, with FinAid and other famous hits packed toward the top of the result list, where they should be.

Use the <u>Narrow Your Search</u> link under the keyword entry form to reach an Advanced Search page with a friendly interface for eliminating undesirable results. (See Figure 14-3.) This page's many options let you define how the keywords are used and how the results are displayed. Scroll down the page to see instructions for each option. Pay particular attention to the Grade Level selection menu, which is useful for defining the age range of your search.

Using the Education World directory

Corresponding to the search engine, Education World maintains a searchable directory of education sites. It's a good one. On the home page, click the <u>Browse by Category</u> link to display the Education Topics page. (See Figure 14-4.) This directory is informed by an extremely broad range of educational resources and levels. It covers both teacher resources and

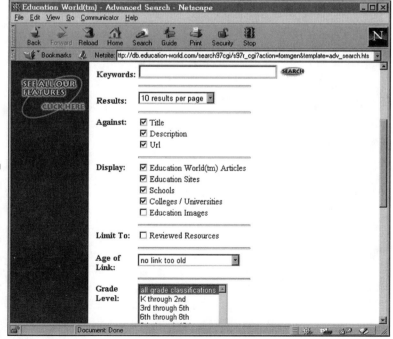

Figure 14-3:
The Advanced Search page of Education World helps narrow your search results.

student search topics. In many cases, the directory reaches down several levels, presenting subtopics along the way. Not every site has a description under its link, but all sites are well-chosen.

Added features of Education World

Education World maintains a weekly update schedule (more frequently on some pages) and is stuffed with content features. Here are the highlights:

- ✔ E-mail newsletter that describes new content at the site. Sign up for the newsletter at the following link:

  `www.education-world.com/maillist.shtml`

- ✔ Lesson plans and activities:

  `www.education-world.com/a_lesson/index.shtml`

- ✔ New and notable books in education:

  `www.education-world.com/a_books/index.shtml`

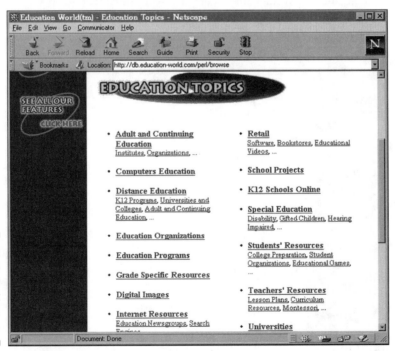

Figure 14-4:
The directory page at Education World.

✔ Monthly list of educational site reviews, sent to your e-mail box:

```
www.education-world.com/maillist.shtml
```

✔ Reports of new curriculum projects (for teachers):

```
www.education-world.com/a_curr/index.shtml
```

U.S. Department of Education

```
www.ed.gov/index.html
```

This government site doesn't coddle the user or fluff up its pages (see Figure 14-5), but it is tremendously helpful and informative. Without a doubt, it's one of the best U.S. government sites. Not meant as a general Web-searching tool, all searches at the Department of Education site are limited to departmental content of one form or another — site pages, government-sponsored sites, press releases from the agency, or other electronic publications produced by the department.

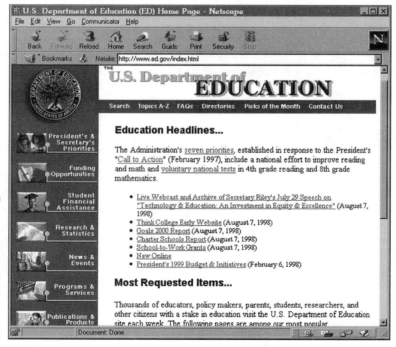

Figure 14-5:
The
Department
of Education
site is
forthright
and rich with
information.

Searching the U.S. Department of Education

On the home page, click the <u>Search</u> link to see the keyword entry form and instructions for using it. The instructions are good, including a practical tutorial on search operators and how to use them at this site. (Bravo! If only more search sites, including the big search engines, provided such clear and visible guidance.) Note the drop-down list above the keyword entry form. Use it to define the realm of your search.

Scroll down the keyword page for a short but essential directory of Internet resources provided by the Department of Education. This list alone is worth a trip to the site.

Added features of the USDE site

On the home page, the left-hand navigation bar furnishes links to a variety of information related to education news, financing, special projects, and Department of Education publications. The <u>Student Financial Assistance</u> link may be of interest to many people; it links to information about the Federal Student Aid program, the Direct Loan Program, tax credits for college costs, and other essential government information for U.S. citizens.

The <u>Research & Statistics</u> link displays an incredible resource of information about education in the United States.

College Express

`www.collegeexpress.com/index.html`

High-school juniors and seniors (and their parents) face a daunting challenge in finding the right college. Of the thousands of higher education institutions, which few have the right mix of features, class offerings, athletic teams, and extracurricular activities? College Express comes to the rescue with a searchable database that lets you dive into a broad range of information from several angles. Besides that, it has a cool home page, as you can see in Figure 14-6.

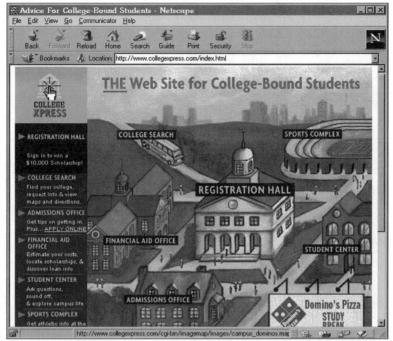

Figure 14-6:
College
Express
helps find
the right
college
through
easy and
powerful
search
tools.

Searching with College Express

You can use keywords at College Express, but it may be more helpful to use one or more of the preset tools that the site provides. Whatever methods you choose, your search results always contain colleges and nothing but colleges. Searching for other types of educational sites should be accomplished with the other search tools described in this chapter.

One of the beauties of College Express is that it doesn't rely on the Web sites of colleges themselves. (Good thing, because many college and university Web sites are in a sad state of irrelevance.) Instead, College Express builds beautiful and informative Web pages for each college in its database. That's what you see when you click any college name in a search results list. If you want to hear from the college itself, check the little box next to the link on any results page. (See Figure 14-7.) That results in a display of an elaborate registration form requesting, among many other bits of information, your mailing address. You end up getting mail from the colleges you've checked. The registration process is one of the most involved I've ever seen at a Web site, but it seems worth it to me.

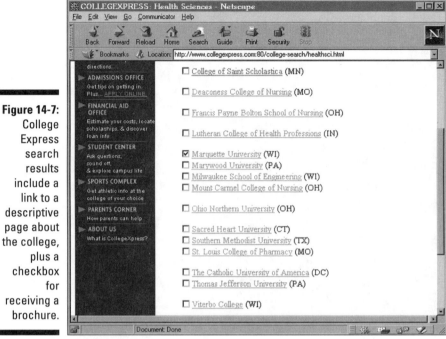

Figure 14-7:
College Express search results include a link to a descriptive page about the college, plus a checkbox for receiving a brochure.

Click the College Search link on the home page to reach the keyword entry form. Here, you can enter keywords related to your desired fields of study. Alternatively, and perhaps more productively, you can use the Advanced Search page (click the Advanced Search link). The Advanced Search page allows you to define geographic location, student population, tuition range — all by clicking radio buttons. You may also type desired religious affiliation and sports teams. This one page may be all you need to begin narrowing your college choices. Combined with the excellent descriptive pages provided by College Express for each college, the Advanced Search page is one tremendous tool.

Go back to the College Search page to see other searching alternatives. You may search by region or by one of several preset special interests. These tools are nice, but really just subsets of the Advanced Search page. That page is the gem of the whole site.

Added features of College Express

As if sophisticated searching weren't enough, College Express throws some other goodies your way. Here's a quick rundown of what you can link to from the home page:

✔ **Admissions Office.** Tips on getting in. After you've found the schools you want to apply to, this portion of the site leads you through the admissions process.

✔ **Financial Aid Office.** Tutorials and calculators about financial aid.

✔ **Student Center.** The community center of College Express includes message boards and articles, but no chat rooms.

✔ **Sports Complex.** This area helps you link up colleges with the sports programs they offer.

Petersons.com

www.petersons.com

Peterson's, the famous college guide company, enables you to access its database of information related to all kinds of education: from kindergarten, to graduate schools, to distance learning. A slight learning curve is required to make the most of the Peterson's resource, but the time required to figure out how to use the site is well spent if you're conducting serious research into educational options. Families who need information on colleges — the database area that put Peterson's on the map many years ago — will want to add this site to their hotlist.

Searching at Peterson's

At Peterson's, you can search alphabetically, geographically, by college type, and by religious affiliation; and you can even read campus news from many schools. Peterson's doesn't like keywords much, preferring to supply highly specific directories that provide common search angles. But one search engine at the site accepts keywords and uses them to search through the undergraduate and graduate descriptions provided to Peterson's by colleges and universities.

The site doesn't exactly hold your hand, and it may seem difficult to get started. Here's what you do:

1. **On the home page, click the <u>Colleges & Universities</u> link.**

2. **On the Colleges & Universities page, click one of the College Searches on the left sidebar.**

3. **On the next page, select a specific search topic from the selection menu, and then click the Submit Selection button.**

4. **On the search results page, choose a college from the selection menu, and click the Submit Selection button.**

   The next page displays information about the college you've chosen, with links, where available, to related portions of the Peterson's database.

The upshot at Peterson's

Is using this site better than just buying a Peterson's book? It depends. You have more flexible search options with a computer, and the online version is certainly cheaper. You also can get your hands on information about high schools, summer programs, careers and jobs, language study, distance learning, continuing education, educational vacations, vocational schools, and testing — all in one place.

On the other hand, the site is veering toward obsolescence in its design and in the way the database is presented to the user. It's clunky by modern standards of Internet searching. The quality of the Peterson's database isn't in question, and that quality continues to make this site essential. We can only hope the company will make it more user-friendly.

Other Useful Education Sites

The following sites don't have advanced searching features but are useful in other ways. Each contributes valuable content to the field of education information on the Internet.

College Board Online

www.collegeboard.org

When I first entered the College Board site, I was intrigued by the link to an SAT Question of the Day from a College Board exam. (Scroll down the home page to see the link.) I went right to it, viewed a picture of a complexly folded piece of paper, read the question about centimeters and edges, puzzled over the impenetrable problem, took a short nap, and awakened with fresh resolve to write this paragraph and get away from the site! Fortunately, my college days are behind me. But for those facing the challenge, this site is a great (and actually nonintimidating) way to get to know how the College Board operates and when you can catch the next test.

You can even register for SAT testing online (though you can't take the tests on your computer). The site also has information geared to counselors, faculty, and admissions staff.

CollegeNET

www.collegenet.com

A glaringly ill-designed home page detracts from this otherwise excellent college search resource. Your first experience of CollegeNET will be tempered by a server system that pushes graphics into your computer even if you're running your Web session with graphics turned off (which I generally recommend). So you must wait a bit for the page to appear, and then you'll strain your ocular limits reading the white-on-black links. But no matter. After you get past the front page, the design normalizes, and a terrific search engine opens for your use. You can search for colleges by location (states in the U.S.), enrollment numbers, tuition amounts, and majors offered. You can search also by name, of course. The results link to college Web pages, where available.

FinAid

www.cs.cmu.edu/afs/cs/user/mkant/Public/FinAid/finaid.html

The Financial Aid Information Page offers a clearinghouse of information for college students who need tuition help. Maintained by the author of a book on the subject, FinAid contains an astounding wealth of information. Glossaries; FAQs (Frequently Asked Questions); special topics, such as international and disabled students; links to financial aid Web pages, books, videotapes, and consultants; and much more combine to create a one-stop resource page. This one's a keeper.

Digital Education Network

www.actden.com

A slick (if slightly unreadable) home page greets you at the Digital Education Network, whose acronym (DEN) provides the motif for various site features: MathDEN, NewsDEN, WritingDEN, and so on. You must register to use this site, but it's free and relatively painless (except for the continued legibility problem caused by the black backgrounds). After you're a member, various tests, games, and other features ensue. It's a good site for kids who are motivated to learn.

The Global Schoolhouse

`www.gsn.org`

Operated by the Global SchoolNet Foundation, a nonprofit organization, Global Schoolhouse is a site designed to link kids together in the spirit of learning. Teachers may be interested in this site for its curriculum ideas. Global Schoolhouse contains a search engine, but it's limited to the site itself, not outside Internet locations.

Chapter 15

Foraging for Files

● ●

In This Chapter

▶ Discovering files

▶ Using Gopher to find software

▶ Trying out keywords to find software

▶ Great shareware Web sites

● ●

*I*n the old days of the Internet, before the World Wide Web was born, most people logged on so that they could rummage through file libraries. (The Usenet newsgroups were popular, also.) Internet file libraries contained text files and software programs, and they were generally shared for free. (*Shareware,* the honor system of software purchase, wasn't as prevalent back then.)

In these new days of the Web-centric Internet, files and file libraries are still great things to log on for. And searching for text files and programs is far easier than it ever was, thanks to the Web's simple navigation, as you find out in this chapter. The greater range of file types also adds to the fun. With multimedia on the Internet scene in a big way, you can now download pictures, sound recordings, and even short movies from the Web. (Admittedly, with *streaming* files such as RealAudio and RealVideo becoming common, downloading multimedia is on the wane. But downloading software programs is popular.)

Downloading simply means acquiring something from a computer that stores files. The file must be located on a server (a type of computer) that allows downloading. You don't need to know anything to recognize a downloadable file or the type of server it's on — the Web page you're visiting should explain it to you. In fact, downloading was never so easy before the Web. In most cases, the Web site from which you're downloading gives you a hyperlink to initiate the download. Click the link, and within a few minutes (depending on the size of the download and your connection speed), you have your file.

What's So Exciting about Files?

The word *files* brings to mind images of office filing cabinets and endless manila folders. Not exactly what the allure of the Web is all about, you may think. Although the Web has become popular because of its graphics dazzle and hyperlinked pathways, it's also a great place to augment your computer's supply of manila folders (on your hard drive, that is).

Files is technospeak for the stuff that makes computers fun. Your favorite software program is a file. If you create a party invitation on your computer, that's a file. When you see a video on your screen, your computer is playing a file. Files either make your computer do things or are the result of what you do with your computer.

On the Web, you can find three main types of files:

- ✔ Programs
- ✔ Information files
- ✔ Multimedia files

Read on to find out exactly what each of these types give you.

Programs

People search primarily for program files on the Web because programs allow users to get the most out of their computers. Computer software (programs) turns your computer into a new device. When you acquire a new game program, suddenly your computer transforms into an arcade machine or a flight simulator. When you get a graphics program, suddenly your computer morphs into a hi-tech digital painting device. You can download just about any kind of program from the Web by using your Web browser (which is also a software program) to place the program directly on your hard drive. Following are the three main kinds of software available for downloading:

- ✔ **Shareware:** Shareware is commercial software that you try out at no charge and then pay for if you decide to keep it. The distribution of shareware runs on an honor code and to everyone's advantage. Software authors can distribute their products inexpensively online, and customers can browse shareware products by the thousands right from home and try them at no cost. Some shareware programs offer limited functionality, and to get the fully functional version, you need to register and pay for the program. Other programs have built-in time bombs (which are harmless to your computer) that kill the program after it has been on your hard drive for a certain number of days. Still others flash registration pleas on your screen insistently until you pay for a guilt-free version. But many programs are full-fledged versions of the commercial program, and you are simply on your honor to pay for them if you decide to continue to use them.

✔ **Freeware:** As the name implies, these programs are yours for the download, no strings attached. Download them, use them, keep them forever at no charge. Naturally, the old rule sometimes applies: You get what you pay for. Freeware programs are usually not powerful, complex, deeply resourceful productivity tools. They tend to be small utilities that fill a niche for some computer users. However, don't write off freeware! You can find some great free programs out there. Some of them are provided by major software companies, such as Microsoft (the Internet Explorer, for example, is freeware). Other excellent utilities are authored by professional programmers who create programs for their own use and then make them available to the public in the traditional Internet spirit of sharing.

✔ **Demos:** Some software houses don't want to distribute their programs as shareware but do want to take advantage of the online customer base. They take a middle road by providing demonstration (demo) versions of their programs for downloading. These programs are never fully functional. Usually, something crucial is missing, such as a Save feature; you can test the program indefinitely and try out its many aspects, but you can't save any of your work to a file. Obviously, such software is useless as a productivity tool, but it works well to demonstrate the program.

Information files

The Internet is the world's largest library, and the Web offers the easiest way to access information files. I want to emphasize that much of the Web's informational resources are embedded directly into Web pages. In other words, you can get most of the information you need by visiting Web sites, without downloading separate files of any sort. You can also access and download many information files through Web sites, and these files are well worth acquiring so that you can refer to them after you leave the sites from which you got the files.

References and links to FAQ (Frequently Asked Questions) files spring up all over the Web. These files are text documents, without graphics, and they usually do a good job of explaining basic information about a topic in question-and-answer format. You can find FAQ files that explain how to navigate the Internet, how to use Usenet newsgroups, how to fix computer and software problems, what Java is and how to use it, and probably even how to scramble eggs, if you look hard enough. The truth is, you can find FAQ files for darn near everything, especially computer-related topics. The three proven ways of finding FAQ files are as follows:

Downloading: What's the delay?

When you begin a download with your Web browser, you may experience delays, and getting the file may take longer than it should. Why the delay, and how can you tell if a delay is stalling your download?

Download delays can be caused by a few things. If you're trying to get your hands on a popular file, such as the latest beta-test version of Internet Explorer, many other people may be downloading the file at the same time. If too many people access the server (the computer storing the file) simultaneously, everyone experiences a slowdown. You have no way of knowing how many other users are reaching for the same file as you, but if you're logging on during Internet prime time (such as late Friday evening), chances are good that you have lots of company.

Other bottlenecks can occur. The file has to travel over the phone line from the server upon which it is stored to your Internet service provider (encountering a few switching points along the way). Then it has to go through your service provider's Internet gateway, over more phone lines, through your modem, and into your computer. Telephone line noise and Internet traffic can interfere with the process at several stages.

How can you tell whether your download is delayed? If you're using an external modem, keep an eye on the RD (Receiving Data) light. If it doesn't blink, nothing's happening. Most people have internal modems, though, and in that case you have to rely on your Web browser to tell you what's going on (unless your system displays modem lights in a corner of your screen — check the Windows 95 task bar). Most browsers display a status panel (a small window that opens on top of the main browser window) telling you how big the file is, how much has been received, and how much time remains. If the status panel doesn't show any change for about 15 seconds, you're stalled. Sometimes (if you have something else to do, for example), you can just let the download proceed slowly. (If a download stalls for too long, however, your ISP may disconnect you from the Internet. This *timeout* function prevents you from accidentally staying online for days on end.) Alternatively, you can stop the download and try again later. Sometimes trying again immediately works too. No matter what you try, yelling a few choice words can help — or at least make you feel better.

✔ **Stumble across them:** Obviously, this method offers the least organized way of finding FAQ files. But it often works when you least expect it, so keep your eyes open for links to FAQ files on Web pages.

✔ **Ask for them:** To ask for a FAQ file, you go to a Usenet bulletin board, find a newsgroup on the topic in which you're searching, and post a message asking whether anyone knows the Internet location of pertinent FAQ files. You often get good results within a day or two.

Beware, though, that some irascible newsgroup veterans get impatient with seeing FAQ requests over and over, and they may respond in a surly fashion if your particular request is at the end of someone's bad day. It's wise to make the effort to read current newsgroup postings to see whether your request has already been answered in the last few days.

✓ **Type** FAQ **in your keyword string.** If, for example, you're searching for basic information about VRML, the Virtual Reality Modeling Language sometimes found on the Web, you can get good results by using **vrml faq** as a keyword string in any of the major search engines.

Multimedia files

Multimedia refers to any computer experience that goes beyond reading text. Multimedia files include pictures, sounds, and movies. The Web is a multimedia playground, and most of its multimedia files come bundled right in the Web pages. But you can also find stand-alone files of pictures, sounds, and videos that can be accessed and downloaded through your Web browser.

Arguably, the best way to experience multimedia files is through *streaming media*. Streaming music and video require a free browser plug-in that matches the format of the streaming file. RealAudio is the most popular and prevalent such plug-in — the recent version is called RealPlayer and includes RealVideo capability. When you download RealPlayer, you get RealAudio and RealVideo in one package. This plug-in and others like it from other companies empower your computer to play sound and video files without downloading them first. The quality is not too bad — faster connections get better quality. Audio works much better than video.

Gophering for Files

Before Gopher, chaos reigned on the Internet. Although the Internet provided a rich resource of information and files, finding anything was a nightmare if you didn't know your way around. And who could possibly know the entire landscape of something as immense as cyberspace? Then Gopher swooped on the scene and gave organization to the chaos. Gopher was the Internet's first popular and effective directory system. When it was established, Internet users could use directory menus — similar to the multilevel Web directories everyone uses now — to travel methodically from a grand overview to a specific file. It was Gopher that first made the Internet a friendly place and first attracted the attention of the general public.

Gopher had a short day in the sun, though. Before long, the Web was stealing headlines with its super-friendly point-and-click hyperlink navigation. Although less organized than Gopherspace, the Web has the star appeal of bright graphics and ease of use. Did it spell the end of Gopher? No, it merely relegated that industrious animal to the background.

Gopher directories still work, and you can access them through your Web browser. Gopher has become a Web tool the way that DOS has become a Windows tool that you access through Windows.

You can find all kinds of files through Gopher: programs, texts, sounds, pictures, and movies. It is especially good for accessing libraries and card catalogs at universities that allow public access to their Gopher systems. You can view and read the text files directly from the host server, without downloading them. You have to download most of the others and then view them (or listen to them) from your own hard drive with the correct utility software.

Getting going with Gopher

You can easily get started with Gopher on the Web. Just enter the address for a main Gopher directory (I give you a good starting place in this section — just look down a few paragraphs for the address) and click your way through the directory levels, just as you do in Yahoo!, Excite, or Lycos.

Gopher menus look stark (see Figure 15-1), completely lacking in pretty graphics and flashy advertisements. You can decide for yourself whether this sparse appearance is an advantage or a drawback.

Hundreds of Gopher servers exists throughout cyberspace. Some are planetary in scope, and others pertain just to the institution that houses the server. Many colleges, for example, maintain Gopher servers for storing files relevant to the curriculum and campus.

Gopher is just a system of organizing files. Whether someone applies that system to the entire Internet or a single office is the free choice of whoever runs the Gopher system. The upshot of this? Just browsing Gopher servers can be an adventure before you even get to the good files!

You should start gophering at the grandfather of all Gopher servers, which is located at the University of Minnesota. Just point your browser to this address:

```
gopher://gopher.tc.umn.edu:70/1
```

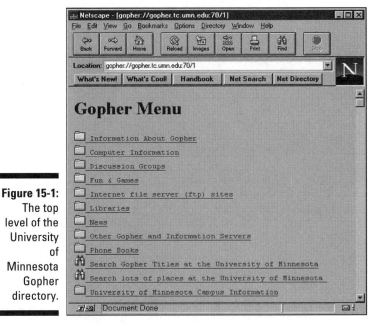

Figure 15-1:
The top
level of the
University
of
Minnesota
Gopher
directory.

Note the `gopher://` prefix. Although you're viewing Gopher through a Web browser, Gopher is not strictly speaking part of the Web. This is the case with all Gopher server addresses.

After you arrive at the main directory page, you can click your way around the Gopher universe. Happy digging!

Using Gopher icons

Several types of small, graphical icons help you navigate your way through Gopherspace. The most common icon is the folder icon, which indicates that at least one more directory level exists beneath that link. The folders resemble the folders in the Windows and Macintosh computer desktops: They represent a collection of files, or more folders, or both files and folders.

File types have their own special icons, which make it easy to identify text, sound, graphics, movie, and MIDI files.

Working with Gopher keywords

Some Gopher listings have a little pair of binoculars next to them. The binoculars indicate that you can conduct a keyword search at that Gopher page. Indeed, if you click the hypertext link next to the binoculars, you see a keyword entry form that invites you to enter one or more words for searching.

In most cases, in Gopherspace, you search for directories, and the search engine at a Gopher site matches your keywords against words in directory names — not against the body of any text files you may be searching for. Accordingly, you should keep your keywords general. If you're searching for medical files about vitamin supplements for heart murmurs, for example, use *nutrition* or *heart* as a keyword, rather than *heart murmur* or *palpitation,* because you're trying to match against a directory name. After you get a list of relevant Gopher directories (with folder icons), you can click your way to more specific files.

Finding Files on the Web with Keywords

Searching for files with keywords is a special challenge. Files are downloadable objects, but most keyword searches investigate topics and subjects. You can stumble across files in any topical search, but finding a specific file with keywords is hard unless you know the exact name of the file.

However, when you search for files, you can use keywords for one handy shortcut. When you want to find a certain *type* of file, you can include the file extension for that type in your keyword string. (The *file extension* is the three-letter suffix that follows the period in a filename.) For this shortcut to work, you also need to use the wildcard asterisk (*) in place of the filename before the extension. Here's an example:

```
*.wav
```

As a keyword, this string matches all files that have a wav extension, no matter what comes before the period. (The wav extension indicates an audio file.) Of course, the results list would be immense and practically useless. To narrow it down, include other keywords in the string and tell the search engine to match *all* of them, like this:

```
*.wav AND grateful AND dead
```

This string returns a list of matches to all three words and includes sites containing audio files of the Grateful Dead.

One easy, if not foolproof, way to find multimedia files lies in the HotBot search engine. (See Chapter 10 to read all about HotBot.) In HotBot, you can designate the type of file you want to locate by using checkboxes. The search results don't point you directly to the picture, film clip, or sound file itself in most cases; instead, HotBot links you to the Web site containing such files, and you must locate them within the site. Still, HotBot offers a quick, nontechnical way to get pointed in the right direction.

Combing Shareware Sites

A few commercial Web sites serve as virtual software stores that specialize in downloadable shareware. Don't let their commercial nature fool you — the sites don't cost a dime. They have advertisements, but there's nothing unusual about that. Like real software stores, the Web versions divide their inventory into categories based on computer type and program type. These categories differ from one site to the next, but a few basic types of shareware appear time and again:

- **Games:** A lot of replication exists among shareware games. You can find dozens of examples of computer versions of board games, such as chess, checkers, and backgammon, plus games that carry on the tradition of the old arcade diversions, such as Pong and Breakout. In most cases, you can download these small files quickly, so you can test several of them to find one you really like. You also can find and acquire larger-scale adventure games for a bigger investment in download time. You may have difficulty downloading high-intensity graphical powerhouses because they are so big, so don't expect to find games that rely on video footage. For those, you should shop in a CD-ROM store.

- **Personal:** Personal shareware includes all kinds of programs that defy easy categorization, including shareware for personal learning or entertainment, as opposed to productivity. Some examples are astrology calculators, science programs, weather forecasting software, genealogy applications, and shareware books and other electronic publications.

- **Computer utilities:** One of the largest groups, these programs tend to be small, with narrowly specific purposes, such as alarm clocks. Because programmers find so many little ways to enhance a computer, miniature utilities spring up everywhere. They're fun to look for, too — and finding just the right utility can really make a difference in your overall computing experience.

One common and prevalent type of shareware utility is the compression/ decompression program. Because almost all program files are compressed and must be decompressed after downloading, just about everyone who downloads files needs one of these programs. ZIP programs (for Windows) and SIT programs (for the Macintosh) are the most common.

Many people also like to download screen savers, which create moving graphics on your monitor when the computer is idle and may protect your screen from burn-in damage while entertaining or dazzling you. You also can find desktop organizers (for the desktop of your operating system — it's up to you to keep your real desktop neat); calendars and clocks; computer diagnostic programs; and too many other types to list. It's a browser's paradise out there.

✔ **Productivity:** Shareware offers a much less expensive alternative to the big, famous, elaborate, powerful, and costly programs for writing, painting, and organizing. Word processors, graphics art packages, and database programs are three of the foundation pillars in the software world. The best, most professional versions of these applications can cost hundreds of dollars. Although these tools are fantastic and worth the investment if you need to generate professional output, for many people they are a little too much bang for the buck. Furthermore, unless you read magazine reviews voraciously, you never know whether you're going to like a program until you invest in it.

Enter shareware to save the day. You can download a simple word processor, graphics viewing program, desktop publishing software, computer paint application, or database organizer without any charge. Often, the online descriptions come complete with pictures of the program's windows, helping you decide which to try. You can test programs until you find the right program level for your needs and then register and pay to keep it. Furthermore, some of the shareware files now in circulation are powerhouses in their own right. But because of the relatively inexpensive means of online distribution, they are less expensive than store-bought programs.

✔ **Internet navigation:** Everyone on the Web has one thing in common, at least to some degree: an interest in the Internet. So it stands to reason that Internet software would be a likely candidate for shareware distribution on the Web. The most obvious examples are the mainstay Web browsers. You can get Microsoft Explorer free just by downloading it, and you can sometimes get Netscape Navigator for free from its Web site. In addition, you can find dedicated Usenet newsgroup readers, e-mail programs, other Web browsers, and many HTML-authoring applications for creating Web pages.

How do you find good shareware sites? It's easy — I've already found some of the biggest ones for you. Just type the address for each of the selected Web stores listed in the following sections, and check them out for yourself. Visiting and downloading from these sites doesn't cost you a penny! The programs aren't free, however, in the long run. You can test them without expense and then register and pay for any programs you decide to keep.

Jumbo

```
www.jumbo.com
```

Not known for its modesty, Jumbo splashes an even mix of self-proclamations and shareware categories in your face as you enter the home page. At last count (it wasn't me who counted them), almost 60,000 programs were available for downloading from Jumbo. The main classifications (dumbly called channels) are Business, Games, Home & Hobbies, Utilities, and Multimedia/Fonts. Jumbo also offers a Shopping Center for buying commercial software, books, and music. Each category is further divided according to the operating system platform (Windows 3.*x,* Windows 95, Macintosh, and so on), which is standard for a software directory.

A few problems besiege the Jumbo experience. For one thing, the sheer size of the program lists makes navigation through the site slow going. Some of the pages are so enormous that it takes a while for Jumbo to load into your browser. If you experience a delay, or if the page stalls for some reason, you can't see the entire list. (Breaking the lists into smaller pages would help.) Furthermore, the promised descriptions of each program often turn up missing, which is frustrating. (Would you want to download a 1.5MB game without seeing a description?) Finally, the downloads are sometimes slow, perhaps due to the well-justified popularity of the site.

But Jumbo is well-named and is one heck of a fun place to browse if you're a software addict or looking for something in particular. The previous elephant motif is gone from Jumbo's pages, and I can't decide whether I miss it.

Shareware.com

```
www.shareware.com
```

Shareware.com enables you to browse, search with keywords, and check out the shareware pick of the day. The site offers one of the most respected download galleries on the Web. The home page includes a keyword search form that helps you find what you're looking for among the 250,000 files. If you don't want to be that efficient, you can just browse by category. The program descriptions are as brief as can be, and the shareware is not critically reviewed. But you are told the size of the shareware, and even how long it will take to download (assuming ideal conditions) with various types of modems. Unfortunately, the site depends heavily on its graphics, which slows down the proceedings when you are moving from page to page in this enormous collection.

When it comes to downloading, Shareware.com has a good system. Rather than keeping its own cyberinventory of shareware programs, the system connects you to one of several Internet sites where you find the program you want. The Shareware.com page remains on your screen during the download, but your browser pulls the files down from another Internet computer in most cases. Because it doesn't matter where you get the program from, Shareware.com links you to several possible transfer sites for each of its programs. These alternatives are great because you can try one, and if the download isn't going quickly enough or is locked in a stalled mode, you can abort it and try one of the other sites. The instructions and page layout make it clear how to switch to another site — it's as easy as a few mouse clicks.

I like browsing for downloads, rather than searching with keywords, and Shareware.com makes browsing a beautiful experience <sniff>. Well, it's not all that soul-stirring, but I like the directory. (See Figure 15-2.) The entire directory is divided by PC and Mac computer platforms through all the subject headers. The Most Popular heading focuses on programs that have gained lots of word-of-mouth download traffic.

Figure 15-2:
The
Shareware.
com
directory
of file
downloads.

Shareware.com creates an electronic newsletter called Shareware Dispatch, which notifies subscribers of the latest additions to the library. It's free and delivered to your e-mail box. Scroll down the home page until you see the e-mail address entry form on the right, and subscribe by entering your address and clicking the Subscribe button.

ZDNet Software Library

`www.hotfiles.com`

PC Magazine is renowned in part for its excellent software reviews and monthly freeware offerings. *PC Magazine* is published by Ziff-Davis, the creator of ZDNet. By this lineage we may assume that ZDNet Software Library, otherwise known by its URL-inspired Hotfiles nickname, is a high-quality software warehouse. Indeed it is.

The site takes a stab at standard directory organization in the left-hand navigation bar, where several subject headers are listed. (See Figure 15-3.) The typical categories are there: Games, Internet, Utilities, Home & Education, Small Business, Graphics & Multimedia, and a few others. But most of the home page is organized like an ezine, with editorial picks and feature selections. This makes returning to ZDNet Software Library an inviting proposition, because you never know what you may find there.

Figure 15-3:
The ZDNet
Software
Library is
like an
ezine for file
downloads.

Forget about keyword searching. ZDNet Software Library is for browsers. The generous descriptions of the programs are welcome, and the operating requirements are clear and complete. One complaint: The download process takes too many mouse clicks and page views.

Shareware Online

www.bsoftware.com/sonline.htm

Shareware Online is a dual-purpose site that serves both shareware customers and program authors. It encourages dialog between these two groups by inviting visitors to place Want Ads requesting specific software program types. Programmers who have relevant programs can then get in touch with them. I can't say whether this system is of any practical value, but I can verify that Shareware Online has a good (if not overwhelming) selection of titles for downloading. You can browse by category, but you can't search for keywords.

Screen Savers from A to Z

www.sirius.com/~ratloaf

If you think that the best thing about computers is what happens to the screen when you're not using it, you *must* visit the Screen Savers from A to Z site. Even if you're only moderately hypnotized by pictures and designs that play across your monitor when the computer is idle, you may want to enhance your collection with a few well-selected downloads from this site. And if you're currently stuck with the factory screen savers that came with your new computer, then you really must test the waters with a new saver program or two. Okay, I admit it, I'm a hopeless screen saver zombie. But you don't have to be like me to enjoy the large catalog of screen savers here. Many are small, quick downloads, so within minutes you too could be wasting most of your time gazing helplessly at colorful animations.

Chapter 16

Investigating the News

● ●

In This Chapter

▶ Discovering the news on your computer

▶ Finding headlines for quick news

▶ Exploring selected news searching sites

▶ Saying goodbye to microfiche

▶ Discovering great news sites

● ●

*I*n August of 1998, when U.S. President Bill Clinton testified before a grand jury, some news sites on the World Wide Web experienced almost a 50 percent increase in visits. Apparently, when news is breaking, the Internet provides news coverage that appeals to many people.

The computer offers an immediacy that satisfies newshounds who must remain up-to-the-second with world events. Even if you're not regularly a news fiend, sometimes an unfolding news story catches your attention and you want to get the latest developments without waiting for TV reports or — even more impatiently — the next day's newspaper.

On the other hand, computers have neither the convenience nor the ambiance of newspapers — carrying a laptop and mobile phone around isn't quite as handy as buying a newspaper — and Web sites certainly aren't as personable as your favorite toothy TV anchorperson. What to do?

Strike a balance. Use computers for their strengths, and balance the equation with traditional news media. The World Wide Web offers a few terrific ways of not only staying informed but being *better* informed than ever before, as you discover in this chapter. If you can integrate a few Web habits into your news-gathering routines, you may find yourself more deeply knowledgeable on general news items and a downright expert on issues of particular interest.

Some of the unique qualities that the Web brings to the news include the following:

- ✔ **Continual updates:** Broadcast schedules and printing deadlines don't exist on the Web. Different news sites handle this glorious liberation in various ways, but generally news gets updated online mighty fast. Logging onto a Web-based source of headlines unquestionably provides the quickest way to get breaking developments.

- ✔ **Variable depth:** News on the Web offers you more control over how much news you get. Of course, you can scan headlines in a newspaper. But the Web makes that simple task easier by organizing the headlines into lists that link to summaries and complete stories. By and large, after you know your way around, you can get the exact level of information you want more quickly.

- ✔ **Links to related information:** This feature proves perhaps the best one of all for people who like to search deeply into a topic. Hyperlinks (usually called links) are the defining characteristic of the World Wide Web. Hyperlinks for news items can take you to sites that give background on a story, to e-mail addresses with which you can contact people involved in the story, to discussion groups for meeting other people following the story, and to various other innovations that get more imaginative every month.

- ✔ **E-mail delivery:** A number of Web news services offer e-mail subscriptions. Some provide ways to tailor the news so that you get an electronic newspaper custom-adapted to your interests. Although such deliveries don't arrive with the reassuring *thump* of a newspaper landing on the front steps (or the heartwarming *crash* of it flying through the front window), e-mail news deliveries still come in handy.

- ✔ **Pushed news:** You can get news *pushed* to your computer from the Web from PointCast, Yahoo!, or some other Web-based news source. See Chapter 12 for more information about *push* and *pull* on the Web.

Gleaning Headlines from the Search Engines

At the time of the first edition of this book, search engines made attempts to provide some kind of headline news coverage. When I wrote the second edition, those same sites had improved their news coverage and vied with each other to provide the best current events features. Now, the race is in earnest. Search engines are in desperate competition to provide the most added features, particularly news.

News headlines in search engines furnish one of the best and easiest ways to grab quick news on the Web.

News in Yahoo!

Yahoo! displays news faster than the other search engines, thanks to its almost-no-graphics page design. Yahoo! has expanded its traditional wire service reports with news sources specific to certain categories, such as the Sporting News for sports and Hollywood Reporter for entertainment.

You can see the Yahoo! Daily News directory by clicking the <u>Daily News</u> link from the Yahoo! home page, or by surfing directly to

```
dailynews.yahoo.com
```

As you can see in Figure 16-1, Yahoo! News operates like a small version of the main Yahoo! directory, with top-level subjects leading down to headlines. The subheads you see under each directory topic also lead directly to headlines. Each headline is accompanied by a short summary of the news item, and each headline is a link. Click on a headline to see any full story. In most cases, Yahoo! keeps you within its site, but in some cases, you are tossed out to the source site and can read the story there.

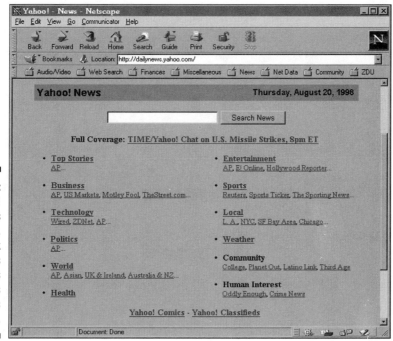

Figure 16-1:
The Yahoo!
News
directory.
Each link
displays
news
headlines
within its
topic.

I use Yahoo! news headlines just about every day. It makes sense to book-mark your favorite headline pages so that you can go to them directly from your browser's hotlist.

The ezine style of Lycos news

As I describe in other chapters, the Lycos directory has the sensibilities and design features of an electronic magazine, and the same holds true in the news department. You can see what I mean by surfing to the Lycos home page at this address:

```
www.lycos.com
```

The home page usually contains some top news headlines to whet your appetite, plus a buzz of colorful features that may just prove distracting at first. The news headlines are hidden in the Lycos directory — click the <u>News</u> topic of the main directory on the home page. The Lycos News directory appears, with ten main news topics. (See Figure 16-2.) The News directory is easy to get around in, thanks to the navigation bar on the left that keeps the top-level topics available no matter how far you drill down.

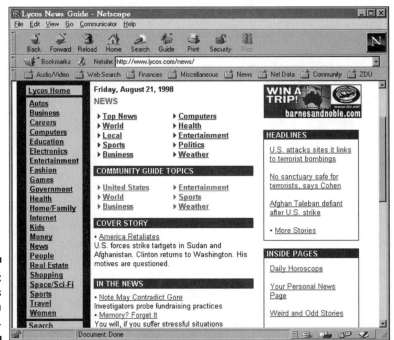

Figure 16-2:
The News directory in Lycos.

Lycos relies on the Reuters wire service for most of its news and keeps you within the Lycos site as you scan headlines and read stories. The busy, cluttered, magazine-style page design persists through the News directory, making headline-surfing a little more confusing than in Yahoo! — but the style may be preferred by some people over the slate-gray, unenhanced design of Yahoo!

The latest news at Excite

www.excite.com

Excite, alas, has become more confusing over time. Still, the news features at this venerable search engine are outstanding. The Excite home page provides a splash of news right off the bat, under the My News banner, if you scroll down far enough to see it. Once you find the headlines, click the Top Stories link. This link displays the Excite News page (see Figure 16-3), which you may want to bookmark.

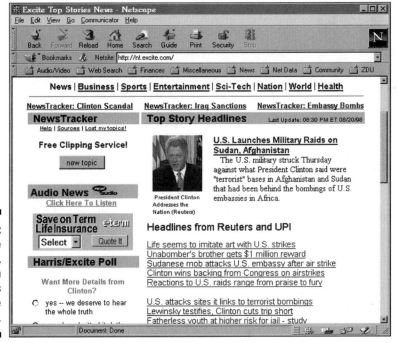

Figure 16-3: The Excite News page, which includes several fine features.

Excite is generous in providing many headlines, most of which are culled from the Reuters and UPI news services. If you don't see what you want, Excite invites a more customized experience with the NewsTracker feature. NewsTracker lets you set up a virtual clipping service (one topic only) based on keywords, and scans over 300 news sources (newspapers and magazines) to stock its database of headlines and stories. Click the New Topic button to fill in your topic and keywords — Excite has set up a good instructional page that walks you through the process and even provides some template topics for your use.

The Audio News feature requires the RealAudio plug-in *and* the Shockwave plug-in to activate RealAudio — whew. Too many plug-ins, just to get some news. Audio news goes against the grain when you're surfing for headlines because it slows down your session drastically.

Scroll down the Excite News page to find a wealth of links to ongoing coverage of long-term stories, and to news sources around the Web. Of all the search engine news pages, this may be the one to bookmark.

News Index

www.newsindex.com

News Index hypes itself as "The most comprehensive, up-to-the-minute News Search Engine on the planet." It may be true. Certainly, the site earns worthy bookmark status by providing a keyword entry form and comparing your words to the content of over 300 newspapers and other sources.

Figure 16-4 shows you the News Index home page, with its keyword entry form. Type keywords as usual, and use the little drop-down list beneath the main form to instruct News Index to find matches to *all* your keywords (resulting in a smaller number of hits) or *any* of your keywords (resulting in more hits). The search results list contains headlines and the first paragraph (approximately) of the story; click the headline to display the full story at the source site.

The left-hand sidebar at the home page provides a nifty feature. Each headline link in that sidebar leads to the results of topical, current, preset search strings. The link displays not one story, but several headlines, as if you had conducted the search yourself.

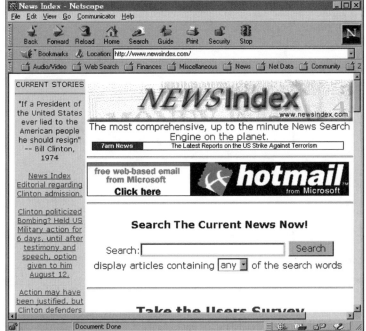

CNN Search

www.cnn.com/SEARCH

CNN, the justifiably famous news organization and cable channel, has one of the landmark news sites on the Web — CNN Interactive. CNN Search is part of that site and has a few unique features. You can limit your search to CNN material, but you don't have to.

Figure 16-5 shows the CNN Search home page, with the keyword entry form. Above the keyword entry box are two radio buttons, which determine whether you want results from only the CNN family of sites or from the entire Internet. Choosing the latter selection opens the doors to some peculiar results, especially when you use broad keywords. There is value in taking this route, however, not to mention the charm of discovery. The search engine displays results in the order of relevance — that is, the sites with the greatest number of matches to your keyword(s) are listed first. Those high-match results may not be recognized news sites, and you may find yourself surfing to an individual's political research site or a sports fan page.

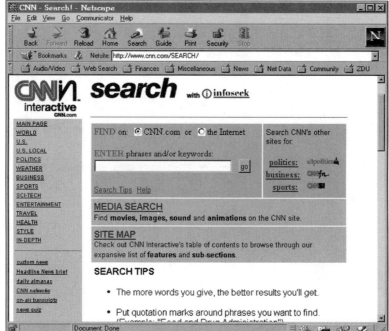

Figure 16-5:
The CNN
Search
home page.

Searching within CNN (choosing the first radio button) guarantees professional news on the results page and is the choice when you're in a hurry or in a serious mood. (You can return later for more leisurely explorations.) If you're prowling through CNN's offerings, be sure to check out the two features linked below the keyword entry form. First, the Media Search. CNN produces lots of audio and video, and much of it is used by the Web site. Clicking the Media Search link takes you to a separate search engine for finding video clips, audio presentations, pictures, and animations. (See Figure 16-6.)

CNN does not use RealAudio or RealVideo for multimedia recognized by this search engine, which is inconvenient. You need the Vivo video plug-in to see CNN video clips, and your browser needs to be configured to understand WAV or AIFF sound files to hear audio.

Beneath the Media Search link is the Site Map link — highly recommended for an awesome glimpse of the vast CNN Interactive Web empire. Every item of the site map is a link, so you can use the page as a hub for finding content on CNN Interactive. Bookmarking that page wouldn't be a mistake.

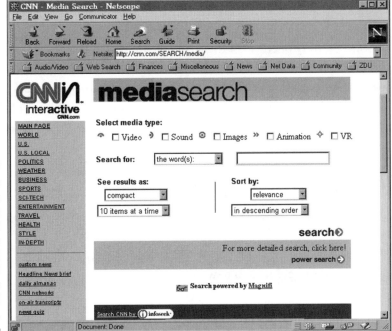

Figure 16-6:
The <u>Media
Search</u> link
of CNN
Search lets
you find
video and
audio clips
produced
by CNN.

MSNBC

Microsoft and NBC got together one afternoon to build a fort and ended up
with a hybrid TV-Internet channel called MSNBC. It's a domineering site,
intensely graphical (warn your modem), and not many people know how to
search it by keyword. I'm here to tell you. Point your browser to the
following address:

```
www.msnbc.com/find.asp
```

MSNBC is one of the most demanding sites on the Web. By *demanding,* I
mean it demands a lot of your modem by squeezing tons of graphics
through it. It is s-l-o-w. Furthermore, MSNBC wants you to download a
special plug-in that makes navigating the site easier (if you use Netscape
Navigator). It tries to push this plug-in down your pipes no matter what page
you enter the site on, even the search page. You don't need to take it!
Everything, except a few special features, works fine without the plug-in.
The plug-in requires a download, then shutting down your browser, then
installing the plug-in manually, then restarting your browser, then performing a *second* download, and then finally enjoying the benefits of your labors.
Is this obnoxious process worth it? Only if you have a fast connection to the

Internet — at least a 56K modem, preferably ISDN or cable access. If you have a slower connection and decide to resist the plug-in, you will be hounded about it every time you revisit MSNBC. I know people who avoid MSNBC entirely because of this issue. If you do get the plug-in, the added navigation menus are very helpful.

The keyword search engine at MSNBC is operated by Infoseek (whose brand you see on each page), but it searches only among MSNBC articles and features.

Searching Newspapers

A few major online newspaper editions provide excellent search tools that prowl through the papers' archives. It used to be that you'd have to make a trip to the local library's microfiche stacks to conduct such an archival search. The following paragraphs point you to what, in my opinion, are the best and most useful such newspaper sites.

Searching the *Christian Science Monitor*

The *Christian Science Monitor* (CSM) has maintained a decades-long reputation for journalistic excellence and fine international news coverage. The *Monitor* jumped into the Internet early and has had time to evolve a top-flight Web site that's worth browsing through, even aside from its archival searching feature. Figure 16-7 shows the CSM's home page, located at the following address:

```
www.csmonitor.com
```

Scroll down to the bottom of the home page and click the <u>Archive</u> link to find the search page. You have a choice between text searching and graphics searching; text goes back to 1980, and graphics goes back only to 1997. If you want to search deeply in time, or if you have a slow modem, or if you're in a hurry, choose text. The following address takes you directly to text searching:

```
www.csmonitor.com/archive/archiveavascii.html
```

As you can see in Figure 16-8, you have two choices when text searching. In the first option, you manipulate the date fields to select an edition of the newspaper, and the search results include every article in that day's paper. The second option invites you to enter keywords, and matches articles from all papers since 1980 that match your words.

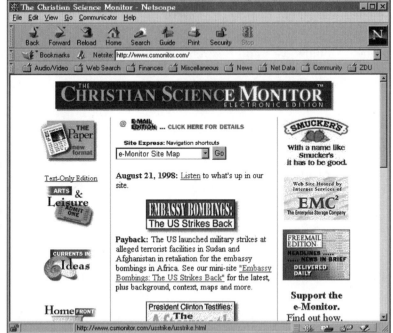

Figure 16-7:
The
*Christian
Science
Monitor.*
Scroll way
down the
page for the
Archive
link.

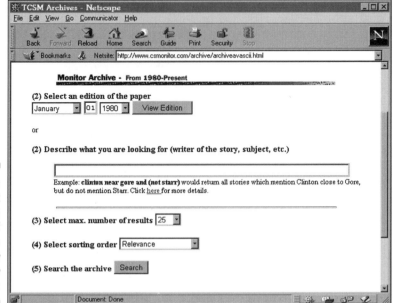

Figure 16-8:
The text
search
engine of
the
*Christian
Science
Monitor.*

Searching USA Today

It makes sense that a newspaper with so much information — so much pure data — would have a good search engine on the Internet. *USA Today* comes through with flying colors, which you'd be able to see if Figure 16-9 weren't in black-and-white. Finding *USA Today*'s search engine from the newspaper's home page is tricky, so go directly to this address:

```
search.usatoday.com
```

USA Today divides its main newspaper sections — News, Sports, Money, Life, and Weather — into separate databases and lets you search them individually. It also provides other topical databases such as Movies, Music, and Travel. Fortunately, you may select more than one database to search with any keyword string. The engine accepts and understands all standard search operators. (See Chapter 3.)

The search results page includes only headlines, without any helpful descriptions or summaries. You must click to the full story to read more.

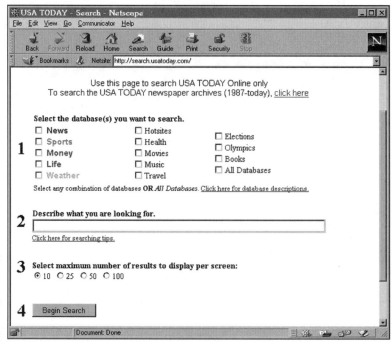

Figure 16-9:
The search
engine of
USA Today.

Searching the New York Times

The *New York Times* has recently redesigned its Web site, dumping the sluggish, unattractive layout that dragged down every visitor's Web session. The site is now a treat. Along with its facelift, apparently, came some daring pretensions. Namely, that viewers like you and me are willing to pay for the privilege of searching the paper's archives. I am not including this site by way of recommending the subscription to the archive service, but I would be remiss not to point it out. Here's the address for the archive search engine:

```
archives.nytimes.com/archives
```

During a recent visit, I noticed a free trial offer, in which you can perform a certain number of searches, constrained to the last 36 days of the newspaper. It's a decent way to try out the service, though the time limit seems parsimonious.

In the meantime, if you decide against the expensive archive service, you can search the current *New York Times* Web content free of charge. Go to the home page at this address:

```
www.nytimes.com
```

Scroll down to the Search the Site keyword entry box. Nothing's fancy about it; just type in a keyword or two and click the Search button.

Flipping through News Sites

News comprises such a significant part of the information superhighway that making suggestions about newsworthy Web sites presents a predicament. It's like recommending certain gas stations to someone who's embarking on a 3,000-mile car trip. Some have clean rest rooms; others offer great prices; and still others boast excellent convenience stores. You can fuel yourself with current events in many ways during your Web travels. You get a mixed selection of news sites, as well as directory pages that link to many other current events Web stops. Be sure to check Chapter 19 for a selection of great Web newspapers and magazines.

News on the Net

```
www.reporter.org/news
```

News on the Net attempts to combine two worlds: news delivery and news linkage. The entire site appears compactly on a single Web page, which makes navigation quick even if you turn on your graphics. At the top of the page, you see major headlines with an emphasis on technology news. The headlines link to outside Web news sources, not to wire service reports in the News on the Net site. Some of these links take you to C/Net, GNN, PCWeek, and other Web domains that provide great news services you should check out.

A bit lower down, a directory of news sites splits into political news, financial news, international news, computer news, and so on. Each category lists links to online newspapers, magazines, and other electronic news sources. The News on the Net directory offers an excellent resource for building your own news hotlist. Of all the many and varied news sites, I gladly recommend this one as an excellent starting place for beginning and veteran searchers alike.

GNN News

```
reuters.gnn.com
```

You find Reuters NewMedia wire service reports in abundance in several prominent Web locations, including Yahoo! and some of the other main directories. The Reuters news headlines and stories are especially well-implemented in the GNN site, which, among other features, lists the time of posting next to each headline. The site archives stories for about a week, and you can look back to headlines of previous days. A lack of breadth may be this site's only fault. The site presents only four sections: Top News, International, Politics, and Entertainment. A popular Web location, GNN News gets slowed by traffic, causing pages to load only partially. This problem, of course, is common all over the Net.

The Omnivore

```
way.net/omnivore
```

Speed. That's what the Omnivore is all about. Speed and global reach. From its graphics-stripped, fast-text interface to its emphasis on headline news sources to its QuickNews trademark, the Omnivore aims to point you in the right direction and get you on your way in a hurry. Not that it carries any news services of its own. Instead, it links you to an impressive array of international sites, such as the *New York Times,* the Africa News Service, China News Digest, Global News Service, and Associated Press (AP) wire reports from the *Boston Globe,* Radio Free Europe, and others. The list isn't long, but it sure is well-chosen.

The Virtual Daily News

```
www.infi.net/~opfer/daily.htm
```

Blending an easy-on-the-eyes, attractive home page with tons of links to news sources around the Web, the Virtual Daily News provides an alluring home base from which to discover online news publications. Set up in typical Web-directory style, with top-level categories leading to a second level of more categories and links, this site goes pretty far toward living up to its motto: "The best free news links . . . comprehensive and convenient." Keyword entry forms for Yahoo!, AltaVista, and Excite add to the convenience, in case you're beset by the irresistible urge to search the Web.

World Wide News Sources on the Internet

```
www.discover.co.uk/NET/NEWS/news.html
```

Wow! The World Wide News Sources on the Internet site slakes any news shark's thirst. When they say *World Wide,* they're not fooling around. Each page of this alphabetically hyperlinked directory struts listings of online news agencies and publications from around the world. Tune in your shortwave radio while surfing to this site for a true global village experience. And a no-nonsense experience as well — hardly a single graphic slows down the quick display of pages here, which generally is a benefit when you search for news.

From the Afghanistan News Service to a newspaper from Zambia, the world is well represented, *except* for the United States. No matter — you can get U.S. news anywhere. Ever wondered what the Bulgarian financial press has to say? This resource links you right to *Pari (Money),* the Bulgarian financial and business news daily. I won't spoil the site by giving away much more, but be sure to check out the news from Latvia while you're there.

NewsLink

www.newslink.org

Another astonishingly good launching pad for news explorations, NewsLink is particularly thorough at linking to newspapers in the United States and abroad. You can browse by state or by country. NewsLink, however, does not slight magazines, radio stations, TV stations, or other online resources. *American Journalism Review* brings you NewsLink, and you can search the site, browse it, subscribe to the print version, and read its articles and columns. NewsLink deserves every one of its many awards.

Chapter 17
Pursuing People

World Wide Web searching is mostly about finding Web pages, information, and files. Cruising around the Web to look for stuff is usually a solitary preoccupation, and you can easily forget that people create the sites. Think of the Web as a giant, planetary movie set — a global array of facades, storefronts, and fake residences erected by people you don't see in the actual movie. But real people lurk behind the Web pages, e-mail addresses, and Usenet postings that make up the World Wide Web experience. And the Web has search tools that you can use to find these people.

This chapter introduces you to sites and techniques that help you locate people. Links to e-mail addresses of people you once knew, still know, or want to know are everywhere — in online white pages, chatting directories, and the Deja News newsgroup search engine, which is where this chapter starts. Read on.

Finding People through Deja News

The Deja News searching service searches Usenet newsgroups (the bulletin boards of the Internet) by keyword. You can use Deja News to find any article (message) posted to any newsgroup bulletin board in the last year. Chapter 11 describes this terrific service in detail. Right now I want to let you in on a few tricks that enable you to search through the Deja News site for the people behind the articles. Naturally, because Deja News looks only in newsgroup postings, you can find someone only if he or she has contributed at least one message to a public newsgroup in the past year.

The first trick involves finding someone by subject. This trick works best when you know for sure that the person you're looking for participates regularly in Usenet discussions on a certain subject.

 Don't use this method when trying to find long-lost college buddies whom you haven't spoken to in 20 years and you have no idea what their current interests or occupations are. Use this method when searching for individuals you *don't* know yet but want to make contact with, such as medical experts. You also can use this method to make new e-mail pen pals if you go about it the right way.

Follow these steps to locate someone on the Web. You may want to log onto the Web and follow along "live" with your Web browser.

1. **Go to the Deja News Power Search page at this address:**

   `www.dejanews.com/home_ps.shtml`

2. **Type one or more keywords in the Search For box.**

   Your keywords should reflect the subject of interest or expertise within which the person you seek participates. In other words, be as detailed as possible in two or three words. The site matches your keywords against the actual texts of newsgroup messages.

3. **Adjust the Search Options.**

   I suggest, on the first run, setting the Results per page option to 50 and the Sort by option to date (as in Figure 17-1). Leave everything else where it is. These settings give you results pages with the largest number of different people from which to choose. If you need explanations for the other Search Options, please refer to Chapter 11.

4. **Click the Find button.**

5. **When the Search Results page appears, click on any article to read it.**

   Use this page to actively search for the people with whom you want to make personal contact. Read the articles until you find someone whose message grabs you.

6. **Click either the <u>Author profile</u> or <u>Email reply</u> link to the right of the page.**

   You have a choice here. The <u>Author profile</u> link displays a list of that person's collected Usenet messages to all newsgroups in the database. You can get to know a person a little better by reading through the list. The <u>Email reply</u> link brings up your browser's e-mail window, where you can write a letter directly to the person's e-mail address.

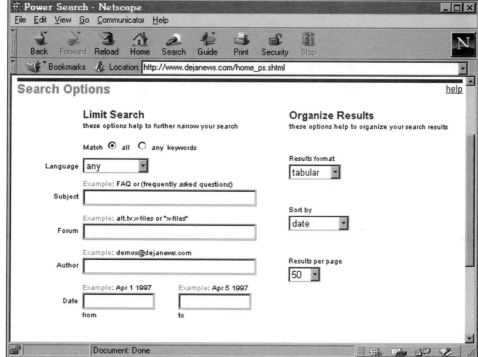

Bookmarks   Location: http://www.dejanews.com/home_ps.shtml

Search Options   help

Limit Search   **Organize Results**
these options help to further narrow your search   these options help to organize your search results

Match ⦿ all ◯ any keywords

Language [any   ▼]   Results format
                                               [tabular ▼]
          Example: FAQ or (frequently asked questions)
Subject   [   ]

          Example: alt.tv.x-files or "x-files"   Sort by
Forum   [   ]   [date   ▼]

          Example: demos@dejanews.com   Results per page
Author   [   ]   [50 ▼]

          Example: Apr 1 1997   Example: Apr 5 1997
Date   [   ] [   ]
          from   to

Document: Done

Figure 17-1:
Preferred
settings
when
searching
for a person
in Deja
News.

Remember that when you send e-mail to a stranger whom you've found through this method, you are a total unknown to this person, even though you've become a little bit acquainted with him or her. Take some time in your letter to introduce yourself and explain how you found the person. Ask whether the person would like to correspond; don't assume it. You need to be more cautious when intruding in a person's e-mail privacy than when posting a message to that person on a bulletin board. If you'd prefer to establish contact through the newsgroup in which you found the person, use the Post Reply link instead of Email reply.

Finding People with Four11

www.four11.com

The oddly named Four11 search service (see Figure 17-2) specializes in finding people on the Web. A well-rounded service, Four11 offers an e-mail address finder, as well as a Web version of a white pages telephone book for the United States. Beginning a search for an e-mail address or a phone number is a simple matter. Follow these steps:

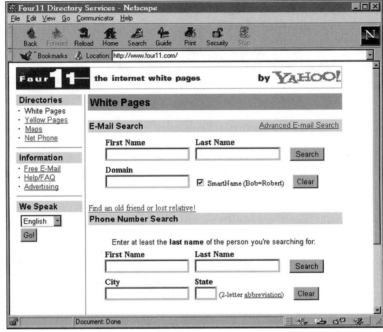

Figure 17-2:
The home
page of
Four11,
showing the
keyword
search
forms.

1. **On the home page, type the first and last names of the person you're searching for.**

   All fields are optional, so you don't have to type both a first and last name, if you don't know them both. Typing only a first name, however, is useless in both e-mail and telephone searches. In the Phone Number Search fields, type the city and state if you know them. The more fields you fill in, the more useful your search results are.

2. **In the E-Mail Search form, type the domain name, if you know it.**

   Domain names are the portion of e-mail addresses after the @ symbol. In most cases, you won't know the domain name, so just leave that field blank.

3. **Click one of the Search buttons.**

   You can search for either an e-mail address or a phone number, but not both at the same time.

As you can see in Figure 17-3, you have quite a few options on the Advanced Search screen for e-mail. The Four11 Internet White Pages Directory boxes ask for the name, city, state or province, and country of the person you're looking for. Easy enough to understand. Two other boxes may require some explanation:

✔ **Current Organization.** In this box, you may enter the company name where the person for whom you're searching works.

✔ **Domain.** The domain is part of the e-mail address you're searching for. You may know, for example, that the person uses Earthlink as an ISP, and that the domain name is *earthlink.net*. In this case, you have simply forgotten the person's user name — the portion of the *username@earthlink.net* address that comes before the "@" symbol.

You see the most intriguing selections to the right of the search input boxes. These options can help you can track down long-lost acquaintances according to the personal information they have entered in their registration forms. The options can be used whether or not you have filled in some or all the forms.

When Four11 searches for someone by using personal information, such as the person's current job or old high school, it can't locate anyone on the Internet who has not registered in the Four11 service. Nobody has to register such personal information to be on the Web or the Internet. Four11, a private service, has a pretty big membership, and it's growing as more people find out about it. If you don't find that old college buddy right away, keep trying every now and then — you never know when that friend from your past will get online and find Four11.

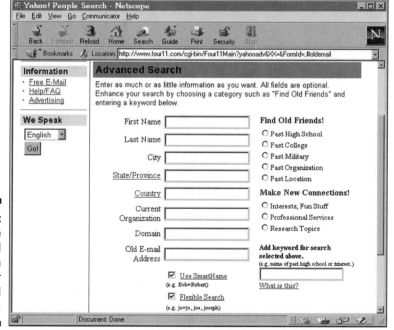

Figure 17-3: The Advanced Search form for e-mail addresses.

Unfortunately, you can search with only one selection at a time. In other words, you can't give a high school name and a college name simultaneously. Try a search based on one of these options by following these steps:

1. **Select one of the Past options by clicking the radio button next to it.**

   You can search for people you went to high school or college with, served in the military with, worked with (Past Organization), lived near (Past Location), and so on.

2. **Type one or more keywords in the Add keyword for search form below the radio buttons.**

   Type the school, military division, company name, or city. Use as many words as needed, such as *University of California at Berkeley.* The search engine understands the phrase as long as you don't add extraneous words.

3. **Click the Search button.**

   You see a new page that shows the search results: a list of hyperlinked names.

4. **When you recognize a name, click it to see that person's entire profile (the information entered during registration).**

You can follow the same process to select the Make New Connections! options. These options enable you to search for people who have listed special interests, affiliations with professional services, and favorite research topics.

You can mix search requirements from the past and present portions of the search forms. For example, type a name in the top, present portion (or fill in all the fields). Then type the high school or college that person attended in the keyword entry box to the right, near the bottom. Click the Search button, and Four11 returns all the members who match both requirements (probably not too many, unless the name is very common).

You can't combine a Find Old Friends! option with a Make New Connections! option. This makes sense because the options define the area that your keyword(s) will search. The search engine wants to search only one topic at a time, and there's no way to force it beyond that limitation.

Bigfoot

`www.bigfoot.com`

Bigfoot (Figure 17-4) has aspirations to be more than just a people finder. The site strives to be a full-service e-mail service site, offering free e-mail accounts to members, a directory of other members, e-mail reminders of important dates, and a few other features. But the main service of the site is helping you find e-mail addresses.

Getting started with Bigfoot is simple. I am concerned with only the people-finding features of Bigfoot. The site also provides a Yellow Pages section and a search engine for finding Web sites. Both of those features can be accessed from the home page, using the tabs above the keyword input box. To get started finding people, leave the People tab selected, as it is by default, and proceed with these steps:

1. **Above the keyword entry field, check whether you are searching the E-mail directory or the White Page directory of phone numbers.**

2. **Type a name into the keyword space.**

   Both first and last names are preferable, because just a last name creates a deluge of results that you may never escape from.

3. **Click the Search tab.**

My favorite way of testing the people-finding search engines is to run a search on myself, because I have many e-mail boxes and phone numbers. It's a brutal test to find them all, and I've never encountered a search engine capable of turning in a perfect score. Bigfoot does a more than decent job with the simple e-mail search — better, in fact, than it does with the Advanced Search tools (which I describe next). It even turns up one of my long-discontinued mailboxes, which is either admirable diligence or behind-the-times sloppiness. Searching the White Pages with just a name for a keyword is asking too much — the results list is huge as Bigfoot scours the entire United States for listings (and displays them alphabetically by state). Nevertheless, Bigfoot found my main phone number.

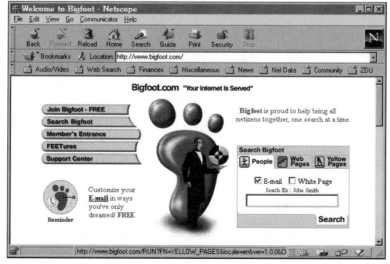

Figure 17-4: Bigfoot, where you can search for e-mail addresses or phone numbers.

Click the <u>Advanced Directory Search</u> on the left-hand portion of the page for a better way to search for people. Nothing is too advanced about the new keyword forms; they let you enter a city and state. That addition makes all the difference. Even just placing a state into the keyword string helps enormously. Oddly, when I enter my own name plus city plus state, Bigfoot finds only a single e-mail box, and it's not mine. Apparently, I don't really exist — at least, not in Bigfoot's advanced directory. The engine does just fine locating my address and phone number, though.

You may search for Web pages through Bigfoot, which turns the site into a general Web searching tool, in a rudimentary sort of way. Bigfoot borrows the LookSmart search engine, and accepts simple keyword strings.

Internet Address Finder

`www.iaf.net`

With almost 7 million listings, Internet Address Finder (IAF) claims to be "the easiest and most comprehensive" white pages service for e-mail addresses on the Web. It certainly is easy. From the home page, just type a last name and a first name and let the search engine do its work. As the name of this service implies, its strength lies in finding Internet e-mail addresses. It doesn't work as well if you want to find an America Online (`aol.com`) or CompuServe (`compuserve.com`) address.

Internet Address Finder found only one of my e-mail addresses in the grueling Brad Hill test. This anemic batting average can be partly attributed to its lack of indexing power over CompuServe and AOL addresses and the fact that it doesn't seem to find Web-based e-mail addresses (such as Hotmail or Yahoo! e-mail).

As with Four11, the site encourages registration by making it free. You can list all your e-mail addresses, as well as personal interests and present work organization.

WhoWhere?

`www.whowhere.com`

Another e-mail location service, WhoWhere? takes free registrations and provides a dead-simple search engine that's impossible to get lost in. The service offers more than just e-mail tracking. You also can look up real world addresses (yes, Virginia, there is a real world), telephone numbers, companies on the Internet, and personal home pages (see Figure 17-5).

Figure 17-5:
The
WhoWhere?
home page,
showing
keyword
entry forms.

Going even further, WhoWhere? attempts to be an all-purpose Internet portal by providing free e-mail accounts.

You can find e-mail addresses from the home page pretty easily by clicking the E-Mail radio button and entering a first and last name in the keyword forms. You may attempt to find a street address by clicking the Phone & Address radio button, but it's a hopeless task without the city and street. To enter that information, you need to click the Advanced link, which takes you to the advanced search keyword forms.

Nothing about the advanced keyword forms is too special, except you can enter a city and a state. Give it a try, remembering to put in a person's name, too. (Try your own if you can't think of anyone else. But don't tell your friends you couldn't think of them.) In my test, WhoWhere? still lists an address I moved from a year and a half previously. In the e-mail search, WhoWhere? found a few of my addresses, including one unusual address on the server of a company I consult to — very impressive. It didn't find my CompuServe or AOL addresses.

One interesting aspect of the street address search results: They contain links to maps of the neighborhood you've just found, plus driving directions. This means you can not only locate old friends through WhoWhere?, you can also drop in on them unexpectedly (which may be why they stopped being your friend in the first place).

ICQ

www.mirabilis.com

ICQ (as in I Seek You — get it?) locates friends who are logged on to the Internet at the same time you are. ICQ requires you to download a program and then register yourself in the system. After you do that, you can receive a notice when any individual from a predetermined list logs on to the Net, and you can also chat with that person in real time.

ICQ is the Internet global chatting program of choice. I also like (prefer, actually) the Yahoo! Pager, which provides the same basic functions in a clearer interface. ICQ has more members, though, so if you're out to meet lots of new people, it could be the better choice. In Yahoo!'s defense, its Pager system has better profiles of its members. You may want to try both, if you like the idea of chatting while surfing the Net. Here's the link to the Yahoo! Pager:

pager.yahoo.com/pager

Chapter 18

Finding Finances

• •

In This Chapter

▶ Using keywords to find financial sites on the Web

▶ Using Deja News to find Usenet financial communities

▶ Covering the financial news with CNNfn

▶ Cruising a directory of finance sites with Economics/Markets/Investments Index

▶ Divulging the definitive source of company information: Hoover's Online

▶ The Motley Fool isn't

▶ Finding commentary and information in the attractive Smart Money site

▶ Gossiping at the Silicon Investor site

▶ Browsing the popular Yahoo! Finance site

▶ Exploring favorite financial sites

• •

*P*ersonal finances show up in cyberspace in a big way. Perhaps your bank has recently sent you a notice offering a modem-based checking account that would enable you to balance your checkbook by accessing the bank's records through your computer. Or maybe you've submitted your tax return through an online service. If you're an investor, you may have considered transferring part of your portfolio to a virtual brokerage and trading stocks through the Web.

As this chapter illustrates, it has never been easier for the financial novice to get a handle on the ropes or for a veteran to expand financial options. The Web brings a great deal of information and a constantly evolving set of tools directly into your home. This chapter provides several starting points.

Financial Keywords

As always with keywords, you first need to formulate short phrases that represent your interest and search goals. But the trick is not to be too broad. Keywords such as *money, finance,* and *banking* deliver gigantic search results, many of them irrelevant. Think how often any of those words could be found in Web pages that don't have anything to do with finances, and you get the picture.

The following basic keyword combinations work well:

- ✔ **Interactive finance:** When you use this string, be sure to put the AND operator between the words (AND is sometimes represented by a + sign) to avoid having nonfinance pages match the word *interactive.* Most services, though, list matches to both words first, so you'd have to scroll through a lot of links before hitting the unwanted matches.

- ✔ **Personal finance:** This keyword string generally delivers large results, but the string offers a more streamlined approach than merely browsing through Yahoo! or Lycos for personal finance sites.

- ✔ **Financial services:** Using this keyword combination tends to pull up a lot of company home pages. Financial service companies in the real world use the Web as an advertising medium. Accessing them provides a way for you to find out about a company and also get an idea of what to look for in other companies.

- ✔ **Stock trading:** Surprisingly, this combination sometimes works better than keyword strings using the word *brokerage.* Be careful about inadvertently getting matches on the word *stockholm,* though. Choose exact matching features, whenever possible, on the word *stock.*

One great way to get new keyword ideas involves a bit of harmless thievery. When you see a word or word combination that catches your eye in a good Web site, use those words in your next search. Chances are good that the engine matches your keywords with other, similarly useful sites. If, for example, a site charts dividend results for various stocks and you'd like to find other pages with that feature, try the keyword string *chart dividends.*

Finances in the Newsgroups

The Usenet newsgroups — the thousands of bulletin boards that make up the community portion of the Internet — offer a great information resource for money and investing. They are especially rich in information about securities trading, with investors from all over the map asking questions about individual issues, sharing experiences and information about companies, and pointing each other to various resources. Even though stock trading is the most competitive area of the financial world, the newsgroups have a feeling of camaraderie and mutual support.

The many newsgroups are divided by topic and Usenet directory. The most popular financial bulletin boards are in the `alt` and `misc` directories. They include the following:

```
misc.invest.funds
misc.invest.stocks
misc.invest.futures
misc.invest.canada
misc.invest.real-estate
alt.invest.penny-stocks
alt.invest.technical-Analysis
```

Deja News searches Usenet. When using Deja News to find financial articles in newsgroups, you get better results if you choose keywords a little differently than the way you choose them in a Web searching service. Remember that you are searching the text content of bulletin board messages. The writing is conversational, informal, and colloquial. You need to think in those terms when you formulate keywords. Keyword strings that work well for Web pages may not turn up many matches when Deja News searches newsgroup messages.

Everyone can participate in Usenet financial newsgroups, but take care to heed the unwritten rules of protocol. Specifically, don't use the groups to promote your own stock agenda, such as talking up your favorite stock in order to attract investors and affect the price. This is called *hyping,* a universally maligned practice. The Internet veterans who populate the newsgroups, especially those in `misc.invest.stocks`, the largest of them, have short fuses when it comes to hyping, and practitioners of Internet stock manipulation usually get flamed to a cinder.

CNNfn

```
www.cnnfn.com/search
```

CNNfn is the financial news station of the CNN news network. The CNNfn Web site supports station programming without imitating it too much — a tricky blend attempted less successfully by the MSNBC and CNBC sites (`www.msnbc.com` and `www.cnbc.com`, respectively). CNNfn presents consistently excellent text-based financial news coverage. Its search engine generously goes beyond the four walls of the CNNfn site or decorously stays within those walls — your choice. As you can see in Figure 18-1, you choose by selecting one radio button or the other.

Figure 18-1:
The CNNfn
search
form.

CNNfn's search engine is provided by Infoseek (see Chapter 9). If you search with the Internet radio button selected, you are basically searching with Infoseek. The search results page is inside the Infoseek site. Because no differences exist between searching the Web (even for financial pages) from within CNNfn and from within Infoseek, what's the point? Good question. Your best bet is to use the other radio button and search for material within CNNfn. The results are gratifying.

The CNNfn site is nothing if not prolific. A search for *russian currency devaluation* recently returned 2,392 articles. Broader searches can be overwhelming — a search on *mutual funds* matched more than 5,000 articles. The database of archived articles is enormous, and the CNNfn search engine can take you on a tour of the whole thing. Note, though, that when search results number more than 500 articles, CNNfn makes available only the 500 most recent matches.

Search results are arranged chronologically — newer articles first. As you can see in Figure 18-2, you get a linked headline and article summary. The headline links to the complete story.

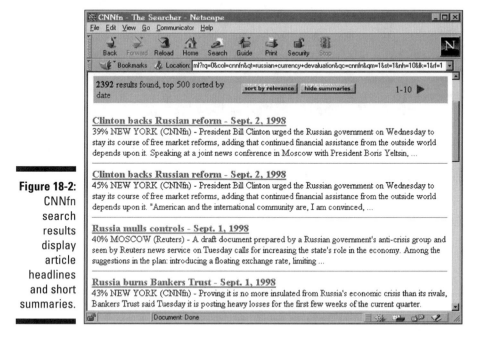

Economics/Markets/Investments Index

```
www.mlinet.com/mle/searchk.htm
```

Economics/Markets/Investments Index: Don't let the daunting site title put you off! This site is a hidden directory of finance sites — hidden, that is, because you can't browse it in the typical fashion with top-level subject headers and underlying levels of subtopics. The directory is there, containing site links and descriptions, but you can access it only with the site's search tools.

The URL (address) takes you to the keyword searching form (see Figure 18-3). This page isn't the only way to search the site, but it's the best way to begin and is the most targeted way to search. Simply type a keyword or three, and click the Perform Search button.

You can modify the search with the three options below the keyword form:

✓ **Results:** Click a radio button to choose the length of the summaries included with each search result. The Long setting displays lengthy and spacious descriptions. Too lengthy. Too spacious. I recommend the Summary setting.

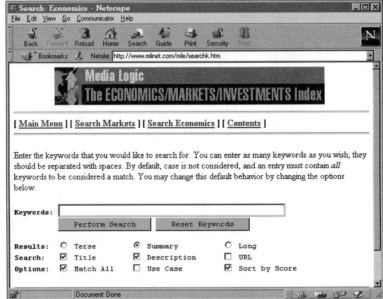

Figure 18-3:
The
Economics/
Markets/
Investments
Index
search
form.

✓ **Search:** This option tells the engine where to search. Selecting Description broadens your search; deselecting Description and selecting either Title or URL has a narrowing effect on your search results. You may choose more than one of the checkboxes; choose all three for the broadest results.

✓ **Options:** Choose the Match All option to force the search engine to match sites that contain *all* your keywords. The Use Case selection recognizes uppercase and lowercase (capital and non-capital letters), and matches accordingly. The Sort by Score option lists search results with the best matches first. Normally, you want to select Match All and Sort by Score.

Above the keyword entry form is a link called <u>Search Markets</u>. Clicking it displays the Markets/Investments page — another way of angling into the database. (See Figure 18-4.) Simply click the checkboxes that represent your searching interest and then click the Perform Search button.

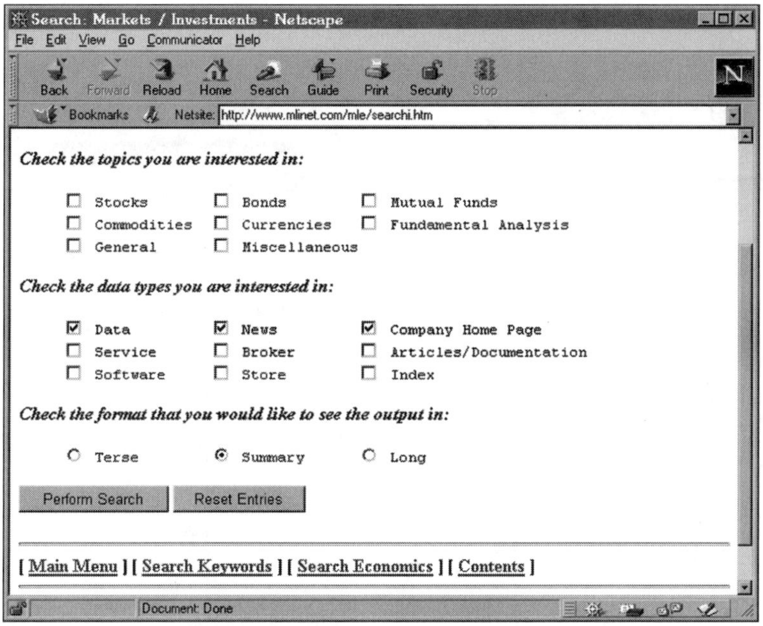

Figure 18-4:
Another
way to
search the
Economics/
Markets/
Investments
Index.

Hoover's Online

www.hoovers.com

Hoover's calls itself "The Ultimate Source For Company Information." The claim is no grander than the company's excellent reputation, and this site gives you access to quite a bit of that information. Searching at Hoover's is free and easy, though a subscription is offered for access to the database of In-Depth Company Profiles. The free profiles are impressive enough for most people doing basic investment research; the In-Depth profiles are almost overwhelming in their detail and comprehensiveness.

Start your exploration of Hoover's on the home page, shown in Figure 18-5. As you can see, it has three keyword entry forms. Use the Company Name field if you know the exact or partial name of a company. (Partial names display a list of possible companies, from which you can link to profiles.) Use the Ticker Symbol form if you know the stock exchange symbol for the company. (You need the exact 3-, 4-, or 5-letter ticker symbol.) Use the Keyword Search form to find companies by concept or product, such as *internet software*.

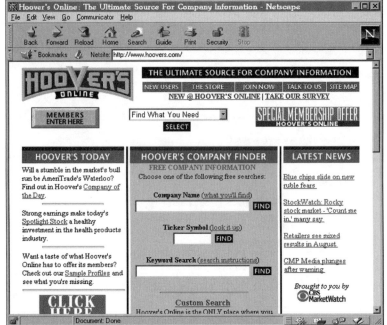

Figure 18-5:
Hoover's
Online is a
definitive
source of
company
information.

The information provided by Hoover's is geared toward investors. A good
deal of it relates to the company's financial statements and stock position. In
addition, miscellaneous bits of data are splashed on the screen, including
number of employees, the company address, and many links to company
Web pages that divulge further information. At the center of it all is a one-
paragraph summary of the company's products, services, market share, and
whatever else gives a quick overview of the firm. Figure 18-6 shows part of a
free company profile on Microsoft.

The free profiles are divided into pages, accessed by the blue tabs right
below the company name (see Figure 18-6). The first page you see in
response to your keyword search is the Company Capsule, from which you
may click to Financials or News. The Company Profile tab leads to the more
detailed information for subscribers only. Figure 18-7 shows what the
Financials section looks like and illustrates the detail of that page. The News
section is organized in an interesting and unusual way. Instead of listing
headlines related to the company, the page links to search results pages on
other sites (SmartMoney, Stockprofiles.com, company press releases, and
other sources) where the relevant headlines are located.

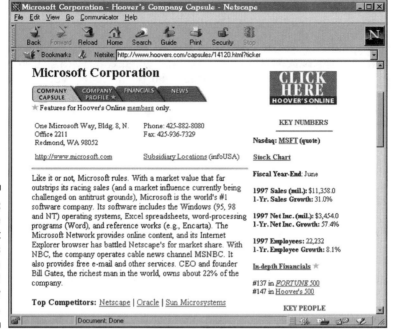

Figure 18-6:
Free
profiles at
Hoover's
provide a
detailed
company
snapshot.

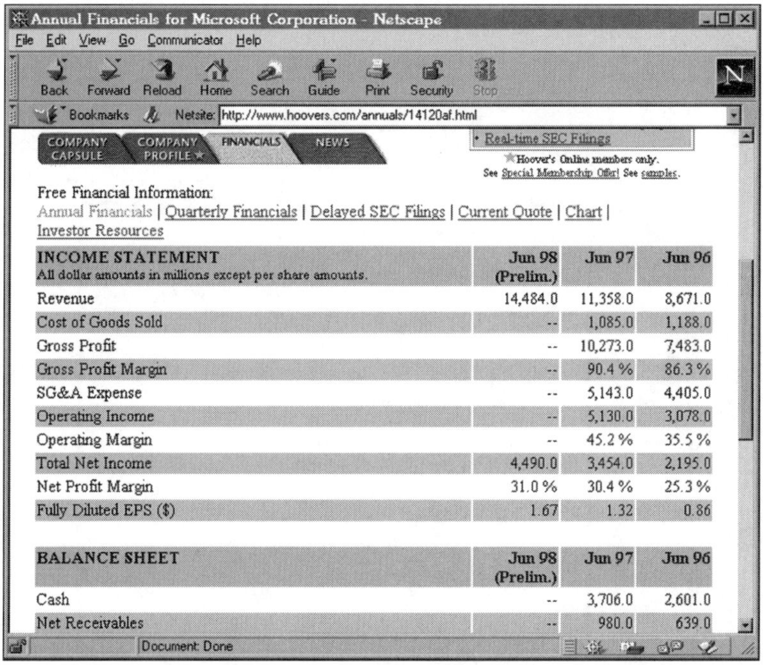

Figure 18-7:
Company
financials
as
displayed in
Hoover's.

Just to tempt you further, let me describe another feature of a Hoover's subscription membership. (Seriously, subscribing makes sense only for professional, semi-pro, or extremely devoted investors.) On the home page, a Custom Search link displays an astonishing page of search features. (You can view the page as a non-member, but when you try to search it asks for a member name and password.) This great resource lets you use drop-down lists and selection boxes to conduct a company search by city, state, or country; by public or private status; or by financial indicators. You can also list the results in various ways. For active, serious investors looking for new opportunities, this is a resource to be reckoned with.

The Motley Fool

www.fool.com/search/search.htm

The Motley Fool has become a media powerhouse and almost qualifies as an entertainment product. The "Fools" began with a modest site on America Online, offering lighthearted investing advice. The advice was serious; the style was capricious. Immense popularity ensued. The Fools moved to the Web, radio, and TV. The Web site is a blend of information and opinion, with some areas available only to paying members. Much is free, though, including a good search engine. (See Figure 18-8.)

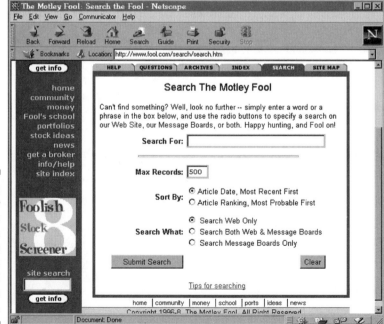

Figure 18-8: The Motley Fool search engine prowls the site's pages and message boards.

The Motley Fool search engine restricts your searches to the Fool site, but still offers some flexibility. You can search Web pages only, or the text of messages posted to the site's community bulletin boards, or both. Just select the radio button that corresponds to your choice. Choose also whether you want the results sorted by date or match ranking.

When searching Motley Fool material, it's best to sort the results by Article Ranking, Most Probable First when using several keywords. The reason is that Motley Fool publishes a huge amount of material on its site, and sorting your results by date is bound to return many articles posted on the current day and the day before that only marginally match your keywords. When searching broadly — for example, using a company name or stock ticker as your keyword — it's fine to sort by date, because you probably want the most recent news. But more detailed searches deserve the most relevant matches, no matter when they were posted.

SmartMoney

`www.smartmoney.com`

SmartMoney is the Web version of a magazine of the same name, and it's chock full of unique information in a beautifully organized site (see Figure 18-9). Not an electronic reprint of the magazine, SmartMoney presents an aggressive editorial mix of information and commentary. As a comprehensive financial news site, SmartMoney provides a nice service by letting us search the dickens out of it.

SmartMoney doesn't make a big deal out of its search engine. The keyword entry field is located on the home page, but it isn't what you'd call obvious. Look at Figure 18-9 — see it down the page on the right? Just a keyword box and some radio buttons. It's easy to use and delivers high-quality information for stock and mutual fund investors.

The keyword entry form works like any other, with one special feature: You may type the ticker symbol for any stock instead of the name of the company. Please note, however, that mutual fund symbols aren't always recognized by the search engine, so it's best to type the name of the fund. The radio buttons initiate the following functions:

✔ **Stock Snapshot:** This radio button requires only a single company or stock symbol to work correctly. In return, it displays a range of financial information about that company and its stock, including a slightly delayed stock quote.

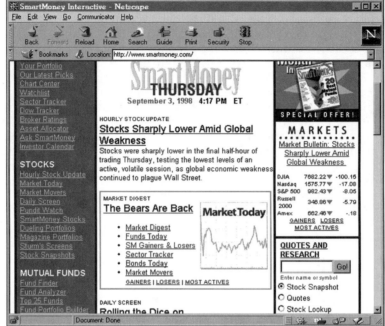

Figure 18-9:
Smart-
Money
buries its
search
engine
amidst the
clutter of its
home page.

✔ **Quotes:** For just a stock quote, without any other financial data, choose this radio button.

✔ **Stock Lookup:** If you don't know the ticker symbol for a company, Stock Lookup can find it for you. You do need to know the name of the company. Don't enter a ticker symbol when this radio button is selected because it will return a blank, quizzical page.

✔ **Fund Snapshot:** The Fund Snapshots are very nice pages of information that give you a basic overview of any mutual fund's financials. Unfortunately, no information about the fund manager is forthcoming, unlike the magazine's emphasis on the personalities behind the funds.

✔ **Fund Lookup:** The most pointless of the radio buttons, Fund Lookup searches for the fund ticker symbol if you know the fund name. But since you can't reliably use fund ticker symbols in this search engine, using this option is a futile exercise — and not particularly fun.

✔ **News Search:** As you might expect, using this radio button lets you search the SmartMoney archives for relevant news stories from various sources of financial news.

✔ **Site Search:** Use this option if you want to search within the SmartMoney site for any topic or company.

Silicon Investor

```
www.techstocks.com/~wsapi/investor/stocktalk
```

Sometimes you tire of slick financial sites, searching for press releases, and all the rest of the information glut surrounding the subject of money on the Net. You just want to find out what other people think about a stock, a fund, or a piece of financial software. At that point, you have a few choices. You can resort to the financial Usenet newsgroups that I list previously in this chapter. You can dive into Web-based messaging communities found on many sites, such as `www.quicken.com` and `www.ragingbull.com`. But the one community you must know about, the single most important watering hole for financial discussion, gossip, and speculation, is Silicon Investor. The site is unique and uniquely valuable.

Silicon Investor is only partially free. You may browse messages to your heart's content, but to post a message you must become a paid member. Try reading for a while and see if the urge to contribute motivates you to pull out the ol' credit card.

Figure 18-10 shows the home page of the Silicon Investor message boards. This page is what you see when you go to the preceding address. The boards are only a portion of a larger investment site, found at the following:

```
www.techstocks.com
```

Don't be fooled by the address or the Silicon Investor title — the message boards deal with all kinds of stocks and securities, not just technology companies. In fact, there is very little that *can't* be found on the vast, thorough message boards, largely because members have the power to create new discussion topics. Many hundreds of such topics exist, covering blue chips, penny stocks, option trading, mutual funds, investing software, and philosophical discussions of economic forces.

Silicon Investor provides extensive searching tools for finding message topics, company information, and individual members. Some of these tools are available only to subscribers, but anyone can search for discussion topics from the beginning. Look again at Figure 18-10 — you can see a keyword entry form. (Disregard the <u>Login</u> link when you visit the page, unless you obtain a membership.) Type a company name or ticker symbol in the form and click the Search button. The results point you to discussion threads related to your keyword. (See Figure 18-11.)

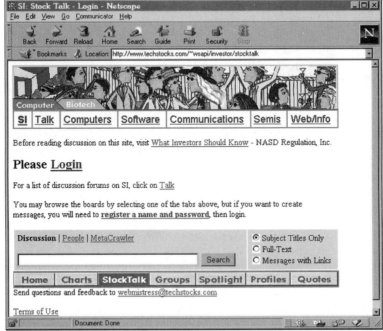

Figure 18-10:
The home
page of the
Silicon
Investor
message
boards.
Members
log on, but
visitors can
browse
messages.

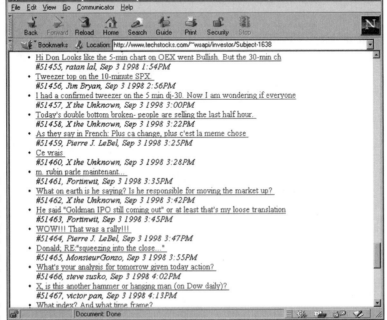

Figure 18-11:
A partial list
of messages
in a popular
Silicon
Investor
discussion
thread.

The <u>People</u> link above the keyword entry form should be ignored by non-members. If you click it, your computer will explode. Wait! Just kidding. If you click it, Silicon Investor takes you down a search path, but thwarts your results at the last minute because you're not a member. Subscribers use the People search to find individuals who have posted messages on certain topics.

The radio buttons next to the keyword entry form are handy. With them, you may select to search in the following ways:

- ✔ **Subject Titles Only:** Silicon Investor searches only the titles that head up entire discussion threads. It does not search through titles of individual messages.

- ✔ **Full-Text:** This option sets Silicon Investor to search the entire textual database of messages. Almost 6 million messages are posted, so this type of searching takes a little longer.

- ✔ **Messages with Links:** Because members can use HTML tags when writing messages, it's possible to include links to outside Web sites in a message or even links to other Silicon Investor messages, the latter being a popular practice. This setting searches only for messages with some kind of hyperlink.

Yahoo! Finance

`quote.yahoo.com`

Perhaps the most widely used financial information site on the Internet, Yahoo! Finance is more for browsing than searching. The keyword entry form, shown in Figure 18-12, is only for getting stock quotes. Yahoo! Finance has no other keyword form for searching the site at large, but it does have an extensive financial directory, as you can see in the figure. Take note that the directory points only to content pages within Yahoo! Finance, and not to outside Web sites. Yahoo! Finance is arrogant enough to think you can find anything you need without leaving the site, and I'm not sure that isn't true.

Keyword searching for stock quotes can deliver more information than you might expect, if you make good use of the drop-down list next to the Get Quotes button. The following choices await you:

- ✔ **Basic:** This choice returns a simple, unadorned stock quote, plus headlines to relevant news stories below the quote.

- ✔ **DayWatch:** This selection results in a slightly more elaborate stock quote, showing pricing indicators for the current or most recent trading day plus the news headlines.

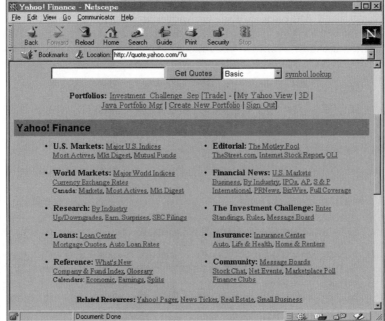

Figure 18-12:
Yahoo!
Finance, one
of the most
popular
financial
sites.

✓ **Fundamentals:** This option shows a basic stock quote with a few bits of company earnings information. Below are the ever-present news headlines.

✓ **Detailed:** The most elaborate stock quote appears when this option is selected, and the steadfast news headlines remain below (see Figure 18-13).

✓ **Chart:** This selection gives you a Detailed stock quote, followed by a chart of the last year's price movements, followed by — what else — the news headlines.

✓ **Research:** The final radio button displays a table with company financial information of interest to investors. Clicking the Detailed Research link on the quote page gives you more financial information than you may want to know.

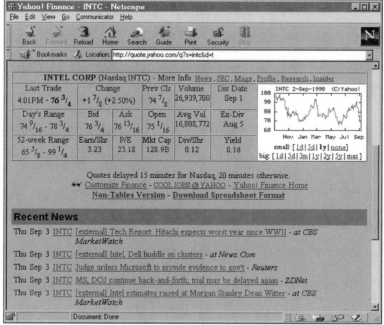

Figure 18-13:
Searching for a stock quote in Yahoo! Finance delivers news headlines as well.

A Few Other Favorite Financial Sites

The Web has so many great sites about money and finances that highlighting examples is almost pointless. Almost. I can't resist, though, showcasing a few particularly excellent ones, which are my personal favorites. With a little dedicated searching, you can build your own list of favorite sites.

Microsoft Investor

```
investor.msn.com/contents.asp
```

Microsoft Investor earns a high grade in my book for attempting to provide a wholly integrated financial service site — and largely succeeding. You get tons of information, company research, an excellent portfolio system for managing your accounts, links to online brokerages, financial commentary, money news, and a dynamite page layout making the whole thing easy to navigate.

The World Wide Web Virtual Library Finance

`www.cob.ohio-state.edu/dept/fin/cern/cernnew.htm`

If you cruise to the World Wide Web Virtual Library Finance site and maximize your Web browser so it fills the entire screen, you find roughly 20 screens worth of links here. The site doesn't organize the links, however, which is kind of fun if you're browsing, but purgatory if you're searching. (But in that case, you should be using a keyword site.) Some of the links do offer paragraph descriptions.

DBC Online

`www.dbc.com`

The DBC Online site has something for both experienced and beginning investors. For the beginner, a financial glossary provides an invaluable education in Wall Street terminology. For the veteran, the site offers Major Market Indexes, an Options Market Summary, and specific exchange roundups. Everyone can use the financial news headlines and a stock quote service — the centerpiece of the site — that gives slightly delayed market prices on stock symbols you type in. You find most of these features under the Quotes & Charts link on the home page.

Investor's Business Daily

`www.investors.com`

The Web edition of *Investor's Business Daily* (IBD) — a well-known daily business newspaper available on most newsstands — is well-designed, informative, and (best of all) free. You need to register to see articles, but registering involves only filling out a form. After you register, a Web design that is heavy on *tables* — the individually scrollable windows that operate simultaneously on a single Web page — makes reading different sections of the publication easy. In addition to the Web version of the newspaper, you can search the IBD database by keyword.

The Wall Street Journal

`interactive.wsj.com`

The interactive edition of the *Wall Street Journal,* the famous financial newspaper, may prove a bit cumbersome in its design, but it contains almost all the articles appearing in the print edition. The site updates articles throughout the day and night. Hyperlinks take you to the home page of any company that the publication mentions. The site may soon begin charging an access subscription rate. For the time being, it's a free ride and a good one — though it would be a faster read if a text-only link enabled you to bypass the intensive graphics.

Part IV
The Part of Tens

The 5th Wave   By Rich Tennant

THE MODERN JAMES BOND

The name is bond.com, JAMES bond.com.

In this part . . .

As anyone who has ever sneaked a peek at a friend's grocery shopping list knows, it's amazing what you can discover from a list. I considered adding my own food shopping list to this part, but I decided that you are probably more interested in reading about Internet searching than about me. Good choice.

Instead, I have collected lists of sites and tips to enhance your searching experience. The sites are unrated, except that they have to be pretty good to make one of these lists.

Leaf through this part when you're in the mood to browse — you're bound to find a hint or a URL that's worth keeping.

Chapter 19

Ten Great Web Newspapers and Magazines

In This Chapter

▶ Exploring online editions of *USA Today* and the *New York Times*

▶ Being dazzled by *HotWired*

▶ Looking at a few great online magazines

A s the World Wide Web has grown more commercial, one of the more interesting developments has been the appearance of newspapers and magazines — online style. A big advantage is that you can't spill your morning coffee on them. A big disadvantage is that you can't tuck them under your arm. Nevertheless, they represent a highlight of the Web and are well worth checking out. Here is a selection of the best of the bunch.

Slate

`www.slate.com`

Slate is a Web-only magazine with highly literary sensibilities and an audience that is split between fierce loyalty and cutting derisiveness. Why derisiveness? Probably because literary values in an *ezine* seem contradictory and pompous. Also, at the beginning of Slate's online publication, it didn't make very good use of the World Wide Web's peculiar graphical possibilities and requirements, attempting a strict translation of print values to the screen. It didn't work. But Slate quickly adapted under the stewardship of its creator and editor, Michael Kinsley, and has evolved into a mature electronic publication. Whatever you ultimately think of it, Slate is a major milestone in the Internet landscape, and you may want to check it out.

Recently, Slate instituted a subscription policy. The site still has plenty of free content, however, including the Today's Papers feature, one of my favorite parts. Check out the table of contents (that, at least, is still free) to get an idea of whether a subscription is in your future.

USA Today

www.usatoday.com

USA Today, the brightly designed, information-rich national daily newspaper, makes a fine transition onto the World Wide Web. Accessing the site with your graphics turned on slows it down a bit but makes for a more pictorial experience similar to the colorful print version. Or if you prefer, do what I do: Zoom through your *USA Today* session with graphics turned off. I have never experienced the slightest delay with this site.

The Web version carries the same content as the print edition (it even includes the sister publication, *Baseball Weekly*) with one important exception — it's updated continuously throughout the day and night. In fact, each page of the site encourages readers to "Click reload often for latest version," and I have had the gratifying experience of checking sports scores late in the evening, clicking Reload just before leaving the site, and seeing updates and new stories appear.

Going to the home page at the address at the beginning of this section is one way to approach the site. But impatient speedsters (like me) may want to heed this hint: Add the index page to your hotlist instead. Here is the address for the index:

www.usatoday.com/leadpage/indexusa.htm

The index is a text list of hyperlinks to the entire contents of the newspaper. From there you can check headlines, the weather, sports scores, and archives of major news topics. Although *USA Today* on the Web is extremely well organized and fastidiously linked within its own complex architecture, it doesn't make the best use of the Web's hyperlinked connectivity. That is to say, you don't find many links to outside sites that relate to the news story you're reading. But no matter. This site is an enormous enterprise, and you can find plenty to read when staying within its boundaries.

Smithsonian Magazine

www.smithsonianmag.si.edu

One of those rare sites that appeals equally to adults and kids (medium-sized kids, anyway), *Smithsonian Magazine* explores the natural world with both sophistication and wonder — and a good dose of fun. Each issue's articles are available on the Web site, and a separate image gallery provides a great browse. There are pleas to subscribe to the print magazine, which may not be a bad idea, and there's also a merchandise kiosk. But avoiding these overt commercials is easy. *Smithsonian Magazine* is beautifully designed (see Figure 19-1) and, like most publication sites these days, offers an e-mail newsletter.

Figure 19-1:
The home page of *Smithsonian Magazine,* which appeals equally to adults and kids.

The New York Times

`www.nytimes.com`

A *New York Times* article about its own online site may carry a headline like this: Venerable Newspaper Makes Dignified Appearance on World Wide Web. The Web edition of the *Times* (as those of us near New York call it) is comprehensive, makes good use of hyperlinks to outside sources, and is considerate of its users' time by remaining graphically lightweight. In fact, for the truly rushed reader, a special low-graphics version is available as a hyperlink from the home page. Furthermore, the online paper is free, and a recent facelift has made it even more attractive than before.

After you register (for free), you can choose from several paths into the site. The address at the beginning of this section takes you to a modified front page, Web style, with hyperlinks to various sections of that day's edition. Another option, which is my personal choice, is to skip right to the index of the day's edition. It is fully functional with graphics turned off, and I find it to be the fastest way to access the entire site. Just add this address to your list of favorites:

`www.nytimes.com/info/contents/contents.html`

Just about everything you expect to see in the print edition is included in the Web site, from the classified ads to the famous *Times* crossword puzzle. Past special reports are archived for later perusal, and the bottom of many stories features links to outside, related Web sites for further background and research. Photos are sometimes included with stories. You can search the site by keyword, take part in a trivia quiz, and use an electronic clipping service. Members can even place a classified ad in the Web edition.

Registration is required at the online edition of the *New York Times,* but it's free. Every time you enter the site, you type in your chosen name and password.

HotWired

`www.hotwired.com`

Regardless of your age, you can join the wired generation by surfing over to *HotWired,* a cutting-edge Web magazine. Owned, designed, and operated by the same organization that produces the print magazine *Wired, HotWired* is a separate publication, with little overlap of content. It has the same techno-hip attitude, though, not to mention similar neon-like design sensibilities.

HotWired must be experienced. It's one of the most advanced and aggressively updated domains on the Web. Free registration entitles you to an occasional e-mail newsletter that informs you of what's new at the site. But try visiting more frequently than that — you'll be surprised at the radical content and design changes. Up-to-the-second HTML design creates such features as a floating remote control (in Netscape Navigator) for cruising through the site's many avenues. You may want to put on sunglasses or turn down your monitor before subjecting your tender retinas to the glare of red-on-yellow text (or whatever the bold colors may be on any given day).

HotWired is worth spending some time in, which is fortunate because you don't have much choice — the server pushes a truckload of graphics into your computer.

U.S. News Online

```
www.usnews.com
```

U.S. News Online is an award-winning, graphically rich, Java-enhanced, beautifully organized Web version of the printed newsweekly. You have a choice between viewing the graphics version at the address at the beginning of this section and the text version at this address:

```
www.usnews.com/usnews/textmenu.htm
```

Both sites are available through links on the main home page, which is the first of the two addresses listed here. The high-graphics pathway trades speed for beauty. It's a dazzling mix of photos and varied fonts, and it takes a while to display, even with a fast modem. I usually choose the text-only path, which doesn't sacrifice any content and is very fast.

I suggest that you register your membership so that you will get e-mail delivery of an occasional *U.S. News* letter that describes what's new at the site. This magazine makes excellent use of hyperlinking to the outside Web and generally provides good coverage of mainstream national news.

San Jose Mercury News

```
www.sjmercury.com
```

One of the first full-scale Web newspaper editions, the *San Jose Mercury News* (or the *Mercury Center,* as it is sometimes referred to) remains a model for other Web publishing enterprises. The project is so extensive that it commands a full directory page of its own in the Yahoo! service.

The site places an emphasis on Silicon Valley news, but the *Mercury News* also covers national and international items. Other good reasons to put the site on your hotlist are its good design and easy navigation. The index feature, with its drop-down lists and Go buttons, is available from every page.

Most of the content is available free, but you need to have a low-priced monthly subscription to get full wire service reports, the comics, some columns, and some other features.

The Christian Science Monitor

`www.csmonitor.com`

Bands of loyal, wired *Monitor* readers were no doubt thrilled when the *Christian Science Monitor* took its highly respected newspaper online. If you're unfamiliar with the *Monitor* brand of journalism, don't be misled by its religious sponsorship. It is a top-flight international news publication that also carries some inspirational material reflecting Christian Science philosophy. The Web version carries forward the *Monitor* ideals of clarity, simplicity, and great writing.

Monitor Radio, a broadcast version of the paper's journalistic resources, is included at the site in RealAudio format. It enables you to hear Monitor Radio programming while browsing the rest of the paper, and even while moving around the rest of the Web. (You need a sound card, speakers, and RealAudio software to hear Monitor Radio.)

The site features a clean design that doesn't take too long to load. Try going through with your browser graphics turned on — the experience is surprisingly undelayed. For my money, the *Christian Science Monitor* site is a perfect blend of attractiveness and efficiency. (The site is free.)

Other features of interest are a bulletin board forum, where you can participate in message-based conversations with other readers about current events; an interactive crossword puzzle; and continuously updated Associated Press headlines.

Utne Online

`www.utne.com`

The *Utne Reader* is as familiar to many as one of the most prominent alternative press magazines. In fact, it's a digest of many alternative press articles found in other magazines, plus some original writing. Because it rounds up and prints the best of hard-to-find articles, many people rely on *Utne* to keep them informed of fringe opinion and nonmainstream viewpoints. *Utne Online* is the Web version — click the <u>Utne Lens</u> link from the home page to see a table of contents. *Utne Online* is alternative journalism at its best — even if the Web is, almost by definition, already alternative. Free registration gets you into Cafe Utne to discuss all kinds of alternative issues with kindred spirits.

The Nando Times

`www2.nando.net`

The *Nando Times,* in consideration of its many readers with varying computer capabilities, offers three levels of access: regular graphics, low graphics, and a Java version that features animation. I have experienced considerable stalling in the regular graphics pathway, probably because the popular Web newspaper handles so much traffic. As a result, I usually cruise through the faster low-graphics route, but take your chances with the pictures turned on — the graphics are worth it.

Divided into typical newspaper sections such as Sports, Politics, Business, InfoTech, Entertainment, and Classifieds, *Nando* is updated aggressively, making it a good site for up-to-the-nanosecond news.

Chapter 20

Ten CompuServe Sites Worth Finding

●●

*T*he CompuServe (CSi) online service has for years stood on its reputation as a *serious* environment for information seekers. CSi has long been the service of choice for business content and database access. CompuServe has developed a range of advanced, sophisticated database search services for a variety of news, business, and health fields, and those services aren't cheap. Many of CompuServe's most valuable information services charge per minute of access, or by the item accessed, or both. In this chapter, I avoid most such services, though I couldn't resist including the Executive News Service. CompuServe has plenty of serious information presented free, and I concentrate on those locations.

Running parallel to the dry databases of information are the extremely interactive, personality-driven CompuServe Forums, deservedly famous as high-quality gathering places for people who share an interest. CompuServe has hundreds of topical Forums, each with an identical structure that includes message boards, conference rooms (chat rooms, basically), and libraries. Each Forum is an incredible resource, staffed by experts in its field, populated by amateurs and professionals, closely supervised and moderated (unlike most community sites on the Internet), and stocked with megabytes of helpful text and multimedia files for downloading (many of which are contributed by Forum members).

CompuServe Forums are free to CompuServe members. Although you have to go through a joining process, it's a one-click procedure that doesn't cost anything and doesn't obtain any personal information.

In this chapter, I recommend a mix of Forums and database sites. If you're not a CompuServe member and would like more information about the service, go to the CompuServe Web site at

```
www.compuserve.com
```

Newsroom

```
Go: NEWS
```

The CompuServe Newsroom (Figure 20-1) is the primary news gathering site of the service, providing wire service reports in various information departments such as National, World, Business, Wall Street, Washington/Politics, Entertainment, Technology, Sports, and Weather. The AP News Summary, updated hourly, is your best bet for a roundup of current headlines. Clicking any of the other departments displays a ton of headlines unorganized by any editorial discretion. Tornadoes could be ripping through Washington, and the National department would still force you to sift through dozens of unrelated articles. There's a certain appeal to this approach, which indiscriminately dumps every wire service report into every folder — it's a relief when a site doesn't tell you what news is important.

The News Clips button moves you to an interesting page where news clips from various countries are available. Double-click any country to view what is essentially a clipping folder of news from that country. The More News Sources button delivers as promised, listing the formidable array of newspaper, wire service, international, and clipping database sources available through CompuServe.

Figure 20-1:
The
CompuServe
Newsroom.

Executive News Service

```
Go: ENS
```

I should disclose right away that Executive News Service is a subscription service in CompuServe. Although I don't feature many paid sites in this book, ENS is such a valuable tool that serious newshounds should be aware of it. Drawing from dozens of wire service sources, ENS organizes the wealth of news in a way that Newsroom (see the preceding section) doesn't. Furthermore, it lets you blaze a trail through the jungle of news by setting up highly specific, keyword-based clipping folders.

It's hard to appreciate the value of ENS until you get into it and set up your own folders. Take note that many Web sites allow you to customize news reports to a certain degree, at no charge. (Many of the search engines described in this book have customizable news services.) Executive News Service is distinguished by the breadth of its sources (many wire services) and the quickness of its operation. You may also arrange to have items in your clipping folder e-mailed to you.

Issues Forum

```
Go: ISSUES
```

For years, the Issues Forum on CompuServe has been a famous virtual watering hole for people who love arguing. These days, during the ascendancy of Usenet newsgroups, where arguing and flaming is a cyber lifestyle, the Issues Forum may seem less remarkable than it was during the pre-Web years.

Personal Finance Center

```
Go: MONEY
```

The Personal Finance Center is much more than just another investment site that serves up stock quotes. A complete financial planning resource, PFC's major departments are Investing, Taxes, News, College, Home, Savings & Borrowing, Retirement, and Forums. (See Figure 20-2.) The Forums button links to all related forums throughout CompuServe, where you can interact with others on message boards and in conference rooms. Each topic area is gratifyingly utilitarian — the Taxes section, for example, includes

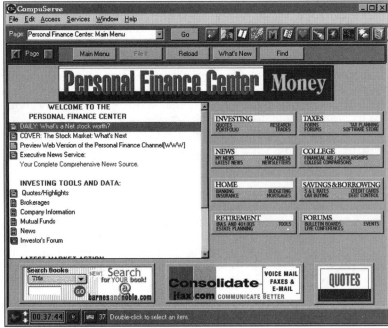

downloadable tax forms in addition to instructions for filling them out. The Investing section bundles a number of tools for viewing a snapshot of current market conditions, assessing stocks, reviewing company information, and screening for investment opportunities.

If I can make any complaint against the basically excellent Personal Finance Center, it's that it moves rather slowly the first time through it. CompuServe pushes graphics into your computer at every step when you first explore the site. Second time through, though, the graphics are pulled up from your hard drive — a much quicker process.

Syndicated Columns

```
Go: COLUMNS
```

CompuServe distributes online versions of several syndicated columns, including Hints from Heloise and Roger Ebert's film reviews. Four topic buttons greet you when you select Go COLUMNS: Opinion & Commentary, Entertainment, Comics, and Home & Family. Past columns are archived in the Opinion Hall Forum (Go: OPHALL) where you can also discuss columns and issues with others.

Roger Ebert's movie review column occupies a special place in CompuServe, perhaps in appreciation of Ebert's long association with the online service. When you double-click his column, a page displays several buttons that dish up his current reviews, past reviews, a link to his Web site, a search engine for all his reviews, and other miscellaneous features.

Clicking the Comics button takes you to the Universal Press Comics Forum (Go: COMICS), where you can view the inked escapades of Doonesbury, Tank McNamara, Bizarro, and several others by accessing comic strips in the Forum library.

Research

Go: RESEARCH

In an online service that emphasizes databases and information, the Research center acts as a hub for all kinds of CompuServe information tools. Figure 20-3 shows the topic buttons on the right and specific databases on the left. Some of those databases are subscription services, though the list doesn't indicate which ones. Take care to read the Agreement statements of these services if you enter them, lest you find your CompuServe account mysteriously billed for services that you didn't know you were paying for.

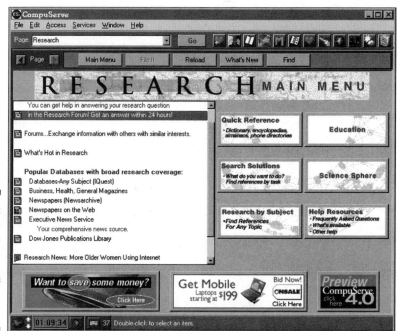

Figure 20-3: CompuServe Research is a starting point for all kinds of information seeking.

The Research site reaches its tentacles into all corners of the CompuServe system to get you what you need. From buying a car to maintaining your computer, from finding a college to finding a person, from looking up a word definition to getting help with science homework — the Research site is a good place for CompuServe members to start.

Fine Art Forum

Go: FINEART

One of the finest features of CompuServe Forums is the file libraries, stuffed with gigabytes of multimedia files for viewing and downloading. The libraries are especially gratifying in the closed CompuServe system, because access times are much improved over the Internet. As a result, viewing graphics files in the Fine Art Forum is a happy experience. All library-stored images may be viewed online or downloaded to your hard drive for local storage.

The Fine Art Forum has more than just stored images — the message boards are an interactive center in which you can get help in using a scanner or mastering photo-finishing software. But the libraries make up the center-piece attraction. From scanned versions of immortal masterpieces to contemporary art displayed in the most recent Winter Park Art Festival, the browsing is rich for art lovers.

Computing Support Directory

Go: SUPPORT

CompuServe began, almost two decades ago, as a handful of Forums providing support to early adopters of personal computers. Throughout its evolution as an online service, computer support has remained a strong point. Not only are the computer Forums populated by unofficial experts in personal computing, but computer companies have taken advantage of the interactive environment by offering customer service through CompuServe. The Computing Support Directory is a nexus for all the computing support services available through CompuServe.

As you can see in Figure 20-4, you can search for the type of support you need in a few ways. An alphabetical database of computer companies is one way. The Quick Search buttons all provide keyword searching by company, product, or concept. The results of your search, in most cases, include Forums devoted to some degree to the company or computing task that you're searching for.

Figure 20-4: The CompuServe Computing Support Directory with its three Search buttons.

Searching the CompuServe Phone Network

Go: PHONES

If you use CompuServe as your Internet service provider, and if you sometimes travel, Go: PHONES is an indispensable resource. The Phones database of CompuServe *nodes* can locate the most local phone number for dial-in access to the service no matter where in the world you happen to be. CompuServe has the finest international network of telephone online access of any online service, making it an ideal Internet solution if you travel. I routinely use my CompuServe account when I'm on a trip, rather than the local Internet service provider I use at home.

You should use Go: PHONES *before* you travel. Otherwise, you are forced to use either your home number, which probably isn't local when you're traveling, or the CompuServe toll-free 800 number, which bills a surcharge to your account — just to get into Go: PHONES and find a better number to use on your trip. A better way is to check Go: PHONES before you hit the road, and travel equipped with every local number you need during the trip.

Health Forums

I want to highlight six health forums that provide excellent support and research features for people dealing with health problems large and small.

The Natural Medicine Forum (Go: NATMED) focuses on alternative healing modalities such as homeopathy, vitamin therapies, holistic diet, and many other off-mainstream approaches to health. The Forum is staffed by medical doctors, who keep the discussions and advice from getting too exotic.

The Health and Fitness Forum (Go: GOODHEALTH) is more mainstream than NATMED, but it still takes a preventive approach to sickness.

The Johns Hopkins Forum (Go: HOPKINS) often devotes forum resources to solving common ailments such as poison ivy. However, as you'd expect from one of the world's leading medical institutions, many more serious conditions are covered as well.

The Weight Management Forum (Go: GOODDIET) offers great support from folks who have succeeded in slimming down and those who are currently in that process. As the Forum name implies, diet is the main topic.

The Chronic Illness Forum (Go: CIFORUM) is a support group (on the message boards) and information resource (in the libraries) for all kinds of chronic conditions. Many participants are family members of sufferers.

The Recovery Forum (Go: RECOVERY) is a supportive "soberspace." Many live chats supplement the support found on the message boards.

Chapter 21

Ten AOL Sites Worth Finding

In This Chapter

▶ Going crazy for entertainment

▶ Managing your money

▶ Spending your money

▶ Exploring cities

▶ Keeping score

America Online is the most widely used Internet service provider in the world, with millions of subscribers logging on to the Web through the AOL system. America Online grew very popular even before the Web was invented.

Although America Online became popular largely on the strength and appeal of its many social aspects, including a vast network of chat rooms, AOL has hundreds of informational sites that are not visible to Web surfers who are not AOL members. This chapter points to a bunch of AOL sites worth finding. They are not the *only* AOL sites worth finding, I hasten to add, but they cover a broad range of important subjects and are a good introduction to the member-only content on America Online.

In each of the following recommendations, I supply the AOL keyword that takes you directly to the site. Press Ctrl+K to display the Keyword entry window, type the AOL keyword, and then press the Enter key. To search all of America Online with keywords of your own, press Ctrl+F to display the Find feature.

Newsstand

Keyword: NEWSSTAND

The AOL Newsstand (Figure 21-1) promotes itself as having more magazines than an airport gift shop, but that claim is ridiculously untrue. The selection is rather small, but I include the Newsstand site in this chapter because of the selection's quality and the coherence with which the online magazines are organized and presented.

Figure 21-1:
AOL's
Newsstand
displays a
coherent
version of
online
magazines
and
newspapers.

Some of the publications featured at Newsstand are more promotional than others. In particular, *Brill's Content,* a new, splashy media watchdog magazine devoted to critiques of how newspapers and television report on current events, offers only a table of contents and a few teasing excerpts in the online version. The *New York Times,* however, presents a full-featured online edition, using the AOL interface to spill out onto the newspaper's Web site.

What's impressive about the AOL version of the *New York Times*, and other publications, is that the contents are organized better than the *Times* does on the Web, so accessing the online edition through AOL can be a better experience than surfing directly to www.nytimes.com.

Other magazines at Newsstand include the *Atlantic Monthly, National Review, Business Week, Entertainment Weekly,* and the *Christian Science Monitor.* In some cases (as with the *Monitor*), the Newsstand simply points you to the publication's Web site.

Entertainment Asylum

Keyword: ASYLUM

Entertainment Asylum is, as the name implies, a site for anyone insane about entertainment. Whether you're nuts about movies, TV, music, celebrities, or games, this AOL watering hole throws more information in your face than you know what to do with. From practical details such as "What's on TV *right now?*" to detail-laden discussions of sci-fi movies, from movie show times to soap operas, Entertainment Asylum covers the bases. Most of the content is in-house and doesn't throw you onto the Web.

One of the best aspects of Entertainment Asylum is the single-window navigation design. If you're an AOL resident, you know how the service tends to open a new window with every mouse click. In this case, the single window remains in the forefront, with a left-hand menu bar for changing the window's features.

Digital Cities

Keyword: [NAME OF CITY]

First, let me explain the bizarre keyword. Digital City has many sites, each devoted to a single metropolis. (At last count, 61 Digital Cities were on AOL.) The keyword for each Digital City is simply the city name.

To see a list of all the Digital Cities, follow these steps:

1. **In the Channels window, click the Find icon.**

   The AOL Find window appears.

2. **In the keyword entry form, type** digital city.

3. **Click the Find button.**

   The list of Digital Cities appears in the results window to the right.

4. **Click the More button until all the results are listed.**

5. **Double-click any city to open its Digital City window.**

Each Digital City is like a virtual magazine of feature articles, sports information about local teams, dining tips, event schedules, nightlife guides, weather forecasts, regional news, classified ads, and cultural hotspots. (Figure 21-2 shows the New York Digital City.) Click the <u>Search</u> link to leap to a related Web site that uses keywords to find restaurants, movies, and events.

Figure 21-2: Digital Cities are well-rounded guides to the attractions and daily life of major cities.

AOL Personal Finance

Keyword: PERSONAL FINANCE

AOL Personal Finance (Figure 21-3) is a complete online resource for almost anyone, from the beginning investor to the veteran stock trader. Tutorials rub elbows with advanced stock tracking tools. In addition to current index prices (Dow Jones Industrial Average, S&P 500, and Nasdaq), ten departments cover business news, the markets, advice, planning, real estate, discussion forums, investment lessons, and a search engine. Four main financial centers explore mutual funds, banking, insurance, and brokerage.

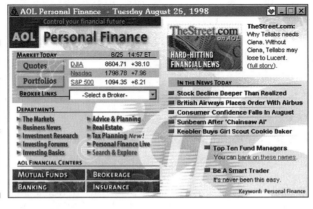

Figure 21-3: AOL Personal Finance stuffs a wealth of content into a small window.

Click the Search icon for a keyword entry form that scours the Personal Finance site. It's a good site, enabling you to determine the time range for the search (material added to the site in the past day, week, or month) and how closely the results must match your keywords.

The site presents TheStreet.com, also found on the Web, which presents sometimes controversial viewpoints and advice about the market and investments. It's a subscription service (both the AOL and Web versions), but a 30-day trial is available at the AOL Personal Finance site.

AOL Scoreboard

Keyword: SCOREBOARD

AOL Scoreboard is a quick way for AOL members to check major sports scores. Don't look for esoteric sports here — NCAA college results are posted and the four marquee team sports (baseball, basketball, football, and hockey), but if you're looking for Frisbee tournament results or national shuffleboard standings, you'll be disappointed.

The scoreboard display is inelegant (that's putting it generously) but efficient. As you can see in Figure 21-4, upcoming evening games are posted during the day. During this time, you may click the I Game Info icon to get player matchups, rosters, and other anticipatory details. Detailed play-by-play information is available during the game, and you can put that information on your desktop, so it's visible as you move to other AOL sites.

Click the Main button to display the AOL Sports site, of which Scoreboards is a part. The main site includes feature articles and more editorial content.

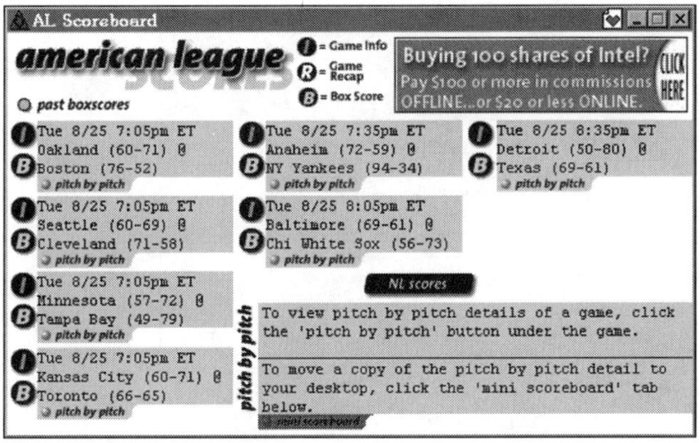

Figure 21-4: The AOL Scoreboard displays upcoming games.

Better Health

Keyword: BETTER HEALTH

A helpfully interactive site, Better Health relies heavily on chats, message boards, and question-and-answer features to convey information. All this is great when you have a specific health question. For more general research, look to the selection menu to the right of the site's main page. Click any information topic, from headaches to sleep disorders, from AIDS to mental health, for an impressive database of related information, presented in a way that may keep you productively learning for hours. Again, the chatting and messaging services are central to each topical database, in addition to an Ask the Expert interactive feature. Each database has a keyword search engine and links to articles, books, and Web sites.

U.S. & World News

Keyword: USWORLD

AOL has plenty of news sites, including the main Today's News feature (keyword: NEWS). I like U.S & World News (see Figure 21-5) for its streamlined, sleek operation and no-nonsense wire news reports. Five main news categories — U.S. & World, Politics, Business, Sports, and Life — are presented with a minimum of graphics. Most of the stories are from wire services such as Reuters and Associated Press, with occasional links to the *New York Times* or ABCNews.com, both of which are on AOL. The Local and Weather sections link to content in Digital Cities (see the Digital Cities listing in this chapter). Best of all, there's a keyword search engine that accepts the AND, OR, and NOT search operators (see Chapters 3 and 4).

Figure 21-5:
U.S. & World News provides searchable wire service reports.

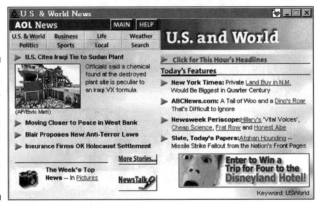

AOL Shopping

Keyword: SHOPPING

AOL Shopping (see Figure 21-6) is a directory of the online merchants who conduct business through America Online. Shopping is obviously taken seriously on AOL; this is one of the most well-developed sites in the service. You can view all the stores alphabetically, but the better way to window shop is by category. All the categories are listed on the left, and they remain there as you browse.

Figure 21-6: AOL Shopping gathers dozens of online merchants into one directory location.

AOL Shopping sometimes throws you onto the Web site of a store listed in the directory. When that happens, it means the store doesn't have an AOL-specific storefront. It doesn't really matter whether you shop inside or outside the AOL fence. You could surf directly to such Web-based merchants without using this site. The valuable aspect of AOL Shopping is that it gathers many online stores into a single directory.

Subscribe to a Free Newsletter

Keyword: NEWSLETTER

I think receiving newsletters is one of the great uses for e-mail — especially when the newsletters are free, as is the case with the almost seventy AOL-sponsored publications. Mutual funds, parenting, entertainment, Christianity, books, cruises, and medicine are a few of the topics represented in these electronic periodicals. Some titles, such as *Insomniac's Asylum,* defy categorization. Finding and subscribing to a newsletter is easy through this site, which automatically determines your AOL address and registers it to receive the newsletter.

The site assumes you want newsletters delivered to whatever AOL address you're currently using. You can subscribe under a non-AOL address or a different AOL address, but doing so requires an additional step. The first thing you receive with each subscription is an information e-mail with instructions for subscribing and unsubscribing. If you're happy receiving the newsletter on that account, do nothing (but save the e-mail against the day you want to unsubscribe). If you'd like to add another e-mail address to the subscription list, follow the subscription instructions.

Club Sinatra

Keyword: SINATRA

Club Sinatra is a memory lane type of site, with more information about Ol' Blue Eyes than any one person can be expected to retain. Divided into the Man, the Music, and the Movies, the site is packed with pictures, celebrity reminiscences, memorials, timelines, discographies, and quite a bit more. The Music section includes album covers, song tracks, and production notes. Chat and messaging forums are provided for those who want to share the memories.

Chapter 22

Ten Internet Portals

*Y*ou may have heard the word tossed around, or this may be new buzzword territory. *Portal* is the name for a site that aspires to be all things to all people. Portals are Web sites with familiar names, especially to readers of this book, because many of them started as simple search engines (the sites, not the readers). Most portal sites contain a similar set of features. A portal has no required features but the following are common attractions that many portals have in common:

✔ **Free e-mail:** Web-based e-mail, stored on a portal's site, can be accessed from any Internet connection in the world, so it's sometimes more convenient than the e-mail account that comes with your Internet service provider.

✔ **Internet search tools:** As mentioned, search engines are prime portals because finding one's way around the Internet is a universal need.

✔ **Community:** Community features include message boards, instant message pagers, and chat rooms, plus some new networking tools that I describe later in the Yahoo! and Excite sections. Whether or not chatting online with strangers seems appealing, Internet community is generally thought to be a desirable feature, and most portals include it somehow.

✔ **News:** Each portal site wants to be your first stop on the Internet, and being your morning newspaper is one way they try to attract you. Headlines abound on portal sites, along with other newsy features such as columns and feature articles.

✔ **Customization:** Portals recognize that they stand a better chance of being your Internet home base if you can create exactly the portal you want. It's sort of like decorating an apartment. Many portals can morph into whatever shape you want by customizing the features that appear when you visit the site. All customization plans require free registration, and the site usually plants a *cookie* (a small packet of identification data) on your hard drive. The cookie notifies the site that it's you whenever you visit, and the portal reconfigures to match your selections.

✔ **Stock market information:** Because the United States is in the midst (as of this writing) of a prolonged stock market boom, and because most major portal sites are American companies, pushing stock market quotes onto the page is a common feature. Market data is part of the news-centric sensibility of most portals.

✔ **Shopping:** Increasingly, portals resemble online shopping malls, and this trend will probably increase. Links to prominent online merchants jockey for position on many portal home pages.

✔ **Regional features:** Classified ads, weather forecasts, and searchable yellow pages fall into this category.

My purpose in this chapter is not to rate a top-ten list, because choosing a portal depends more on personal needs than on portal features. Some portals are targeted to a special interest or lifestyle. Virtual Jerusalem (www.virtualjerusalem.com), for example, may be a more useful, friendly, and familiar portal for an Israeli citizen living in another country for awhile than any of the big, general-purpose search engine portals.

This chapter is more comparative than evaluative. Although I praise good features and criticize bad ones (from my lofty perch as Internet critic at large), the purpose here is to describe a range of features found in the major portals, so you have a basis of comparison when visiting them and know in a general way what to expect.

Not every search engine is an Internet portal, and not every portal is a search engine. HotBot is one major search engine that has not compulsively added features in an attempt to be an all-purpose site. HotBot is for searching only. By the same token, some legitimate portals don't feature search engines as a central attraction, and I include a few of those in this chapter.

Yahoo!

www.yahoo.com

Yahoo! is one of the most recognized Web portals, one of the most visited Web sites of them all, and arguably the most valuable Web site ever built. As a portal, Yahoo! gains points for its consistently fast operation, tremendous breadth and depth of features, and its comprehensive, searchable index of Web sites. (I describe the Yahoo! directory in Chapter 2, and explain how to search Yahoo! with keywords in Chapter 5.)

Does Yahoo! have any downside as a portal? Well, the constant gray background and general lack of graphics makes it a bit depressing visually. (The lack of graphics also contributes to its fast and reliable performance, however.) But if you like your information speedy and lean, Yahoo! has a tremendous grip on the complex universe of information and daily social life played out on the Net. Some of Yahoo!'s strongest features follow:

- ✔ **Community:** Starting with the Classified ad section and including the incredible network of Yahoo! chat rooms, the site knows how to set up online communities. The Yahoo! Pager deserves special praise as a fine example of Internet instant messaging — far better, in my opinion, than the more popular ICQ system. On the downside, the new Yahoo! Clubs feature, providing self-contained mini-communities for families, coworkers, or groups of friends, is much inferior to the new Excite Communities.

- ✔ **E-mail:** Web-based e-mail always has the same basic advantages (easily accessible from any Internet connection) and disadvantages (slower and more cumbersome than standard Internet e-mail), but Yahoo!'s clean interface maximizes the plusses and minimizes the minuses.

- ✔ **Calendar:** An online day planner, the Yahoo! Calendar e-mails your appointments to you and is highly configurable. A nifty feature.

- ✔ **Live Net events:** This daily listing can get you involved in the real-time life of the online experience in a flash. You may not be aware how much interactive socializing occurs every day on the Net, and how many interesting celebs and semi-celebs go online to gab and meet people. Yahoo!'s Live Net events section (the link is at the bottom of the home page) fills you in.

- ✔ **Personalization:** Yahoo!, like any self-respecting portal, allows you to create your own version of the home page, and it's a less painful process than you find in some other portals. The results continue the Yahoo! style of sparse graphics and fast displays.

Excite

```
www.excite.com
```

Consistently one of the most relied-upon portals, Excite furnishes an Internet directory and search engine, which I describe in Chapters 2 and 7. Beyond the Web navigation tools, Excite's portal features are strong on customization, innovative community features, and regional information.

Perhaps the most exciting news to come out of Excite is the Excite Communities, a new community feature. Excite Communities are like free home pages, but with many added networking features and with all the design work taken out of your hands. When you open an Excite Community (it's free), you get a miniature Web site including a home page, message boards, chat rooms, an interactive calendar, space for posting pictures, and the capability to paste notes around the pictures. The idea with these things is to invite groups of friends, family members, or coworkers to develop the site together and communicate with each other in semi-privacy. You have control over who is admitted to the Community. Or, you can leave the doors open for anybody who shares a special interest to join.

Excite Communities are in *beta* phase as of this writing, but may be released as a public feature by the time you read this. If you don't see any mention of the new feature on the Excite home page, try this address to get more information:

```
www.excite.com/communities/new/
```

Excite's customization priorities are clear right from the beginning, since all the information categories are labeled My News, My Chat, My Stocks, My Sports Scores, My This, and My That — none of which is exactly true until you undergo the personalization process. Then all those categories will truly be "Yours." Many of the categories are individually changeable at any time, which is helpful.

Excite has partnerships with many online merchants and features their links prominently. It's convenient to see so many shopping and service features, but always remember that you have other choices besides whatever your portal throws in your face.

Lycos

```
www.lycos.com
```

Lycos is usually in the top-ten list of most visited sites, but just barely. Perhaps if it were better organized, people would be more attracted to it. (Although being in the top ten of all Web sites is an amazing accomplishment!) Personalizing Lycos is highly recommended if you're going to use it as an online home base, so you can impose your own organization to supercede the default semi-chaos. Nothing in the personalization features, however, is even slightly innovative.

Lycos excels in the chatting department. Rather than simply open dozens of chat rooms for general use, some effort is made to schedule live events, on-topic discussions, and celebrity interviews. Message boards are implemented, but there's nothing interesting to report about them.

Two feature warrant special mention:

- ✔ **Lycos Games:** A game center for playing online versions of popular board games, including chess.
- ✔ **Free home pages:** Lycos has partnered with two World Wide Web communities that offer free home pages: Tripod and Angelfire. This feature is a strong incentive to build an online home at Lycos.

Infoseek

www.infoseek.com

The ascendancy of Infoseek during the last few years has landed the site in the middle of the top-ten pack almost every month. The Seekster has earned its popularity with one of the lightest portal touches. The home page doesn't bombard you with information overload or obnoxious come-ons. You get a tasteful degree of news-feeding, plus the opportunity to get more.

Infoseek keeps you clicking for portal-type features. That's part of the site's determination to keep a clean interface. Rather than offer Web personalization tools (a rather surprising omission), Infoseek goes the ambitious route by providing a downloadable toolbar for your desktop called Infoseek Desktop. In addition, Infoseek Quickseek plants a permanent keyword search form in your browser. These innovations are refreshingly original, though they require more work to implement.

A few nice features of the Infoseek portal follow:

- ✔ **Reference:** Click the <u>Reference</u> link for keyword search forms of the Webster Dictionary and the Webster Thesaurus.
- ✔ **People & Business:** A combination white pages and yellow pages.
- ✔ **Maps:** Using keyword address searching, you can view maps and driving instructions.

AOL.com

```
www.aol.com
```

If you're an America Online subscriber, using AOL.com as your portal may be a no-brainer. The entire America Online service may be considered an Internet portal, for that matter, but the AOL.com Web site is a nexus for the entire AOL experience. For non-AOL subscribers, the site still provides a well-organized mix of features. (See Figure 22-1.) No wonder it is frequently the most-visited Web site, especially among users who log on from home. Some features (such as AOL Netmail) are useful specifically to AOL members.

If AOL.com has a downside, it's the glut of graphics-rich information that bogs down the site. The site resorts to a complex directory structure to fit everything in, and thank goodness it's customizable. In fact, you can personalize each directory section separately — a good idea.

AOL is big on shopping, and if you like having links to online merchants gathered into a single place, this may be the portal for you. AOL.com provides a search engine, but it's not front-and-center as in the portals that started as dedicated search engines. The engine is simply a redesigned version of Excite.

Figure 22-1: AOL.com makes a busy and feature-rich portal for AOL members and non-members alike.

ZDNet

I have appreciated the broad range of services at ZDNet for some time, and recently realized that it had gained a footing as a Net portal when I began receiving some e-mail with *zdnet.com* in the return address. If the emphasis of your online involvement is technology, computers, and the cyber experience, ZDNet makes a great portal (see Figure 22-2).

Ziff-Davis Publishing, the home company of ZDNet, brings its publishing resources to bear in providing one of the newsiest portals imaginable (at least when it comes to computer and technology news). The Web directory is entirely a technology directory. Becoming a member of the portal is free, and offers a seductive mix of features including the aforementioned Web-based e-mail, free software downloads (not shareware — the programs are absolutely free), a month's free tuition at ZDU (an online learning environment), and access to technology-related message boards and chat rooms.

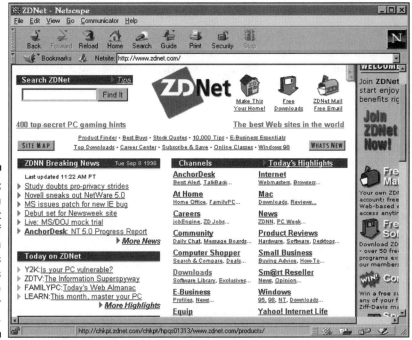

Figure 22-2: ZDNet is an excellent portal if your main interest is computers and the cyber experience.

GeoCities

GeoCities was the first major intentional community on the Internet that built its membership by offering free home pages. The deal is pretty good: You get several megabytes of space on the GeoCities server to build your Internet home, and there is no charge. (GeoCities is permitted to place advertisements and other revenue-generating material on your pages in exchange for the free server space.) Millions of people have responded to this inducement, and GeoCities is a bustling community of families and individuals who call GeoCities their Internet portal.

It really doesn't make sense to use GeoCities as your portal if you don't create a home page there. All the portal-type features relate to GeoCities membership. The site encourages a sense of community by dividing member pages into neighborhoods, streets, and avenues, as if GeoCities were a virtual city. The home page directory is limited exclusively to GeoCities member pages. As such, the place is nice to visit, especially if you enjoy browsing among non-commercial, personal home pages. GeoCities has some great ones, including outstanding hobby and special interest pages.

I'm highlighting GeoCities in this chapter because of its status as founder of the intentional community movement on the Internet, but other, similar community sites serve as portals to their membership. Each offers a slightly different blend of features, though the basic deal is the same across the board.

Hotmail

www.hotmail.com

As long as free, Web-based e-mail is a constant feature among most Internet portals, why not choose a portal that is *essentially* a free e-mail site? That's the reasoning behind Hotmail's new push into portal awareness. Hotmail was one of the first free e-mail services, and its acquisition by Microsoft gives it many more resources to attract visitors.

As of now, a lot of content at the Hotmail site is unrelated to e-mail. Many of the features are Microsoft-created attractions, but you also find a news headline feed and a nice reminder service that shoots notes to your e-mail box. Classified, white pages, and e-mail lookup services round out the features.

Hotmail is a popular e-mail service for people requiring anonymity in their e-mail exchanges. To put it delicately, many sexual liaisons are forged on the Internet using Hotmail accounts. Nothing inherent about the service encourages this, and it has gained this status probably through the simple expedient of being around the longest. Be aware, however, that the `hotmail.com` e-mail address carries a certain racy stigma. This stigma may fade as the service becomes more broadly popular. But for now, if you need a Web-based e-mail account for business purposes, you may want to choose a different provider, such as Yahoo!

Snap!

`www.snap.com`

Snap! is part of C|Net's broad technology site, and competes with ZDNet (which I describe previously in this chapter) as a specialized portal. C|Net's specialties are original reporting of technology news and breadth of coverage of technology issues. Snap's advantages as a portal include fairly fast page operation and a simple, clean interface (see Figure 22-3). Snap! has taken design lessons from Yahoo!, it would appear (not to mention exclamation mark lessons), and the results are pleasing, if unoriginal.

The Internet directory is one of Snap's big selling points. Broadly informed, with a great Oddities category, the directory is enhanced by topical features highlighted as red links next to the main headings. Each of those special links displays a help center in the related topic — as with the rest of Snap!, these centers are nicely designed and quick loading.

Figure 22-3: Snap! mixes clear page design with basic, unoriginal features.

Netscape Netcenter

www.netcenter.com

Netscape is one of the catalyzing companies of the World Wide Web, having invented a browser that almost everyone used a few years ago. Netscape also accelerated the development of HTML, the underlying language code of all Web pages, and in so doing established itself as one of the utterly cool *new media* companies of the early Web. Netscape has stumbled in the face of competition from juggernaut Microsoft, and its newest stab at regained glory takes the form of Netcenter, a portal site (see Figure 22-4).

Netcenter suffers from a needlessly complex registration process (it's free, but it's a labyrinth). After you get in, though, Netcenter delivers all the usual features — free e-mail, a Web directory, news headlines, a keyword search engine, stock quotes, horoscopes, weather, yadda yadda yadda. Basically, it has the same feature set you find in all the mass-audience portals.

Netcenter distinguishes itself in its message boards. Most portals throw up the boards and let members roam around in them at will. Netcenter, however, has created intentional messaging communities with moderators and expert discussion leaders. As a result, Netcenter has some of the most interesting conversations around — quite possibly worth jumping through the registration hoops to access.

Figure 22-4: Netscape Netcenter provides the usual range of portal features, plus great message boards.

Part V
Appendixes

The 5th Wave   By Rich Tennant

KEG BROWSER

"YEAH, I STARTED THE COMPANY RIGHT AFTER I GRADUATED FROM
COLLEGE. HOW'D YOU GUESS?"

In this part . . .

I crammed in some last-minute information, despite the publisher's complaints that the book is getting too big. Appendix A offers a rundown of three Web browsers and related Internet programs. If you don't know whether to use Internet Explorer or Navigator (or a third possibility, Opera, that you may not be aware of), this appendix provides a helpful overview of features. Appendix B describes what's on the enclosed CD.

Appendix A
Choosing a Browser

● ●

A battle has been played out on the Internet between two software companies, each of which wants you to view the Web through its interface. The interface to the Web is called a *Web browser*. The question isn't whether or not you must use a browser (you must), the question is, which one? That question is the battlefield upon which Netscape and Microsoft, the two companies, wage their tug of war.

Netscape arrived on the scene first. Inventing a browser program called Navigator, Netscape helped define what the Web would look like by making its browser capable of displaying certain page layouts that other browsers couldn't handle. Many Web page designers used those special page formatting layouts because they looked so great, forcing most Web surfers to use Navigator to see the Web pages. As a result, at one time, about 90 percent of all Internet surfers viewed the Web with Netscape Navigator.

Microsoft was envious. There's nothing a software company likes better than *market share,* the percentage of a population that uses the company's program. Netscape had what amounted to a monopoly, and Microsoft went to work. Developing its own browser called Internet Explorer (IE, or Explorer, for short), Microsoft began attracting users by providing the browser free. Anyone could download a copy (ironically, using Navigator). The Navigator program cost money at that time (they are now both free). Simultaneously, Microsoft arranged to have Explorer loaded into new computers that also carried Microsoft's Windows operating systems.

This titanic struggle for browser market share continues to this day, with the odds having pretty much evened out. Roughly half the Internet's citizens use one and the other half use the other — and many use both to take advantage of each program's strengths. The purpose of this appendix is to provide a brief guide to the two browsers, and — surprise — to introduce you to a third alternative.

You may have noticed . . .

You may have noticed that all the illustrations in this book show Web sites as displayed by Netscape Navigator. You may deduce from this that I recommend Navigator over the other two browsers discussed in this appendix. Actually, I don't make any such recommendation. Although it's true that I've been using Navigator since its beginning and it's my main browser, I also have downloaded almost every version of Internet Explorer, and currently own the latest incarnations of all three browsers.

I can't say which is the right browser for you, because that choice depends on your needs and tastes. You may end up using more than one or at least trying a browser based on what you find out in these pages.

How to Compare Browsers

All Web browsers (at least, the two main ones and the third alternative I'll introduce later in this appendix) contain similar features. Their functions are essentially the same — to display Web pages. Furthermore, they include additional features for reading and composing e-mail and messages to Usenet newsgroups. (The e-mail and newsgroup functions are combined in the same subprogram in both Navigator and Explorer.)

So if browsers all do pretty much the same thing, how do you compare them? Well, they don't do exactly the same things, as you see in this appendix. Furthermore, the similar features are implemented differently in some cases. The differences are merely stylistic in some cases and more substantial in others. In this section, I indicate some points of comparison to keep in mind.

Speed

Why would one browser, displaying a Web page, load that page onto your screen more quickly or slowly than a different browser displaying the same page? It's a question for the ages — well, it's worth pondering for a few seconds, anyway. The answer is either too technical or simply unknown in most cases. The point is that unpredictable speed differences exist, and you may notice that one browser loads favorite pages faster than another browser (if you have two and compare, that is). For example, one message board site that I visit almost every day loads slowly in Navigator for some reason, so I often go into that site with another browser.

I make some speed observations about the three browsers in this appendix, even though I do not reach a conclusion that one browser is a speed champ over the other two.

Navigation buttons

Web navigation is largely a matter of clicking hyperlinks, but browsers also contribute navigation buttons atop the browser window as shortcuts. These buttons include:

- **Back button** that steps you back to the previously visited Web site and can be used repeatedly to retrace your steps.

- **Reload or Refresh button** that reloads the page you're currently viewing. You might want to reload a page to update swiftly changing information, such as sports scores or to begin again loading a page that has stalled in mid-display.

- **Home button** that returns you to a pre-determined Home Web site.

- **Search button** — relevant to this book — that displays some kind of search engine or directory. Both Netscape and Microsoft have partnership arrangements with search engines to display versions of those engines when you click the Search button.

- **Bookmarks or Favorites button** that lets you access your list of favorite sites. The way in which those lists are created is one of the main comparative features of browsers, as I explain a bit further on.

- **Print button** for — yes — printing a Web page.

- **History button** that is found on the toolbar in some browsers or versions of browsers. Clicking the History button shows you a list of previously visited Web sites that may stretch back several days, depending on your settings. Clicking or double-clicking a site from the History list takes you directly to that site.

Button functions are always replicated in the browser's menus. The buttons just bring certain menu selections to the forefront, where you can easily see and use them.

Creating bookmarks or favorites

Navigator calls them *bookmarks;* Explorer calls them *favorites.* No matter — in both cases they are lists of your favorite sites. You may add to the list as you encounter Web pages you might want to return to. The bookmark (or favorite) does not save the entire Web page; it saves only the URL (address). When you return to that address later, it usually loads whatever changes have been made to the page since you last visited.

If your browser is set up to *cache* visited Web sites in a folder on your hard drive, it may display the page from that stored version rather than from the address of your bookmark (or favorite). In that case, the page won't reflect any changes that may have been made to it since your last visit — you're still viewing the old version as it was stored in your computer. However, the browser regularly checks the address, when you visit it, to see whether changes have been made and updates the cached version accordingly. Furthermore, some Web pages that have constantly updated information force the browser to take the new version.

A good, up-to-date browser allows you to add a bookmark or favorite easily, and to place the address anywhere in your list without a lot of hassle. If you surf often and like to save the locations of pages for future reference, being able to add a bookmark (or a favorite) is an important feature.

Related programs

Modern browsers are part of integrated program suites that include e-mail programs, Usenet newsgroup readers, and sometimes other programs, depending on which browser version you have and what features you downloaded. It's not necessary to use those extra programs. In fact, you can mix and match, using one company's browser and another company's e-mail program. I do such mixing to an almost manic degree, using Microsoft's e-mail program primarily, and Netscape's program for specialized tasks. At the same time, I use Netscape's browser primarily, but resort to Microsoft's browser for certain sites.

Most people don't take such a schizophrenic approach, though, preferring to use a single integrated package. New computer owners especially start using whatever package is supplied with the new computer, and are reluctant to rock the boat by trying bizarre combinations. So it's important that the browser suites work well, each packaged program interacting smoothly and supportively with the others.

Guidance

In the old days of the Web, browsers didn't have any personality or editorial point of view. Some modern browsers, though (depending on company and version), actively help you organize the Internet experience. Pretty nice of them to extend themselves helping you get around, huh? Actually, the browser companies have business arrangements with Web sites in which the browser company gets paid to recommend the Web sites and provide classy-looking links to them. Explorer and Navigator are particularly active in this direction, supplying several *channels* (as if the Internet were TV, which it emphatically is not) of organized Web links. Browser guidance can be a blessing or a distraction, depending on your experience and independence.

Netscape Navigator

www.netscape.com

Navigator is part of a total Internet program suite called Communicator. Communicator includes the following main programs:

- ✔ **Navigator browser**
- ✔ **Messenger** (an e-mail and Usenet newsgroup program)
- ✔ **Composer** (a Web page creation program)
- ✔ **Netcaster** (a channel selection program)

In addition, many plug-ins and utility add-ons come bundled with Communicator. Periodically, you may update your version of the Communicator package by selecting new plug-ins, or other small ancillary programs you'd like to download. The entire shebang, in whole or in part, is free. (Occasionally, Netscape partners with a company to offer a utility with Communicator, and using that utility may cost money. But such an arrangement is rare, and you are always notified about possible expenses.)

As I write this, the newest version of Communicator is 4.5. This appendix explains features from the perspective of the 4.xx series of Communicator programs. Many people still use version 3.xx, and older computers are running version 2.xx. Remember — Communicator is free. If you have the time, hard drive space, and desire to take advantage of the features and designs shown in this appendix, surf over to www.netscape.com and download a new version. (If you use a telephone modem for your Internet access, you may want to accomplish the download during the night while you're sleeping. It's a big 'un.)

The Navigator browser

Navigator seems almost like a stripped-down browser compared to Explorer when you first run it, but it has abundant features that can pump up its appearance and functionality when you dig into it a bit. Navigator has a leaner feel than Explorer, probably due to its longer lineage as a Web browser — in the old days, Navigator was very lean indeed. Figure A-1 illustrates a pumped-up Navigator.

Edit bookmarks   Drag page to bookmarks   Toolbar

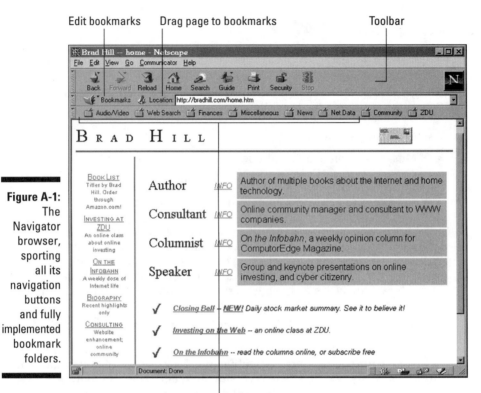

Figure A-1:
The
Navigator
browser,
sporting
all its
navigation
buttons
and fully
implemented
bookmark
folders.

Personal toolbar folders

The Navigator toolbar

Navigator's toolbar, the top panel of the browser window, contains buttons
that help you navigate online. You must be logged on to use all of them
except the Print button. As you can see in Figure A-1, the toolbar contains
the inevitable Back, Forward, and Reload buttons. The Home button takes
you to whatever your Home page is, as defined in the Navigator preferences
(the default Home page is Netscape's site). To change your Home setting,
follow these steps:

1. **Choose Edit.**

2. **Choose Preferences.**

   The Preferences window appears

3. **Select the Navigator category.**

4. **Under Home page, type the URL (address) of the site you'd like to
   display when you click the Home button.**

The Search button takes you to Netscape's Net Search page, which is an
interface to several of the major search engines described in this book (see
Figure A-2).

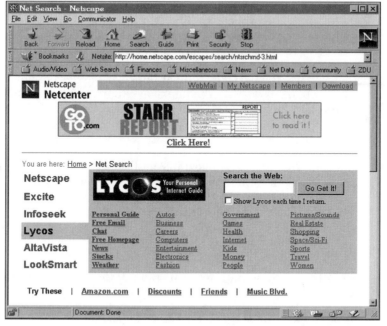

Figure A-2:
The Net
Search
page at
Netscape,
which
appears
when you
click the
Search
button.

The Net Search page is handy, but remember that it doesn't give you access to the more advanced search tools for any of its search engines. Many of the tips and tricks I describe in Part II can be performed only at the main sites of the respective search engines.

The Guide button of the Navigator toolbar takes you to Netscape Netcenter (the company home page), where an Internet directory awaits you. (See Chapter 24 for a description of Netcenter and other portals.)

The Print button prints the currently viewed page in the browser, as long as you have a printer connected to your computer.

The Security button displays a window describing the security features of the currently viewed page. You might use Navigator for years without ever clicking the Security button.

The Stop button halts a current page loading. You may also press the Escape key to stop whatever is going on.

Navigator bookmarks

The Navigator bookmark system is one of its strong points and is a pleasure to use. Version 4.xx of the program implements a new twist to the traditional bookmark list, in the form of personal toolbar folders. You may easily organize your bookmarks into folders, and then force some or all of those folders to appear in a special toolbar (see Figure A-1) for easy access. Having become accustomed to this system, I don't know how I ever lived without it (if you can say that I have a life at all).

Whether you use the personal toolbar bookmark folders or not, you can access your bookmarks with the Bookmarks button. To edit your list, click Bookmarks and then select Edit Bookmarks. The Bookmarks window appears, allowing you to drag bookmarks around with your mouse, create new folders, and delete bookmarks or folders.

It's important that you be comfortable with how a browser lets you create a bookmark. Navigator offers three ways to mark a page on-the-fly:

✔ Click the Bookmarks button and select Add Bookmark. This action throws the page's URL to the bottom of your bookmark list. Later, you can select Edit Bookmarks to organize the links you've collected in this fashion.

✔ Click the Location button (to the right of the Bookmarks button, as you can see in Figure A-1), and drag it to one of your personal bookmark folders, if you are using them. When you drag an address in this fashion, the bookmark folder opens, allowing you to place the new address exactly where you want in that folder's list. This maneuver may take a little practice, but it's handy after you get the hang of it.

✔ Use a combination of the previous two methods. Click the Bookmarks button and select File Bookmark. A menu appears, showing your bookmarks and folders. Use your mouse to move around this menu and drop the new address into a folder or into your unorganized list. You can't see the contents of folders with this method, so it's less precise than the first method, dragging the Netsite URL.

Navigator: The upshot

Netscape Navigator is a venerable browser updated for the modern Web. It has a slim look and feel, especially when compared to the more luxurious Internet Explorer.

Navigator assumes the user has more initiative than Explorer does. It encourages searching rather than browsing. Navigator channels (described in the Netcaster section) must be called up deliberately as a separate program — they are not bundled with the browser. It wouldn't

surprise me if Navigator were the browser of choice among most veteran Internet citizens, and Explorer the choice for newcomers. This is not to say that Navigator is difficult to use. It simply doesn't hold your hand as much as Explorer does.

Bookmarks are one of the program's strong features, although it is not as easy to import bookmarks (or favorites) from another program as it is in Explorer.

Non-browser programs

Netscape Communicator contains a few crucial bundled programs that you may or may not use along with the browser. All of the main subsidiary programs are full-featured pieces of software — far more than mere utilities. They are meant to work in an integrated fashion with Navigator, but you don't have to use them.

Messenger

Netscape Messenger is a combination e-mail and Usenet newsgroup manager. It serves quite well as a stand-along e-mail composer and reader. Or you might want to use it as I do, for newsgroups but not for e-mail. You needn't imitate my whacked-out style; I bring it up only to illustrate how flexible and undemanding Messenger is.

Figure A-3 shows what Messenger looks like as an e-mail program. Rather than use a system of folders, as the Explorer e-mail program does (I describe Explorer and its programs later in this appendix), Messenger uses a drop-down list to reveal your e-mail folders and subscribed Usenet newsgroups. When you drop the list down and select one of your newsgroups, the program retains its same basic appearance, but it is suddenly a newsgroup reader instead of an e-mail reader (see Figure A-4).

Figure A-3:
Netscape
Messenger
is a stand-
alone
e-mail
program.

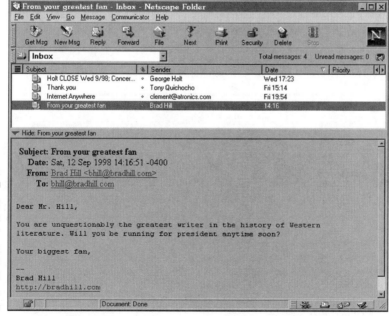

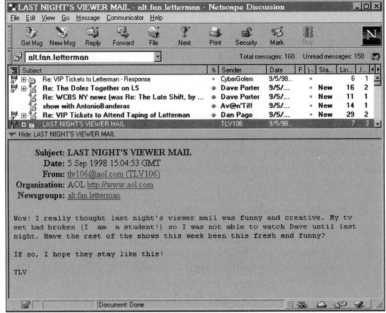

Figure A-4:
Messenger
becomes
a Usenet
newsgroup
program by
using the
drop-down
list to select
subscribed
newsgroups.

Netscape calls newsgroups Discussion Groups, and lets you browse the groups available on your ISP's newsgroup server. Every time you add a newsgroup to your list, it appears on the drop-down list in Messenger. Messenger treats e-mail messages and newsgroup messages equally, which is one of the program's strengths. You can easily copy a newsgroup message into your e-mail Inbox, for example.

The upshot of Netscape Messenger

Messenger is a geek's program compared to Outlook Express, the e-mail program associated with Microsoft Explorer. Not that Messenger requires any special knowledge to operate, beyond the normal learning curve that comes with any new software. But Messenger doesn't hide the details of e-mail transmission to the same degree that Outlook Express does — you see message headers atop e-mails and newsgroup messages. The program has a more industrial look and feel than Microsoft products.

More important than cosmetic differences is whether your e-mail program lets you handle multiple e-mail addresses with ease. That, however, is important only if you have more than one address that you check regularly. Messenger does not shine in that department.

Messenger excels in integrating e-mail with Usenet newsgroup functions. For people who have one main e-mail address and participate in several newsgroups, Messenger makes life very easy.

Composer

Netscape Composer is a Web-authoring program that lets you create Web pages. If you want to put pages up on the Web, you need to check with your ISP to determine whether you have access to server space on your ISP's computer (often, such server space is included with the Internet access account). Consult your ISP's customer service representative for instructions about loading the pages. Netscape Composer can work with your correct setting to upload pages you create in Composer.

Composer is a medium-to-good Web authoring tool. Considering the price (it's free), the program is extraordinary. It lacks some of the power tools needed to create forms and JavaScript elements, but for basic pages it has everything you need. Figure A-5 shows Composer as it looks displaying the page shown in Figure A-1 — each of the outlined areas can be modified in many ways.

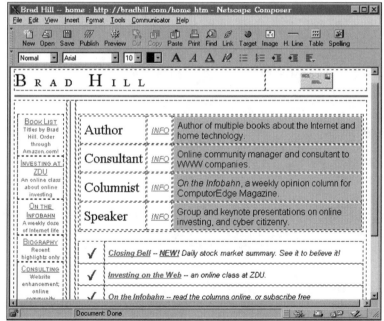

Figure A-5: Netscape Composer creates Web pages.

Netcaster

Netcaster is Netscape's cumbersome attempt to provide surfing channels. Netcaster must be launched as an independent program; it takes forever to load; it intrudes on your screen space; and it gobbles your computer's resources like you wouldn't believe. You can tell I'm a real fan of the feature.

The upshot of Composer

When it comes to the Big Two browsers, Composer is the only game in town. Microsoft has a commercial program called FrontPage that provides powerful tools for Web page creation, but it's not free and doesn't come bundled with Internet Explorer.

Composer is very strong for a basic program. It operates similarly to Microsoft Word, a popular word processor, and makes creating nicely formatted Web pages easy. If you get more ambitious than that, you'll want to graduate to a more powerful and costly software package.

The channels provided by Netcaster include Disney, CBS Sportsline, HomeArts Network, and Money.com. Browsing among the channels involves four Navigator windows popping open on your screen, which is both confusing and stressful. (Confusing to you; stressful to the computer.) Everything you do in Netcaster — even closing the blasted windows — takes a long time.

Microsoft Internet Explorer

`www.microsoft.com/ie`

Internet Explorer is loaded into many new computers as a default browser and is designed to provide a guided Internet experience to the newcomer. With that, the program has all the basic browser features you need to search the Net on your own.

The upshot of Netcaster

Netcaster is a dog. Netcaster should be attempted only if you have a fast, powerful computer and a high-speed connection to the Internet. Even with those power tools, you're in for a baffling and time-consuming experience. Explorer wipes Netscape off the map with its channel experience.

Keep in mind, however, that channels may not be that important to your online venture. I never use channels in Netscape or in Explorer. If you are interested enough in Internet searching to use this book, you may not need your browser to lead you around the Net. Channels do provide some programming not available at regular Web sites, but they are a far cry from television and not what the Internet is best suited for.

Internet Explorer is in the 4.xx series of updates. The descriptions and illustrations in this appendix relate specifically to version 4.71. Upgrades are free, as is the first download of Explorer, and you can obtain a version from the preceding address.

The Explorer browser

Internet Explorer is a smoothly operating browser with a built-in directory of so-called *channels* that provide Web-based programming just for Explorer users. Some toolbar features are designed to suggest links to visit or to give you easy access to channels. Figure A-6 shows what the browser looks like with the channels hidden. (I describe how to reveal the channels a bit later.)

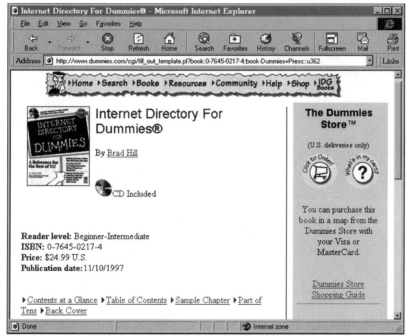

Figure A-6:
Microsoft
Internet
Explorer.

The Explorer toolbar

Besides the usual Back, Forward, and Stop buttons, the Explorer toolbar contains these functions:

✔ The Refresh button reloads the page you're currently viewing.

✔ The Home button has a default setting that takes you to the Microsoft home page. You can change that setting by pulling down the View menu, selecting Internet Options, and typing a new URL.

✔ The Search button works beautifully. Rather than surf you to a new page, it opens up a panel right in the browser. This panel (see Figure A-7) offers an interface for AltaVista, Infoseek, Excite, and Deja News. (See chapters on each of these search engines in Part II.)

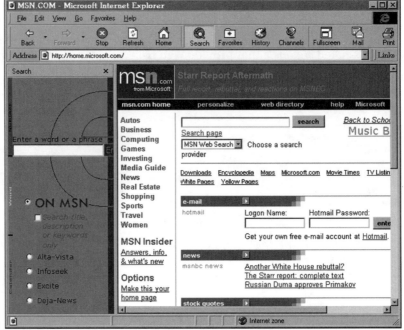

Figure A-7:
The Search panel in Internet Explorer appears when you click the Search button.

✔ The Favorites button is like Navigator's bookmarks feature, but operates quite differently. As with the Search button, clicking Favorites on the toolbar opens a left-hand panel with your favorites listed.

✔ The History button uses that great left-hand panel yet again to display Web sites you've visited recently, in chronological order.

✔ The Channels button makes the most extensive use of the left-hand panel. Figure A-8 shows the channel panel (can you resist saying that out loud?) with the Business topic expanded. Click any channel, and the main browser window surfs to its content.

✔ The Fullscreen button is a nifty and unique feature that expands the browser to its full size, gently removes the left-hand panel (it drifts out of view like a debutante leaving the ball), and eliminates the toolbars. This button is wonderful for Web pages that extend beyond the bounds of a normal browser window and for multimedia sites that require as much screen space as possible.

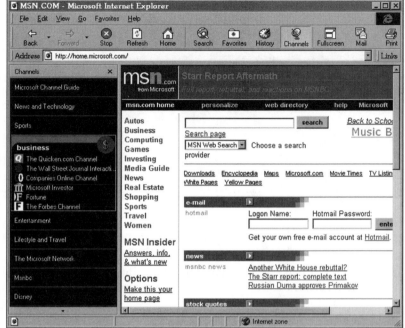

Figure A-8:
The
Explorer
channel
bar is
integrated
into the
main
browser
window.

✔ The Mail button boots Outlook Express, the e-mail program associated with Explorer.

✔ The Print button prints the currently displayed page.

Explorer favorites

In Explorer, favorites make up an organized list of Web addresses. Like Navigator's bookmark list, the favorites list is just a collection of URLs — not the actual pages with their text and graphics. With Explorer, favorites are integrated with Explorer channels; they are all part of the same master list. Fortunately, you can create folders to distinguish your favorites from Microsoft's favorites.

To save a page to your favorites list, do this:

1. **Pull down the F̲avorites menu.**

2. **Choose A̲dd to Favorites.**

   The Add Favorite window appears.

The upshot of Explorer

Explorer has some addictive features. The left-hand viewing panel is a wonderful integration of navigational aids in the main browser window. The Fullscreen button is an excellent idea.

The system of creating and organizing favorites leaves something to be desired and suffers in comparison to Navigator's elegant solutions.

Balancing that drawback, Explorer provides added-value channels in a way that outshines Navigator's awful Netcaster by several megawatts. It all adds up to a browser tailored more for the Internet newcomer who can appreciate the high-quality guidance of a smooth browser.

3. **Select whether or not you want Explorer to notify you of changes to the page, and then click the OK button.**

   Explorer can notify you of changes to the page and even — as a separate choice — download the page for offline viewing. This may be an option worth exploring, but it makes the process of adding a favorite awkward and complex.

Alternatively, you may follow these steps to add a favorite:

1. **Click the Favorites button.**

   Your favorites appear in the left-hand panel.

2. **Click the Explorer icon next to the address of the page you're viewing and hold down the mouse button.**

3. **Drag the icon to the location in your favorites list where you'd like it to reside, and then release the mouse button.**

   This feature is similar to saving a Navigator bookmark, but less precise. The favorite is dumped at the bottom of that folder's list of sites; you can't view the contents of the folder first and decide where to place the favorite.

Non-browser programs

Explorer comes with an e-mail and newsgroup program called Outlook Express. Outlook is an extremely flexible e-mail tool, especially if you have more than one e-mail address.

Figure A-9 shows how Outlook Express appears in one of its configurations. One of the beauties of the program is its capability to reconfigure itself depending on your preferences. The three main windows, and the columns within those windows, are all under your control and can be laid out in different ways. Figure A-10 illustrates an alternative setup.

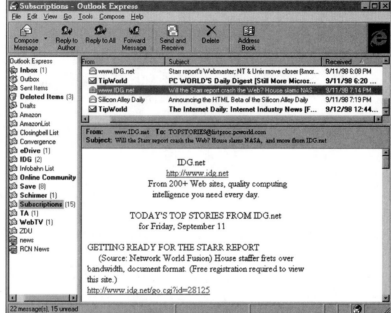

Figure A-9:
Outlook
Express,
the e-mail
program
associated
with
Internet
Explorer.

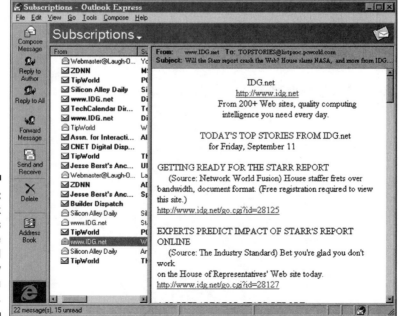

Figure A-10:
Outlook
Express
can be
configured
almost any
way you
please.

The upshot of Outlook Express

Outlook Express is a serious, powerful e-mail program for advanced e-mail users. Don't let that sentence put you off from trying it, however, if you have a single e-mail box that you check once a week. It works perfectly well in simple situations too, and is no more difficult to figure out than any other e-mail program.

Outlook Express hides header information on incoming e-mails, which is cosmetically nice but inconvenient sometimes. If you need to trace the routing of an e-mail, several mouse clicks and a lot of squinting are required.

Speaking of cosmetics, Outlook provides several *stationary* formats that place graphical borders around your outgoing mail. Beware, though, that the pretty borders are visible only by recipients who also use Outlook Express.

The address book in Outlook is the program's weak link. It's very difficult to move an address from a received e-mail into the book, though you can set the program up to automatically place all addresses you respond to in the address book.

Outlook becomes a newsgroup program easily; simply click any subscribed newsgroup in your folder list. The process of subscribing to groups is easy, but not as effortless as in Messenger, the Netscape program. However, dragging messages from one folder to another, or from a newsgroup into a mail folder, couldn't be simpler.

Outlook Express comes to life as a multi-mailbox tool. You can set up an unlimited number of e-mail boxes, each with its own logon name and password, and set up Outlook to check all or some of them automatically at certain intervals. The Inbox Assistant (found in the Tools menu) helps sort incoming mail from different mailboxes into different folders. (Figure A-11 shows the Inbox Assistant configuration window.)

Figure A-11:
The Inbox Assistant in Outlook Express helps sort incoming mail into different folders.

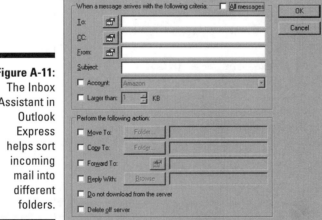

A Third Choice

So much publicity surrounds the competition between Netscape Navigator and Microsoft Internet Explorer that you'd think they are the only two browsers in the world. This section alerts you to a third choice, one that offers distinct advantages. The browser is called Opera and can be downloaded from this site:

```
www.operasoftware.com/download.html
```

I have room in this appendix to only pique your interest in Opera, not to review it comprehensively. The download is free, though Opera is shareware. If you'd like to explore the program on your own, you may use it for 30 days. To keep the program beyond that trial period, you pay the registration fee ($35 as of this writing).

Following are some of the best features of Opera:

- ✔ Perhaps best of all in this era of bloated browser software, Opera is a relatively quick download. After Opera is on your hard drive, it requires much less space than the Big Two browsers. When running the program, it consumes less of your computer's operating resources.

- ✔ Opera uses a program shell that houses multiple browser windows (see Figure A-12). This design is convenient, though it takes up a little more screen space than the competing browsers.

- ✔ Opera loads pages fast! At some sites, such as a complex message board location I frequent, I use only Opera to speed things along.

- ✔ The Hot list (like Navigator bookmarks and Explorer favorites) looks like the Windows File Manager program, making veteran Windows users feel right at home. You can import lists from Navigator and Explorer.

- ✔ A dedicated on-screen button lets you toggle Internet images on and off — a standard feature in early Netscape browsers that I sometimes miss. Turning images off is advisable for people using slower modems, because it speeds up navigation.

- ✔ When you position the cursor on a link, the URL appears next to it. It's a tiny feature, but you'd be surprised how convenient it is.

- ✔ Opera comes with e-mail and newsgroup programs.

It's worth noting one large drawback to Opera, besides the fact that it's not free. Web pages don't always appear as they are supposed to. If you compare the displays in Opera with those in Navigator and Explorer, certain differences are apparent. Colors are translated differently, which is disconcerting if you have designed your own page. Sometimes the layout of page elements is jumbled. Opera definitely needs to get its act together in this regard if it is to compete with the Big Two in any meaningful way.

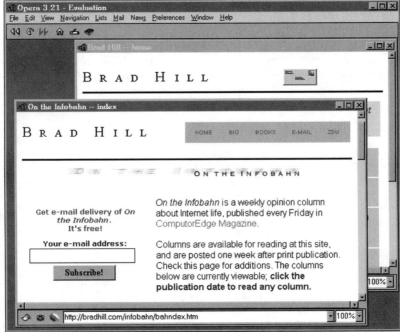

Figure A-12:
The Opera
browser
hosts
multiple
browser
windows in
a program
shell.

For now, Opera is a novelty worth trying and a browser well worth using in
certain Web situations.

Appendix B

About the CD

*Here's some of what you can find on the *Internet Searching For Dummies* CD-ROM:*

- ✔ Several automatic search agents for scouring the Web from your computer desktop and organizing the results
- ✔ A toolkit of Internet utilities
- ✔ Paint Shop Pro, a great shareware graphics program for Windows

System Requirements

Make sure your computer meets the minimum system requirements listed here. If your computer doesn't match up to most of these requirements, you may have problems in using the contents of the CD.

- ✔ A PC with a 486 or faster processor, or a Mac OS computer with a 68030 or faster processor. Some programs require a Pentium processor.
- ✔ Microsoft Windows 3.1 or later, or Mac OS system software 7.5 or later. Some programs require Windows 95, Windows 98, or Windows NT.
- ✔ At least 8MB of total RAM installed on your computer. For best performance, we recommend that Windows 95-equipped PCs and Mac OS computers with PowerPC processors have at least 16MB of RAM installed.
- ✔ A CD-ROM drive — double-speed (2x) or faster.
- ✔ A sound card for PCs (Mac OS computers have built-in sound support) if you want to listen to audio over the Web with Crescendo, VivoLive, or VDOLive.
- ✔ A monitor capable of displaying at least 256 colors or grayscale.
- ✔ A modem with a speed of at least 14,400 bps.

If you need more information on the basics, check out *PCs For Dummies,* 6th Edition, by Dan Gookin; *Macs For Dummies,* 6th Edition, by David Pogue; or *Windows 3.11 For Dummies,* 4th Edition, *Windows 95 For Dummies,* 2nd Edition, or *Windows 98 For Dummies,* all by Andy Rathbone (all published by IDG Books Worldwide, Inc.).

Using the CD with Microsoft Windows

To install the items from the CD to your hard drive, follow these steps.

1. **Insert the CD into your computer's CD-ROM drive.**

2. **Windows 3.1 or 3.11 users: From Program Manager, choose File⇨Run.**

   Windows 95, 98, or NT users: Click the Start button, and then click Run.

3. **In the dialog box that appears, type** D:\SETUP.EXE.

   Replace *D* with the proper drive letter if your CD-ROM drive uses a different letter. (If you don't know the letter, see how your CD-ROM drive is listed under My Computer in Windows 95, 98, or NT or the File Manager in Windows 3.1.)

4. **Click OK.**

   A License Agreement window appears.

5. **Read through the License Agreement, nod your head, and then click the Accept button if you want to use the CD.**

   (After you click Accept, you'll never be bothered by the License Agreement window again.) The CD interface appears. The interface is a little program that shows you what is on the CD and coordinates installing the programs and running the demos. The interface basically lets you click a button or two to make things happen.

6. **The first screen you see is the Welcome screen. Click anywhere on this screen to enter the interface.**

   Now you are getting to the action. This next screen lists categories for the software on the CD.

7. **To view the items within a category, just click the category's name.**

   A list of programs in the category appears.

8. **For more information about a program, click the program's name.**

   Be sure to read the information that appears. Sometimes a program might require you to do a few tricks on your computer first, and this screen will tell you where to go for that information, if necessary.

9. **If you don't want to install the program, click the Go Back button to return to the previous screen.**

   You can always return to the previous screen by clicking the Go Back button. This allows you to browse the different categories and products and decide what you want to install.

10. **To install the program, click the appropriate Install button.**

    The CD interface drops to the background while the CD begins installation of the program you chose. When the installation is complete, the interface usually reappears in front of other opened windows. If the interface is in the background, click anywhere in the interface's window to bring it forward.

11. **To install other items, repeat Steps 7 through 10.**

12. **After you've finished installing programs, click the Quit button to close the interface.**

    You can eject the CD now. Carefully place it back in the plastic jacket of the book for safekeeping.

Using the CD with the Mac OS

To install the items from the CD to your hard drive, follow these steps.

1. **Insert the CD into your computer's CD-ROM drive.**

   In a moment, an icon representing the CD you just inserted appears on your Mac desktop. Chances are, the icon looks like a CD-ROM.

2. **Double-click the CD icon to show the CD's contents.**

3. **Double-click the License Agreement icon.**

   This file contains the end-user license that you agree to by using the CD.

4. **Double-click the Read Me First icon.**

   This text file contains information about the CD's programs and any last-minute instructions you need to know about installing the programs on the CD that we don't cover in this appendix.

5. **To install most programs, just drag the program's folder from the CD window and drop it on your hard drive icon.**

6. **Other programs come with installer programs — with those, you simply open the program's folder on the CD, and then double-click the Install (or Installer) icon.**

   After you have installed the programs you want, you can eject the CD. Carefully place it back in the plastic jacket of the book for safekeeping.

What You'll Find

Here's a summary of the software on this CD. If you use Windows, the CD interface helps you install software easily. (If you have no idea what I'm talking about when I say "CD interface," flip back a page or two to find the section, "Using the CD with Microsoft Windows.")

If you use a Mac OS computer, you can enjoy the ease of the Mac interface to quickly install the programs.

Automated search agents

Search agents are programs that perform the hard work of searching for you. Technically, any online search engine is a search agent, and certainly the meta-search sites that rummage through several search engines are agents. Automated search agent programs differ in that you store the program on your hard drive and launch the search outside your Web browser.

At their best, such search agent programs accept sophisticated keyword strings. Their real strength often lies in how the search results are organized. Complex folder structures sometimes help make sense of search results. Some programs collect the entire site, not just the URL, and store all the text and graphics on your hard drive. Such full-featured programs are complete information management tools.

Is automated searching with these agent programs better than online searching through the engines? Not necessarily. It's largely a matter of taste and convenience. Some search agents can launch a search at a specified time, perhaps during the night, and have the results waiting for you. Others search continuously or frequently, and notify you of new results as they are found. Used in this way, search agent programs can relegate searching to the background of your life, freeing you for other things.

BullsEye

www.intelliseek.com

BullsEye is a professional-level search tool that allows you to track, find, and manage Internet information. The program combines searching, organizing, and bookmarking features into a single desktop package. The CD contains a demo version for Windows 95, 98, and NT 4.0.

Copernic 98

`www.copernic.com/free98.html`

Copernic 98 is a personal search engine. The copy included on the CD is a fully functioning program for Windows 95, 98, and NT 4.0, and absolutely free. Copernic 98 Plus is a beefed-up version with extra features, and that version costs money to own.

CyBot v2

`www.TheArtMachine.com/CyBot.htm`

CyBot claims to find stuff on the Internet 1,000 times faster than you could do manually, using the search engines I describe in this book. That might be the tiniest exaggeration. Nevertheless, CyBot was one of the first automated search agents, and this version lets you use all the features for a 30-day trial period. This program runs on Windows 95, 98, and NT 4.0.

MacroBot

`www.ipgroup.com/macrobot`

This free program specializes in searching the Yahoo! index. What's special about that? It organizes the returns in a map-like way that makes sorting through your matches a much more pleasant experience than using Yahoo! manually. This program works on Windows 95, 98, and NT 4.0.

Mata Hari

`thewebtools.com`

Mata Hari is a feature-rich, intelligent search agent that queries at least 140 Internet search engines in groups that you determine. Fairly complex keyword strings are supported, including strict Boolean operators. The program on the CD is a 30-day trial shareware version for Windows 95, 98, and NT 4.0.

SurfSaver

`www.surfsaver.com`

SurfSaver is an information organizer and search agent built specifically for Microsoft Internet Explorer 4.0 (or later) and Netscape Navigator version 4.0 (or later). SurfSaver saves entire Web pages, complete with graphics, and organizes them into folders. This program runs on Windows 95, 98, and NT 4.0.

Web Whacker

```
www.bluesquirrel.com/whacker
```

Web Whacker is less of a search agent than a browsing agent. It visits predetermined Web sites and collects all their contents, storing them in an organized form on your hard drive. Set it to perform this task before you get to your computer in the morning, and your daily Internet rounds are waiting for you, without the delays of surfing and loading pages. The CD includes trial versions that run on Windows 3.1, Windows 95, 98, and NT 4.0, or the Mac.

Web Bandit

```
www.jwsg.com/webbandit.htm
```

Web Bandit is an automated searcher with some snazzy features. You can set it to pick out certain types of files from around the Net, prowl through search engines, and even strip out e-mail addresses from search results. This demo copy of Web Bandit for Windows 95, 98, and NT 4.0 allows ten full searches before expiring; after that, registration is required.

WebFerret

```
www.ferretsoft.com/netferret
```

This freeware program for Windows 95, 98, and NT 4.0 is a slimmed-down version of a professional model automated Internet searcher. One of several bots on the CD, WebFerret has won several "Best of Bot" awards.

Internet utilities

The following utility programs assist your Internet experience. You may not need them every day, but it's sure good to have them around when you *do* need them.

Acrobat Reader

```
www.adobe.com/prodindex/acrobat
```

Adobe Acrobat is a freeware utility program for reading documents created in the Adobe Acrobat format. It's not often that you find downloadable files in this format, but when you do it's handy to have the Acrobat Reader. I can think of one Internet location where it's essential: at the Internal Revenue Web site, where downloadable tax forms are stored in Acrobat format. The CD has versions for Windows 3.1, Windows 95, 98, and NT 4.0, and the Mac.

Anarchie

www.stairways.com

Anarchie is an upload-download program for the Macintosh that lets you acquire files from FTP sites around the world. Anarchie comes with an extensive list of bookmarks that take you to popular software archives on the Internet. The copy of Anarchie on the CD is shareware.

Catch-IT

www.remotecommunications.com

Catch-IT is an Internet utility for Windows 3.1, 95, 98, and NT 4.0 that can make surfing the Web easier no matter what browser you are using. It helps you remember your favorite Web sites by enabling you to create and organize bookmarks that can be transported not only from one browser to another but also to multiple computers.

Crescendo

www.liveupdate.com/crescendo.html

Crescendo is a musical plug-in that empowers your browser to play MIDI music files that create background music to some Web pages. The program on the CD is free. Crescendo PLUS is a faster-playback version that can be purchased on the Web for $19.95 (U.S.). For more information, check out www.liveupdate.com/proddes.html (the Crescendo product description page). The versions on the CD are for Windows 3.1, Windows 95, 98, and NT 4.0, and the Mac.

Eudora Light

eudora.qualcomm.com/eudoralight

Eudora Light is the dietary version of Eudora Pro, a popular e-mail program. Eudora Light is fully functional freeware with no limited trial period. It is an alternative to the e-mail programs associated with the Navigator and Internet Explorer browsers (see Appendix A), but lacks features of the Pro version. The versions on the CD are for Windows 3.1, 95, 98, and NT 4.0, and the Mac.

Flash 3

www.macromedia.com

Flash 3 from Macromedia is a Web page and animation creation tool featuring vector-based drawing tools (rather than painting tools). It works with a special Shockwave Flash plug-in for Netscape Navigator. The CD has fully-functioning trial versions for Windows 95, 98, and NT 4.0 and the Macintosh that expire 30 days after your installation date.

Free Agent

```
www.forteinc.com/agent/freagent.htm
```

Free Agent is a free Usenet newsgroup reader. It provides an alternative to Outlook Express and Netscape Messenger, the e-mail/newsgroup programs supplied with the Internet Explorer and Navigator browsers. (See Appendix A.) The versions on the CD are for Windows 3.1, 95, 98, and NT 4.0.

GatherTalk

```
www.forteinc.com/agent/freagent.htm
```

GatherTalk is a trial version of a communications product for Windows 95 and 98 that allows users all around the world to communicate with each other using their computers.

HyperACCESS

```
www.hilgraeve.com/ha-win.html
```

HyperACCESS is an Internet utility that can help you get online and make the most of your modem. Its Phonebook can keep track of those important numbers as well as the duration of your calls while the Host manages incoming calls from as many telephone lines as your computer can support. The program on the CD is a demo for any Windows 3.1 machine or later.

HyperTerminal Private Edition

```
www.hilgraeve.com/htpe.html
```

HyperTerminal Private Edition is a more powerful version of the Hyper-Terminal program that comes in Windows 95, 98, and NT 4.0. HyperTerminal Private Edition uses the same interface as the familiar free version, but adds power and capabilities. The program is a speedy 32-bit program that takes full advantage of the Windows interface and key features, such as TAPI (Telephony API) and Unimodem universal modem support.

MindSpring Internet Access

```
www.mindspring.com
```

MindSpring is a complete Internet service provider package for Windows 3.1 or later, and for the Mac, that you can use to get on the Internet for the first time or as an alternative to whatever service you're currently using. This software installs Internet Explorer.

Important note: If you already have an Internet service provider, please note that MindSpring Internet Access software makes changes to your computer's current Internet configuration and may replace your current settings. These changes may stop you from being able to access the Internet through your current provider. Also note that you need a credit card to sign up for MindSpring Internet Access.

VDOLive Player

```
www.vdolive.com
```

VDOLive is a free streaming-video plug-in. When installed in your browser, it plays back Internet video clips encoded in the VDOLive format. The versions on the CD are for Windows 3.1, Windows 95, 98, and NT 4.0, and the Mac.

VivoActive Player

```
mitec.softseek.com/
```

VivoActive is another free video-streaming plug-in (see VDOLive). This one plays clips encoded in VivoActive format. The versions on the CD are for Windows 3.1, Windows 95, 98, and NT 4.0, and the Mac.

WS_FTP LE

```
www.ipswitch.com/Products/WS_FTP/index.html
```

The WS_FTP LE program provides an easy way to make file uploads and downloads to and from UNIX servers. This is a free (for noncommercial use), limited-edition version of a commercial product for Windows 3.1, 95, 98, and NT 4.0. WS_FTP is a common solution for uploading Web pages to a host server. If you have not created a Web site, WS_FTP is probably of no use. Portions of this software are copyrighted, 1991-1997, by Ipswitch, Inc.

Computer utilities

The computer utilities in this section are not specifically related to the Internet or Internet searching, but are part of any computer owner's toolkit.

CleanSweep

```
www.qdeck.com/qdeck/products/cleansweep
```

CleanSweep is a powerful deinstaller utility that removes unused program elements from your hard drive. The copy on the CD is a trial version for Windows 3.1 or Windows 95, 98, and NT 4.0.

FoolProof Security

`www.smartstuff.com`

FoolProof Security is designed for the school environment. With this program, you can prevent users from moving, renaming, or deleting files. That way, you don't have to worry about one person messing up the configuration of a multiuser setup. FoolProof Security has other protective features as well, although the demo version has disabled some of those features. The CD has demos for Windows 3.1, Windows 95, 98, and NT 4.0, and Macintosh. Important note: You must call SmartStuff Software at 800-671-3999 for passwords and installation codes before you can install FoolProof.

Message Server Communication Suite

`www.mawnet.com/products.html`

Message Server Communication Suite is a powerful utility for Windows 95, 98, and NT 4.0 that lets you send fax, e-mail, and voice messages through your computer. This demo of the product can show you how to send messages in multiple formats, compile contacts in a database, and intercept incoming calls.

Paint Shop Pro

`www.jasc.com/psp.html`

Paint Shop Pro is a shareware graphics viewing and editing tool. Versions are available on the CD for Windows 3.1 and Windows 95, 98, and NT 4.0. Check out `www.jasc.com/pspdl.html` on the Web for a full description.

StuffIt ensemble: StuffIt Lite, StuffIt Expander, and DropStuff with Expander Enhancer

`www.aladdinsys.com`

One problem with a Mac is that, after a while, you have lots of folders, files, and programs. What you won't have left, as a result, is sufficient hard drive space to keep more stuff. Here's where the StuffIt line of products enters to help you out. StuffIt Lite is a shareware program that allows you to create StuffIt archives, which are files that contain items you have compressed to save disk space. You can't do anything with the contents of a StuffIt archive until you unStuff (decompress) the archive, which StuffIt Lite can also do.

StuffIt Expander is a free program that lets you drag any StuffIt archive (and a few other archive formats such as BinHex-encoded files from the Internet) and instantly decode (unStuff) the items. DropStuff does just the reverse; it creates a StuffIt archive for any items you drag to it. DropStuff also adds capabilities to StuffIt Expander, such as decompressing ZIP archives, which are the PC's version of StuffIt archives.

WinFax PRO

`www.symantec.com/winfax`

WinFax PRO permits faxing of computer files directly from your computer, by means of your modem. You can activate WinFax PRO directly into file creation programs such as word processors and graphics software, making it easy to create a document and fax it from a single program. The version on the CD is for Windows 95, 98, and NT 4.0, and it's a try-buy deal. If you like it, you can call Symantec with a credit card and get a code to unlock your copy; otherwise, it stops working 30 days after you install it.

WinZip

`www.winzip.com`

WinZip is the most popular compression/decompression program. Essential if you like downloading programs from the Internet, WinZip decodes the compressed file so that it can be installed and run. The version on the CD is shareware.

If You Have Problems (Of the CD Kind)

I tried my best to compile programs that work on most computers with the minimum system requirements. Alas, your computer may differ, and some programs may not work properly for some reason.

The two likeliest problems are that you don't have enough memory (RAM) for the programs you want to use, or you have other programs running that are affecting the installation or running of a program. If you get error messages such as Not enough memory or Setup cannot continue, try one or more of these methods and then try using (or installing) the software again:

- ✔ **Turn off any anti-virus software you have on your computer.** Installers sometimes mimic virus activity and may make your computer incorrectly believe that it is being infected by a virus.

- ✔ **Close all running programs.** The more programs you're running, the less memory is available to other programs. Installers also typically update files and programs. So if you keep other programs running, installation may not work properly.

- ✔ **In Windows, close the CD interface and run demos or installations directly from Windows Explorer.** The interface itself can tie up system memory, or even conflict with certain kinds of interactive demos. Use Windows Explorer to browse the files on the CD and launch installers or demos.

✔ **Have your local computer store add more RAM to your computer.**
This is, admittedly, a drastic and somewhat expensive step. However, if
you have a Windows 95 PC or a Mac OS computer with a PowerPC chip,
adding more memory can really help the speed of your computer and
enable more programs to run at the same time.

If you still have trouble with installing the items from the CD, please call the
IDG Books Worldwide Customer Service phone number: 800-762-2974
(outside the U.S.: 317-596-5430).

Index

IDG Books Worldwide, Inc., End-User License Agreement

READ THIS. You should carefully read these terms and conditions before opening the software packet(s) included with this book ("Book"). This is a license agreement ("Agreement") between you and IDG Books Worldwide, Inc. ("IDGB"). By opening the accompanying software packet(s), you acknowledge that you have read and accept the following terms and conditions. If you do not agree and do not want to be bound by such terms and conditions, promptly return the Book and the unopened software packet(s) to the place you obtained them for a full refund.

1. **License Grant.** IDGB grants to you (either an individual or entity) a nonexclusive license to use one copy of the enclosed software program(s) (collectively, the "Software") solely for your own personal or business purposes on a single computer (whether a standard computer or a workstation component of a multiuser network). The Software is in use on a computer when it is loaded into temporary memory (RAM) or installed into permanent memory (hard disk, CD-ROM, or other storage device). IDGB reserves all rights not expressly granted herein.

2. **Ownership.** IDGB is the owner of all right, title, and interest, including copyright, in and to the compilation of the Software recorded on the disk(s) or CD-ROM ("Software Media"). Copyright to the individual programs recorded on the Software Media is owned by the author or other authorized copyright owner of each program. Ownership of the Software and all proprietary rights relating thereto remain with IDGB and its licensers.

3. **Restrictions on Use and Transfer.**

   (a) You may only (i) make one copy of the Software for backup or archival purposes, or (ii) transfer the Software to a single hard disk, provided that you keep the original for backup or archival purposes. You may not (i) rent or lease the Software, (ii) copy or reproduce the Software through a LAN or other network system or through any computer subscriber system or bulletin-board system, or (iii) modify, adapt, or create derivative works based on the Software.

   (b) You may not reverse engineer, decompile, or disassemble the Software. You may transfer the Software and user documentation on a permanent basis, provided that the transferee agrees to accept the terms and conditions of this Agreement and you retain no copies. If the Software is an update or has been updated, any transfer must include the most recent update and all prior versions.

4. **Restrictions on Use of Individual Programs.** You must follow the individual requirements and restrictions detailed for each individual program in Appendix B, "About the CD." These limitations are also contained in the individual license agreements recorded on the Software Media. These limitations may include a requirement that after using the program for a specified period of time, the user must pay a registration fee or discontinue use. By opening the Software packet(s), you will be agreeing to abide by the licenses and restrictions for these individual programs that are detailed in Appendix B, "About the CD," and on the Software Media. None of the material on this Software Media or listed in this Book may ever be redistributed, in original or modified form, for commercial purposes.

5. **Limited Warranty.**

    IDGB warrants that the Software and Software Media are free from defects in materials and workmanship under normal use for a period of sixty (60) days from the date of purchase of this Book. If IDGB receives notification within the warranty period of defects in materials or workmanship, IDGB will replace the defective Software Media.

    (b) IDGB AND THE AUTHOR OF THE BOOK DISCLAIM ALL OTHER WARRANTIES, EXPRESS OR IMPLIED, INCLUDING WITHOUT LIMITATION IMPLIED WARRANTIES OF MER-CHANTABILITY AND FITNESS FOR A PARTICULAR PURPOSE, WITH RESPECT TO THE SOFTWARE, THE PROGRAMS, THE SOURCE CODE CONTAINED THEREIN, AND/OR THE TECHNIQUES DESCRIBED IN THIS BOOK. IDGB DOES NOT WARRANT THAT THE FUNCTIONS CONTAINED IN THE SOFTWARE WILL MEET YOUR REQUIREMENTS OR THAT THE OPERATION OF THE SOFTWARE WILL BE ERROR FREE.

    (c) This limited warranty gives you specific legal rights, and you may have other rights that vary from jurisdiction to jurisdiction.

6. **Remedies.**

    (a) IDGB's entire liability and your exclusive remedy for defects in materials and workmanship shall be limited to replacement of the Software Media, which may be returned to IDGB with a copy of your receipt at the following address: Software Media Fulfillment Department, Attn.: Internet Searching For Dummies, IDG Books Worldwide, Inc., 7260 Shadeland Station, Ste. 100, Indianapolis, IN 46256, or call 800-762-2974. Please allow three to four weeks for delivery. This Limited Warranty is void if failure of the Software Media has resulted from accident, abuse, or misapplication. Any replacement Software Media will be warranted for the remainder of the original warranty period or thirty (30) days, whichever is longer.

    (b) In no event shall IDGB or the author be liable for any damages whatsoever (including without limitation damages for loss of business profits, business interruption, loss of business information, or any other pecuniary loss) arising from the use of or inability to use the Book or the Software, even if IDGB has been advised of the possibility of such damages.

    (c) Because some jurisdictions do not allow the exclusion or limitation of liability for conse-quential or incidental damages, the above limitation or exclusion may not apply to you.

7. **U.S. Government Restricted Rights.** Use, duplication, or disclosure of the Software by the U.S. Government is subject to restrictions stated in paragraph (c)(1)(ii) of the Rights in Technical Data and Computer Software clause of DFARS 252.227-7013, and in subparagraphs (a) through (d) of the Commercial Computer–Restricted Rights clause at FAR 52.227-19, and in similar clauses in the NASA FAR supplement, when applicable.

8. **General.** This Agreement constitutes the entire understanding of the parties and revokes and supersedes all prior agreements, oral or written, between them and may not be modified or amended except in a writing signed by both parties hereto that specifically refers to this Agreement. This Agreement shall take precedence over any other documents that may be in conflict herewith. If any one or more provisions contained in this Agreement are held by any court or tribunal to be invalid, illegal, or otherwise unenforceable, each and every other provision shall remain in full force and effect.

Installation Instructions

The *Internet Searching For Dummies* CD offers valuable information you won't want to miss. To install the items from the CD to your hard drive, follow these steps if you're using Windows:

1. **Insert the CD into your computer's CD-ROM drive.**

2. **Windows 3.1 or 3.11 users: From Program Manager, choose File⇨ Run. Windows 95, 98, or NT users: Click the Start button, and then click Run.**

3. **In the dialog box that appears, type** D:\SETUP.EXE **and then click OK.**

   Replace *D* with the proper drive letter if your CD-ROM drive uses a different letter.

4. **Read the License Agreement, and then click the Accept button if you want to use the CD.**

5. **Click anywhere on the Welcome screen to enter the interface.**

6. **To view the items within a category, just click the category's name. For more information about a program, click the program's name.**

   If you don't want to install a program, click the Go Back button to return to the previous screen.

7. **To install the program, click the Install button.**

8. **To install other items, repeat Steps 6 and 7.**

9. **When you've finished installing programs, click the Quit button.**

To install the items from the CD under the Mac OS, follow these steps:

1. **Insert the CD into your computer's CD-ROM drive.**

2. **Double-click the CD icon to show the CD's contents.**

3. **Double-click the Read Me First icon.**

4. **To install most programs, just drag the program's folder from the CD window and drop it on your hard drive icon.**

5. **Other programs come with installer programs — with those, you simply open the program's folder on the CD, and then double-click the Install (or Installer) icon.**

For more information, see Appendix B, "About the CD."

Discover Dummies Online!

The Dummies Web Site is your fun and friendly online resource for the latest information about ...*For Dummies*® books and your favorite topics. The Web site is the place to communicate with us, exchange ideas with other ...*For Dummies* readers, chat with authors, and have fun!

Ten Fun and Useful Things You Can Do at www.dummies.com

1. Win free ...*For Dummies* books and more!
2. Register your book and be entered in a prize drawing.
3. Meet your favorite authors through the IDG Books Author Chat Series.
4. Exchange helpful information with other ...*For Dummies* readers.
5. Discover other great ...*For Dummies* books you must have!
6. Purchase Dummieswear™ exclusively from our Web site.
7. Buy ...*For Dummies* books online.
8. Talk to us. Make comments, ask questions, get answers!
9. Download free software.
10. Find additional useful resources from authors.

Link directly to these ten fun and useful things at
http://www.dummies.com/10useful

For other technology titles from IDG Books Worldwide, go to
www.idgbooks.com

Not on the Web yet? It's easy to get started with *Dummies 101*®: *The Internet For Windows*®*98* or *The Internet For Dummies*®, *5th Edition*, at local retailers everywhere.

Find other ...*For Dummies* books on these topics:

Business • Career • Databases • Food & Beverage • Games • Gardening • Graphics • Hardware
Health & Fitness • Internet and the World Wide Web • Networking • Office Suites
Operating Systems • Personal Finance • Pets • Programming • Recreation • Sports
Spreadsheets • Teacher Resources • Test Prep • Word Processing

IDG BOOKS WORLDWIDE
BOOK REGISTRATION

We want to hear from you!

Register This Book and Win!

Visit **http://my2cents.dummies.com** to register this book and tell us how you liked it!

✔ Get entered in our monthly prize giveaway.

✔ Give us feedback about this book — tell us what you like best, what you like least, or maybe what you'd like to ask the author and us to change!

✔ Let us know any other ...*For Dummies*® topics that interest you.

Your feedback helps us determine what books to publish, tells us what coverage to add as we revise our books, and lets us know whether we're meeting your needs as a ...*For Dummies* reader. You're our most valuable resource, and what you have to say is important to us!

Not on the Web yet? It's easy to get started with *Dummies 101*®: *The Internet For Windows*® *98* or *The Internet For Dummies*®, 5th Edition, at local retailers everywhere.

Or let us know what you think by sending us a letter at the following address:

...*For Dummies* Book Registration
Dummies Press
7260 Shadeland Station, Suite 100
Indianapolis, IN 46256-3945
Fax 317-596-5498

...FOR DUMMIES™

BESTSELLING BOOK SERIES FROM IDG